The Complete Guide to
Animation
and
Computer
Graphics
Schools

"As an adolescent I was told that cartoons were for kids—but I never outgrew my love for those films and their stars. Instead, I became curious to know more about them; when they were made, who created the characters, why some series were funnier than others, and why there seemed to be three thousand mice in every Paul Terry Cartoon."

LEONARD MALTIN

The Complete Guide to Animation and Computer Graphics Schools

ERNEST PINTOFF

Watson-Guptill Publications

New York

An Academy Award winner for *The Critic*, Ernest Pintoff is a former animator and film director in motion pictures and television. He is the author of a novel, *Zachary*, and of *Bolt from the Blue*, an autobiographical account. Recently he wrote *The Complete Guide to American Film Schools*. Pintoff is a professor of film at the University of Southern California, and lives in Hollywood with his wife Caroline.

Senior Editor: Candace Raney
Edited by Stacey Guttman
Designer: Jay Anning
Production Manager: Ellen Greene

Copyright © 1995 Ernest Pintoff

Published in 1995 in the United States by Watson-Guptill Publications, a division of BPI Communications, Inc.,
1515 Broadway, New York, NY 10036

Library of Congress Cataloging-in-Publication Data
Pintoff, Ernest
  The complete guide to animation and computer graphics schools by Ernest Pintoff.
    p. cm.
Includes index.
ISBN 0-8230-2177-7
1. Computer animation—Study and teaching (Higher)—United States—Directories.
2. Computer graphics—Study and teaching (Higher)—United States—Directories.
3. Computer animation—Vocational guidance—United States. 4. Computer graphics—Vocational guidance—United States. I. Title.
TR897.7.P56 1995
700—dc20   95-334
                                                                 CIP

Manufactured in the United States

Contents

Preface

by Ernest Pintoff

No single art form utilizes all of man's creative potential quite like animation. It can express so many emotions: happiness or sadness through comedy or drama. It can do it quickly or slowly, with restraint or with dazzling graphics. Children, naive by nature, respond emotionally. Adults, already conditioned by the arts, react intellectually. Yet almost everyone is enthralled.

The options in animation are virtually limitless. The canvas can be enormous, and the miracle of the creator controlling every moment and frame is precise. That precision has been further enhanced by the employment of computers in animation. In fact, the interface of computer and video technologies is allowing for radically new exploration in animation, utilizing computer and video camera-generated imagery as well as video editing. The revolution of the cable industry has also created an expanding market that enables more and more animators to bring their work to the attention of both adults and children. For many years, animation has primarily been the vehicle for light, kiddie fare. However, I foresee animation being used as a medium to express the widest variety of ideas, profound and sophisticated, as well as the frequently mindless action on television.

The recent revival of animation in varying forms, combined with the development of powerful computer software, has created the need for many new concepts that are compatible with both classical techniques and electronic imaging. Computer graphics are used in diverse fields such as scientific visualization, engineering, and design. In fact, many computer graphics professionals are multidisciplinarians. But more and more film, video, and fine arts programs are devoting significant attention to the rapidly-expanding use of computer graphics as an arts discipline.

This book is designed for students seeking programs that develop skills in either character or computer animation—or both—for careers in motion arts media. The guide will also be most useful to graphic designers who in today's market benefit from studies in motion graphics, especially in the field of advertising. In addition, I have included the most prominent computer science programs offering a substantial graphics curriculum, as their work represents the most recent developments in graphics research, such as in interactive media design. Finally, explored are a variety of newly-created programs—thoroughly interdisciplinary in nature—that merge scientific investigation with aesthetic ideals.

Choosing the appropriate school is a challenge. Among other things, you will be evaluating the cost of tuition, location, size, academic opportunities, equipment access, curriculum, general philosophy, and reputation. I realize how tempting it is to concentrate on schools within the major cities, but there are plenty of programs throughout the country that deserve a good look. Depending on your goals, previous exposure, and available time and resources, you might also consider practical alternatives such as seminars, workshops and continuing education programs. Institutions featuring seminars and workshops usually offer a varied curriculum, while continuing education programs generally provide a more structured sequence of studies, often leading to a certificate in film or video.

As an undergraduate, do not overlook the value of studying the humanities and social sciences. Absorbing technical and production knowledge should only be part of your education. Read and write as much as possible. In my opinion, sensitivity to people and awareness of society is essential. At the undergraduate level you will of course be required to take a variety of electives outside your major discipline, many of which will enrich your animation skills. Acting, music, dance, anatomy, costume design, painting, psychology, mythology, history, and writing are all areas of inquiry that will particularly inform your craft. A career in animation can be extremely rewarding, both creatively and financially, and having the right foundation is half the battle.

After completing your education, there are a number of ways to get started in animation. There are no rules. Interning is an excellent way to "get your foot in the door" while continuing to learn in a professional, real-world atmosphere.

You could also create a storyboard and submit it to an agent, producer, or bankable actor or actress. Unfortunately, studios and networks usually turn away unagented concepts, mainly to avoid litigation should they be developing a property along similar lines. Sometimes, though, an eager producer will consider an unsolicited piece because the quest for good material is always high. However, do continue sketching and planning during your struggle to get established.

For those starting out as layout artists, a portfolio that demonstrates strong drawing skills is what those in hiring positions will certainly look for. Another good route to take would be to produce a modest animated production and use it as a showcase or arrange for its distribution yourself.

Academically aquired computer animation skills will open the door to a number of careers at film and video production studios, special effects production houses, television stations, advertising agencies, and areas from video game design to creating animation for NASA.

In any case, I recommend that all animators learn about the business aspects of movies and television. To expect to be presented with a plush assignment, no matter how talented you are, is naive in the media arts. The competition is intense. I can assure you.

My own hands-on introduction to animation began as an in-betweener at United Productions of America soon after earning an M.A. in art history from Michigan State University in 1959. In animation, in-between drawings are the transitional drawings in the cycle of motion between extreme drawings. I learned this from my first job. At the time, there were no animation film courses being offered at any accredited schools. But I had a passionate interest in jazz and cartooning. Subsequently, I was attracted to animation and new horizons in graphics. I was so inspired by UPA's versions of *The Tell-Tale Heart* by Edgar Allen Poe, and *The Unicorn and the Garden* from a James Thurber story that eventually I founded my own commercial studio, producing ads as well as animated and live-action shorts. In 1963, I was fortunate enough to win an Oscar for *The Critic,* a spoof on animated "art films." Following that, I directed numerous dramatic television films and a few theatrical movies. In 1969, I directed and produced the feature film *Dynamite Chicken,* a multimedia concept employing both animation and live-action techniques.

Since 1973 I have lectured and taught film directing, animation, and writing at the School of Visual Arts in New York, the USC School of Cinema and Television, UCLA Extension, and The American Film Institute. This book was written in the hope that the sum of my professional experience might enable me to contribute to the needs of today's animation students. To offer multiple perspectives, I have invited a number of former and current students to express their views. I have also solicited comments from film school graduates and esteemed professionals who evaluate their educational experiences and present their own advice.

In acknowledgment, I wish to thank Patricia Capetola for her expert research and editing. Alan Berger was also of valuable assistance as was Herb Klynn, who hired me years ago as an apprentice in-betweener at UPA. Finally, I want to thank my wife Caroline for her support, affection, and numerous contributions.

Although my professional beginnings were in traditional animation, several years ago when I obtained my first computer, an eager young computer wiz named Sailesh Ranchod installed my system. When Sailesh learned that I was a professor teaching animation writing, he lit up, barely able to restrain his enthusiasm concerning the potentials of computer graphics and animation. Since then, we have become friends and frequently chat about all aspects of animation, teaching, and computer graphics. Sailesh's energy, coupled with his computer animation skills, prompted me to invite him to write this book's foreword.

Foreword
by Sailesh Ranchod

■■■■■■■■■■■■■■■■■■■ ■ ■ ■ ■ ■ ■ ■ ■ ■

My entry into the world of computer graphics and animation happened back in my junior year of high school, when I got my first Apple IIe computer. Ever since I was little, I have been fascinated by the way things work, from tape recorders, to calculators, to light bulbs—just about everything attracted my attention. The computer seemed a very curious box, because it did all these wonderful things that I could control, create, and change. I got some paint programs and, eventually, an animation program called Take-1, and created my first computer animations. They were simple little visuals, but I had a great time making them. I came up with the idea of creating something called CompuGrams, interactive computer greeting cards. Since one of my buddies also had an Apple IIe, I would produce some fun animations and messages and send him the disk.

In high school, we learned how computers can be used to teach concepts and ideas. I recall writing my first Computer Assisted Instruction program on a TRS-80 computer, which taught people how to play chess. I had no idea at the time of the impact computers, graphics, and the possibilities and evolution of this technology was going to have on my life. I just remember how joyful it was to use the computer as a tool.

In college I became fascinated with the Macintosh computer and took a class that really made a difference and set my career in motion. My teacher, Dr. Standish, taught us to program the Macintosh, and our goal was to create some programs to teach people computer concepts. He was a great inspiration, bringing in lively computer animations and games that ran on the Macintosh and getting the class really excited about the possibilities. Our team of four wrote a program called Digital Magic, which was later published and won an Ncriptal Award for distinguished software.

After completing college in 1989, my first job was teaching a class on HyperCard to gifted junior high and high school students. It was pure magic. I had asked the students to write a story about what they wanted to become and where they saw their lives headed. I told them that we would make their stories come to life using pictures, sounds and animation. Though we were only using Macintosh Plus computers, I could not believe my eyes. I showed the kids how to move a little box from one place to another and the next thing I knew, there were spaceships flying, dolphins swimming, and cars zooming. The resulting creative expression, visualization, and interactive learning using computer graphics, animation, and sounds were truly fascinating to see in the hands of these students, some of whom had never used a computer before.

I went on to work as a contractor for a pharmaceutical company to create an interactive marketing program that would introduce one of their latest products at an upcoming ophthalmology conference. I wanted to learn and master this program on animation, and here I was, a few months after graduation, learning this same program and getting paid for it. The work was fascinating. My job was to explore, innovate and develop something that would mesmerize the audience while teaching them about the company's latest product. We used three-dimensional animation with molecules dancing to music and had an interactive part with a palette of all the various pieces that made up the molecule. The conference attendees had to piece it together. It was a huge success. It was 1990, and the multimedia revolution had just begun.

I now work for a firm that builds custom computer-based training applications for large corporations. It is most stimulating to use graphics, animation and video to create effective training applications that are not only entertaining, but also help people to better understand material. My job is to bring into reality the ideas that our artists, writers, and designers develop state of the art technology. We just completed a project for a company in which we used full three-dimensional modeling and three-dimensional animation with rendered images to create a virtual office park complex. It has a mix of real photographs and computer-generated images that create a visually stunning sales learning adventure.

Getting here was not easy. I made many mistakes along the way and suffered quite a few failures. However, my excitement over the possibilities about what this technology can do helped me to move ahead. I have discovered that a formal education is essential to building a strong foundation. But passion, desire, and the willingness to learn and grow are also imperative to succeed in the dynamic field of multimedia. I have also found it important to be well-organized because there is so much information to deal with. In addition, it is vital to keep an open mind because the field is still young.

We are on the dawn of a new frontier that has been dubbed the "Information Age." But information is only useful if it is organized, informative, synthesized, visually accessible, and grasped. Most of all, the presentation of the information has to be enjoyable.

My vision is to one day use computer animation and visualization technology to set up classes in universities, high schools, and junior high schools, for students to describe their dreams and goals, help each other study problem-solving strategies, and brainstorm ideas on how they can achieve their dreams. The class would provide a lab where computer animation and visualization could be taught, so that students could use the computer to make their ideas come to life. Our brain is a fantastic visualizer and now the computer allows us a way to communicate that vision to other people.

When considering animation studies, research all the schools you may wish to attend. Currently, many art and film programs offer a concentration in the new field of computer-generated motion graphics. Other programs focus on studies in character animation. There are new programs that offer substantial training in both techniques and those that are engaged in the active exploration of multimedia art forms. If you decide to explore the subject as a computer science major, you may wish to delve into the explosive field of graphics interactive programming, as I did, studying high-level languages such as Lingo, Supertalk, and Hypertalk. *The Complete Guide to Animation and Computer Graphics Schools* will help you sort out the information you need from this wealth of available programs while providing a helpful reference source, whether you are considering undergraduate or graduate studies, general or intensive media/graphics programs. Use this book to help determine which program is right for you.

After you've pared down your list to a manageable selection of schools you are considering, be sure to send for each school's catalog as well as any supplemental information you can gather about particular programs. If at all possible, try to visit a prospective campus, get a general feel for the school, and talk to faculty and students. Ask questions. For example: What are their alumni doing now? This will give you an idea about the kind of orientation the program has, and if it does in fact suit your goals. Remember, you are interviewing them as much as they are interviewing you.

While examining various programs, you may be heartened to find that some departments allocate money for advanced student projects in animation. But in many such cases, only projects approved by a committee get the nod. This may prove too restrictive for some people. Other students may welcome the chance to make an animated film without going into debt. It is probably a good idea to determine what the school's policy is regarding the rights of the filmmaker. Does the school you're considering retain the rights to student productions? Do such rights revert to the artist, or is there co-ownership of production projects? You may also wish to explore the legal implications of any graphics program you might design and want to patent as a student.

I hope that the use of computers, including graphics and animation, will allow us to communicate more effectively and learn about ourselves and the world we live in. The greatest appeal and magic come from the visual feast that computer graphics and animation satisfy for palettes of all ages. The multimedia field is wide open, with many opportunities and lots of room for creativity. It is an exciting time and I am very happy to be a part of it. I wish you all the best, too.

How to Use This Guide

Each school entry includes the name, address and phone number of the institution, describing its size, location and academic calendar. In addition to indicating relevant degrees offered, information is provided concerning curricular emphasis, facilities and equipment. The "Guide POV," borrowed from the term "point of view," provides a careful overview of studies in animation and graphics at each listed institution, and at times additional information about the school as well as its special offerings are given. The POV is designed to present an analysis of each program based on research from questionaires and information culled from catalogs, interviews with students and faculty, as well as other sources.

Inasmuch as the contents of this book are subject to change, prospective students are urged to contact individual schools for up-to-date information.

The Complete Guide to Animation and Computer Graphics Schools

Alabama

■■■■■■■■■■■■■ ■ ■ ■■■■■ ■ ■ ■ ■ ■ ■ ■ ■

AUBURN UNIVERSITY

Auburn, AL 36849

(205) 844-4080

State comprehensive institution. Coed, small town location. Undergraduate enrollment: 21,500. Graduate enrollment: 3,000.

Calendar: Quarters.

Degrees Offered: B.S., Computer Science and Engineering.

Curricular Emphasis: Studies in hardware and software components of computer graphics systems; display files; two-dimensional and three-dimensional transformations; clipping and windowing; perspective; hidden-line elimination and shading; interactive graphics; survey of applications; computer vision.

Facilities/Equipment: Computer graphics lab with variety of systems and software.

Guide POV: Auburn University offers computer graphics studies within the context of a broad computer science and engineering curriculum that includes structured programming; software engineering; parallel processing; artificial intelligence.

UNIVERSITY OF ALABAMA AT BIRMINGHAM

1300 University Blvd., Birmingham, AL 35294

(205) 934-2213

State comprehensive institution. Coed, suburban location. Undergraduate enrollment: 12,000. Graduate enrollment: 4,000.

Calendar: Quarters.

Degrees Offered: B.S., M.S., Ph.D., Computer and Information Sciences; B.A., Art.

Curricular Emphasis: Computer and Information Sciences Department— course listings include Computer Graphics I and II, Geometric Modeling; Independent Study; Thesis Research. Art Department—course listings include Intermediate Graphic Design I and II (Macintosh); Graphic Design for Advertising; Advanced Graphic Design; Advanced Studies.

Facilities/Equipment: Computer majors utilize a graphics lab featuring Silicon Graphics Indy, Indigo2 Extreme, and Sun workstations; in addition, a computer graphics lab for art students carries a variety of systems and software, including Macintosh, which are geared for graphic design applications in both print and video; video outlet.

Guide POV: Computer and Information Science majors may pursue graduate-level graphics projects emphasizing biomedical visualization, geometric modeling, and image processing; many projects actively involve the university's medical school, especially in the areas of crystallography, cardiology, neurosurgery, and biomedical engineering. Art majors are introduced to the Macintosh as a graphic design tool, emphasizing conceptual problem solving in both two- and three-dimensional forms; students explore advertising concepts, copy and compositional rendering for print and video; emphasis on portfolio development.

UNIVERSITY OF MONTEVALLO
Montevallo, AL 35115
(205) 665-6030
State comprehensive institution. Coed, small town location. Undergraduate enrollment: 2,400.

Calendar: Semesters.

Degrees Offered: B.A., B.S., Communication Arts

Curricular Emphasis: Communication Arts Department—Basic principles and practices of graphic design for video on the Macintosh as well as IBM and dedicated graphic computers are undertaken as part of a broad video production curriculum

Facilities/Equipment: Computer graphics lab.

Guide POV: Graphic design for video is studied within the framework of a comprehensive television broadcast curriculum; computer graphics curriculum stressing design offered through Art Department.

UNIVERSITY OF NORTH ALABAMA
Florence, AL 35632
(205) 760-4318
State comprehensive institution. Coed, urban location. Undergraduate enrollment: 5,600. Graduate enrollment: 200.

Calendar: Semesters.

Degrees Offered: B.A., B.S.

Curricular Emphasis: Communications and Theatre Department—Studies in computer graphics applications for video production include titling; special effects.

Facilities/Equipment: Computer graphics lab.

Guide POV: Video production students are offered computer graphics training through the Communication Arts Department, which enjoys newly redesigned facilities; in addition, the Art Department offers computer graphics courses emphasizing original design and composition, and the Computer Science Department offers an advanced course that explores techniques used in interactive computer graphics.

UNIVERSITY OF SOUTH ALABAMA
AD 182, Mobile, AL 36688-0002
(205) 460-6141
State comprehensive institution. Coed, urban location. Undergraduate enrollment: 9,000. Graduate enrollment: 2,000.

Calendar: Quarters.

Degrees Offered: B.F.A., M.F.A.

Curricular Emphasis: Art/Graphic Design—undergraduate and graduate course listings include Computer Art I/II; Advanced Computer Art; 2-D and 3-D Computer Art; Special Effects.

Facilities/Equipment: Computer graphics lab with Macs; 386/486s; Wavefront; additional on-campus facilities in Computer Science building.

Guide POV: Art students may study all aspects of computer art through the solid Graphic Design concentration, including motion graphics for video; additional graphics training through Computer Science Department with special attention to computer-aided design; applications to business and engineering.

Alaska

UNIVERSITY OF ALASKA AT ANCHORAGE

3211 Providence Dr., Anchorage, AK 99508
(907) 786-1800
State comprehensive institution. Coed, urban location. Undergraduate enrollment: 15,000.

Calendar: Semesters.

Degrees Offered: B.A., B.S., Computer Science. B.A., B.F.A., Art

Curricular Emphasis: Computer Science Department—course listings include Computer Modeling and Simulation Techniques; Computer Graphics; Design and Analysis of Algorithms. Art Department—course listings include Computer Art and Design; Advanced Graphic Design

Facilities/Equipment: Computer graphics lab with variety of systems and software

Guide POV: Students choosing the Computer Science major may study graphics in terms of display devices, display processing, transformation systems, interactive graphics, three-dimensional graphics, graphics system design and configuration, low- and high-level graphics languages, along with a variety of applications; in addition, the art major explores digital imaging to create graphic designs with an emphasis on print media.

Arizona

ARIZONA STATE UNIVERSITY
Tempe, AZ 85287
(602) 965-7788
State comprehensive institution. Coed, urban location. Undergraduate enrollment: 24,000.

Calendar: Semesters.

Degrees Offered: B.A., M.A., Studio Art (emphasis in Computer Art). B.S., Manufacturing and Industrial Technology (Option in Interactive Computer Graphics).

Curricular Emphasis: Art Department—sequential courses in both computer art and computer animation; other courses include animation and special effects; computer imaging; video art; film genres.

Facilities/Equipment: Computer graphics labs are generally microcomputer-based with a variety of software and peripherals for animation, video, photo manipulation, interactive media and print industry applications; mainframe computing is available through the network; independent study can be arranged on high-end SGI animation systems.

Guide POV: Computer animation training is offered through the Art Department with additional electives in design and photography; in addition, the Manufacturing/Industrial Technology Department offers an interactive computer graphics option for technical designers.

NORTHERN ARIZONA UNIVERSITY
Flagstaff, AZ 86011-4084
(602) 523-5511
State comprehensive institution. Coed, small town location. Undergraduate enrollment: 12,000. Graduate enrollment: 4,500.

Calendar: Semesters.

Degrees Offered: B.F.A.

Curricular Emphasis: School of Art and Design—special emphasis in computer art with course listings that include Computer Art I to IV; two-dimensional studio exhibition.

Facilities/Equipment: Computer graphics lab with variety of systems and software.

Guide POV: Studio art majors may explore animation, multimedia and modeling concepts through a special sequence of computer art courses; in addition, training in computer graphics programming is offered through the Computer Science and Engineering Department.

PHOENIX COLLEGE
1202 W. Thomas Rd., Phoenix, AZ 85013
(602) 285-7282
State two-year institution. Coed, urban location. enrollment: 3,000.

Calendar: Semesters.

Degrees Offered: A.A.S., Computer Graphic Design; certificate program available

Curricular Emphasis: Computer Graphic Design—required courses include two-dimensional computer design; electronic publishing design; computer-photographic imaging; computer aided graphic arts; variety of electives include courses in computer animation design.

Facilities/Equipment: Computer graphics lab includes Power Macintosh series Color Systems; Apple Laserwriter IINTX Printer; Paintjet Color Printer; Free-hand; Tektronix Phaser Illustrator; Photoshop; Quark XPress; Scanjet; framgrabber; scanners; film recorder; video equipment.

Guide POV: This lively, two-year professional certification program offers training in all aspects of computer graphics; flexible program features a variety of electives; practical career training in computer animation and TV graphic design as well as design and illustration for print media; computer art; prepress courses.

SCOTTSDALE COMMUNITY COLLEGE
Scottsdale, AZ 85250-2699
(602) 423-6337
State two-year institution. Coed, urban location. enrollment: 3,000.

Calendar: Semesters.

Degrees Offered: A.A., Art.

Curricular Emphasis: Computer Art/Graphics—course listings include Introduction to Computer Graphic Arts; 2-D Computer Design; 3-D Computer Design; Computer Art; Design Tools.

Facilities/Equipment: Computer graphics lab includes Amiga; Xerox 4020; film recorders; video toasters; software.

Guide POV: Scottsdale Community College offers thorough computer graphics instruction to artists seeking practical training for careers in graphic design and illustration.

Arkansas

■■■■■■■■■■■■■■■■■■ ■ ■ ■ ■ ■ ■ ■ ■

ARKANSAS STATE UNIVERSITY

P.O. Drawer 2160, State University, AR 72467

(501) 972-3024

State comprehensive institution. Coed, rural location.

Undergraduate enrollment: 9,500. Graduate enrollment: 1,000.

Calendar: Semesters.

Degrees Offered: B.S., Radio-Television; M.S.M.C., Radio-Television.

Curricular Emphasis: Department of Radio-Television—news production, cable/alternate technologies, corporate video, telecommunications research.

Facilities/Equipment: Complete video production and postproduction includes chromakey capability; special effects and other graphics potential; compact disc technology and satellite down-linking capability.

Guide POV: Students who choose the Radio-Television major at this state university gather hands-on experience producing a variety of telecasts; diverse course listings; digital special effects graphics and titling for television; additional graphics studies through Department of Computer Science, Mathematics and Physics.

ARKANSAS TECH UNIVERSITY

Russellville, AR 72801

(501) 968-0343

State comprehensive institution. Coed, small city location. Undergraduate enrollment: 4,000.

Calendar: Semesters.

Degrees Offered: B.S., Computer and Information Science.

Curricular Emphasis: Computer and Information Science Department— studies in applied computer graphics.

Facilities/Equipment: Computer science laboratory with advanced systems and software.

Guide POV: Students undertake projects in applied computer graphics; there is a strong design orientation; instruction in developing algorithms to do line drawing, two- and three-dimensional displays, clipping and windowing, and hidden line removal; other areas of exploration include display processors and data structures for graphics.

HARDING UNIVERSITY

Searcy, AR 72143

(501) 279-4000

Private comprehensive institution. Coed, small town location. Undergraduate enrollment: 4,000.

Calendar: Semesters.

Degrees Offered: B.A., B.S.

Curricular Emphasis: Department of Communication—hands-on training is available to introduce the broadcasting student to computer graphics techniques for video.

Facilities/Equipment: Macintosh computer lab for computer-aided graphic design work; 22 Macintoshes linked in an AppleTalk network; various microcomputer labs; Amigas; video cameras; video toaster.

Guide POV: Computer graphics training is available to video production students; additional courses stressing design applications available through the Department of Art and the Department of Mathematics and Computer Science.

UNIVERSITY OF ARKANSAS AT LITTLE ROCK
2801 S. University, Little Rock, AR 72204
(501) 569-3000
State comprehensive institution. Coed, urban location. Undergraduate enrollment: 10,141. Graduate enrollment: 1,500.

Calendar: Semesters.

Degrees Offered: B.A., Radio-Television-Film; B.S., Engineering Technology.

Curricular Emphasis: Radio/Television/Film Department—production; performance; broadcast journalism; computer graphics for television. Engineering Technology Department—specialized training in engineering design graphics.

Facilities/Equipment: Complete television production and postproduction; computer graphics lab with PCs and Suns.

Guide POV: Media students are engaged in a variety of programming projects and use techniques of computer graphics to produce special effects; the Engineering Technology Department offers advanced training in design graphics.

California

ACADEMY OF ART COLLEGE
79 New Montgomery St., San Francisco, CA 94105
(415) 274-2200
Private comprehensive arts institution. Coed, urban location. Undergraduate enrollment: 600.

Calendar: Semesters.

Degrees Offered: B.F.A., M.F.A.

Curricular Emphasis: Motion Pictures Department—character as well as experimental and computer generated animation may be explored in the context of the fine arts.

Facilities/Equipment: Single-frame capable 16mm cameras; computer graphics lab.

Guide POV: Founded in 1929, this fine arts academy offers studies in cel animation and computer art within the context of a film production major; in addition, an expanding computer graphics laboratory is used by students in illustration, advertising, design, and photography.

ALLAN HANCOCK COLLEGE
S. College, Santa Maria, CA 93454
(805) 922-6966
District/state two-year institution. Coed, suburban location. enrollment: 3,000.

Calendar: Semesters.

Degrees Offered: A.S., Applied Design/Media; Certificate in Film and Video Production.

Curricular Emphasis: Applied Design/Media—training in both film and video animation is offered within the context of a general program in video production.

Facilities/Equipment: Animation stand; 3/4" video animation; postproduction lab.

Guide POV: A two-semester program in animation featuring small classes and using both 16mm and computer-controlled video is offered at this community college.

ANTELOPE VALLEY COLLEGE
Lancaster, CA 93536-5426
(805) 943-3241
State two-year institution. Coed, suburban location. enrollment: 9,700.

Calendar: Semesters.

Degrees Offered: A.A., Computer Graphics, Computer Imaging, and Electronic Presentations; certificates in computer graphics, digital imaging, electronic presentations.

Curricular Emphasis: Computer Graphics—students learn to produce computer animated graphics to create video shows.

Facilities/Equipment: Computer graphics facility with 12 computer laboratories and an open laboratory for students; equipment includes Power Macintosh CPUs; CD-ROM Towers; Servers; Color and Black and White Laser Printers; Thermal Image Printers; Dye-Sublimation Printers; Ink Jet Printers; Plotters; Film Printers; Slide Scanners; Flat Bed High Resolution Scanners; Digital Cameras; complete production and postproduction for film/video including stand; video frame editing; design center.

Guide POV: This two-year college offers a full major in computer graphics for those students pursuing careers in video art/production, with additional electives in high-resolution graphics, commercial illustration, interior design, electronic publishing and photographic imaging; expanding program offers sequential studies in digital video editing and digital animation.

ART CENTER COLLEGE OF DESIGN

1700 Lida St., Pasadena, CA 91103
(818) 396-2373
Private comprehensive arts institution. Coed, urban location. Undergraduate enrollment: 1,200. Graduate enrollment: 85.

Calendar: Trimesters.

Degrees Offered: B.F.A., Art/Fine Arts; Graphic Arts; Film Studies; Photography; other areas; M.F.A., Interactive Design and Computer Graphics.

Curricular Emphasis: Computer graphics classes include Introduction to Computer-Based Design; Digital Design; Computer Imaging; Interactive Media Tools/2-D Animation; 3-D Modeling (SGI); 3-D Animation; 3-D Modeling; Color Separation; Advanced Digital Designing; Interactive Media Production; Computer Imaging; Advanced 3-D Modeling (SGI). Illustration—course listings include Film/Video Graphics; Experimental Illustration.

Facilities/Equipment: Complete production and postproduction for film/video includes animation stand; video frame-by-frame recording equipment; General Motors Computer Graphics Laboratory includes Silicon Graphics (SGI) Personal Iris workstations; Alias Studio Software; Indigo; 310 VGX machines; Full Color Publisher; Mac IIci; Macintosh Quadra 700; Macromind Director (animation software); Supercard; MacPluses with selection of software; plotters; color scanners; gray scale scanners; laser printers; color printers; MIDI sound lab.

Guide POV: At the undergraduate level, students may take a wide variety of computer graphics classes within their own major department; such classes provide multidisciplinary training in the fields of computer animation, filmmaking, art, design, advertising, photography, and illustration; there is a graduate program focusing on interactive design and computer graphics; the Film Department provides full character animation training; Art Center affiliate campus in La-Tour-de-Peilz, Switzerland.

BROOKS INSTITUTE OF PHOTOGRAPHY
Alston Rd., Santa Barbara, CA 93108
(805) 966-3888
Private three-year professional institution. Coed, suburban location. Undergraduate enrollment: 500.

Calendar: Six seven-week sessions per year.

Degrees Offered: B.A., M.S., Film/Video.

Curricular Emphasis: Film and video production featuring several courses in character animation techniques.

Facilities/Equipment: Animation stand; film and video equipment.

Guide POV: Students attending this professional arts institute may study cel animation while developing technical and creative production skills in both film and video.

BUTTE COMMUNITY COLLEGE
3536 Butte Campus Dr., Oroville, CA 95956
(916) 895-2288
Two-year comprehensive institution. Coed, rural location. enrollment: 9,300.

Calendar: Semesters.

Degrees Offered: A.A., Communication Arts and Technology.

Curricular Emphasis: Video Production Option—practical training in television and corporate video production including digital graphics. Video Graphics Option—aside from electives in video production, there are additional course listings in design; drawing; illustration art; technical drawing; graphic design; desktop publishing.

Facilities/Equipment: Television—studio; audio bay; control room; 15 Amiga computer graphics systems.

Guide POV: This two-year college provides a diversified degree program with special options in video graphics and video production; emphasis on practical training within the context of emerging technologies.

CALIFORNIA COLLEGE OF ARTS AND CRAFTS
5275 Broadway, Oakland, CA 94618-1487
(510) 653-8118
Private professional arts college. Coed, urban location. Undergraduate enrollment: 1,100. Graduate enrollment: 70.

Calendar: Semesters.

Degrees Offered: B.F.A., M.F.A.

Curricular Emphasis: Film/Video/Performance—an Animation Workshop covers the basics of film animation and its applications to video and computer graphics, teaching the fundamentals of cel animation in conjunction with other methods such as claymation and exploring both commercial and fine arts applications; Computer Mediated Postproduction and Image Creation examines the use of computer-based tools to coordinate and control multiple tracks of sound, image, and visual effects, and also includes basics of 3-D modeling and animation.

Facilities/Equipment: Computer Center includes multiple Macintoshes with Premiere, Quark, Director, and Photoshop software; Newtek Video Toaster; separate lab contains J/K Animation stand with Thing M controller, a J/K dual optical printer with Thing M controller, a NewTek Video Toaster in a multi-format editing suite; Rutt Etra video synthesizer; Sandine Image Processor; 4-track and 8-track analog audio recorders; Macintosh with Protools digital audio system.

Guide POV: This is a highly selective arts college that offers advanced training in experimental film and video production and postproduction as well as in computer-aided design.

CALIFORNIA INSTITUTE OF TECHNOLOGY
Pasadena, CA 91125
(818) 356-6811
Private comprehensive institution. Coed, urban location.

Calendar: Semesters.

Degrees Offered: B.S., M.S., Ph.D.

Curricular Emphasis: Computer Science—studies in the design and analysis of computing structures; areas explored include computer vision; computer graphics; computer-aided design; VLSI Design Laboratory; advanced projects; related imaging studies through the NSF Science and Technology Center for Computer Graphics and Scientific Visualization, and the Biological Imaging Center.

Facilities/Equipment: Computer graphics lab includes 10 Hewlett-Packard RISC-based graphics workstations; an AT&T Pixel Machine ray-tracing engine; and a complete system for generating computer animation, using a VPR-3 one-inch videotape recorder or a digital magnetic video disk recorder; parallel supercomputers; laser printers; color plotting devices; libraries of advanced computer graphics routines.

Guide POV: Students attending this top-ranked institution who possess a strong background in mathematics and physics are offered thorough computer graphics training with an emphasis on the creation of realistic images and models for a variety of scientific applications; advanced research facilities.

CALIFORNIA INSTITUTE OF THE ARTS
McBean Pkwy., Valencia, CA 91355
(805) 253-7825
Private comprehensive arts institution. Coed, suburban location. Undergraduate enrollment: 700. Graduate enrollment: 350.

Calendar: Semesters.

Degrees Offered: B.F.A., M.F.A., Film/Video; B.F.A., M.F.A., Art.

Curricular Emphasis: Animation Program—there is a concentration in character animation with a core curriculum including Life Drawing; Character Design; Character Animation; Basic Color and Design; Layout; Story Development. Experimental Animation Program—courses include Computer Graphics; Animation Sketchbook; Computer Animation and Music/Iris-Wavefront;

Advanced Computer Graphics/Video Studio; Motion Control; Oxberry Camera Operation; Optical Printer Operation; Direct Animation. Art Department—both the Art and Graphic Design programs offer the courses Advanced Digital Synthesis; Motion Graphics.

Facilities/Equipment: Students in both animation programs use Amiga and Iris/Wavefront computers; motion control camera; computerized optical printer; standard and computer controlled animation stands; video studios with CMX video-editing computer; several cuts-only editing bays with the ability to mix digital and analog video; video synthesizer; MIDI; Center for Experiments in Art, Information, and Technology; in addition, students in computer graphics design may utilize two computer animation laboratories with eight Mac SE's; two SE/30's; two color IIs and a IIci; two Laser Writers IIntx's; image scanning and both black/white and color video digitizing equipment.

Guide POV: Founded in 1961 by Walt Disney, Cal Arts offers separate, complete degree programs in character animation and experimental animation through its well-equipped School of Video/Film; computer graphics training also available through the School of Art, the Music Department and the Critical Studies Department; strong emphasis on production of innovative works.

CALIFORNIA STATE UNIVERSITY, LONG BEACH
Bellflower Blvd., Long Beach, CA 90840-2803.
(310) 985-5471
State comprehensive institution. Coed, suburban location. Undergraduate enrollment: 26,000. Graduate enrollment: 7,000.

Calendar: Semesters.

Degrees Offered: B.A., M.A., Radio, Television and Film. B.F.A., Art.

Curricular Emphasis: Art Department—animation graphics; computer graphics. Radio, Television, and Film—character and computer animation.

Facilities/Equipment: Animation stand; film and video cameras; computer graphics lab includes IBM AT/EGA; Amiga2000; NeXT; Apollo 3500; variety of other systems and software.

Guide POV: Both cel and computer animation may be studied through the Radio, Television, and Film Department; in addition, the Art Department offers sequential training in computer graphics and animation for those students pursuing careers in commercial design; advanced undergraduate and graduate research in computer graphics through Computer Science and Engineering Department.

CALIFORNIA STATE UNIVERSITY, LOS ANGELES
5151 State University Dr., Los Angeles, CA 90032
(213) 343-2752
State comprehensive institution. Coed, urban location. Undergraduate enrollment: 15,200. Graduate enrollment: 5,900.

Calendar: Quarters.

Degrees Offered: B.F.A., Art.

Curricular Emphasis: Art Department—there are sequential courses in computer graphic design as well as a course in 3-D computer animation; special projects.

Facilities/Equipment: Computer lab features VAXs; Mac IIs; NeXT; TARGA; videodisk; video cameras available.

Guide POV: Students in the Art Department may pursue training in computer graphics for careers in the fine and motion graphic arts as well as for commercial design and advertising.

CALIFORNIA STATE UNIVERSITY, NORTHRIDGE
18111 Nordhoff St., Northridge, CA 91330-8300
(818) 885-2242
State comprehensive institution. Coed, suburban location. Undergraduate enrollment: 26,000. Graduate enrollment: 6,100.

Calendar: Semesters.

Degrees Offered: B.A., M.A.

Curricular Emphasis: Art/Video Production—courses in animation graphics and computer graphics are offered.

Facilities/Equipment: Computer graphics lab; video cameras.

Guide POV: Both art and video production students may receive hands-on computer animation training.

CALIFORNIA STATE UNIVERSITY, STANISLAUS
801 W. Monte Vista Ave., Turlock, CA 95382
(209) 667-3122
State comprehensive institution. Coed, rural location. Undergraduate enrollment: 3,000. Graduate enrollment: 1,300.

Calendar: Semesters.

Degrees Offered: B.A., Art; B.S., Computer Science.

Curricular Emphasis: Art Department—course listings include Filmmaking and Animation; Electronic Art and Design. Computer Science Department—Computer Graphics I and II; Seminar; Selected Topics.

Facilities/Equipment: Computer graphics lab; basic film and video production and postproduction; animation stand.

Guide POV: Art majors may pursue projects in both traditional and computer-based animation; personal and group film animation projects; students creating computer-based art explore techniques of electronic painting, image-capture from video, animation, color, and laser printing techniques; computer art class is geared to both computer science and art majors; in addition, computer science majors examine advanced topics in three-dimensional computer graphics; emphasis on producing high quality images on raster devices; studies in animation; ray tracing; object modeling; advanced graphics hardware.

CENTER FOR ELECTRONIC ARTS
950 Battery, San Francisco, CA 90032
(415) 956-6550
Continuing education courses with variable enrollment.
Curricular Emphasis: Computer graphics in the context of film and video production training.
Facilities/Equipment: Computer graphics lab includes MS DOS computers; Macs; Symbolics; Lumena; Aurora.
Guide POV: For those considering either a career change or updated training, this center provides a practical hands-on approach to graphics instruction geared to the working adult.

CHAPMAN UNIVERSITY
333 N. Glassell St., Orange, CA 92666
(714) 997-6815
Private comprehensive institution. Coed, urban location. Undergraduate enrollment: 2,000. Graduate enrollment: 300.

Calendar: Semesters.

Degrees Offered: B.F.A., Art. B.F.A., Communications; B.A., Communications; M.A., Communication (concentration in Film Studies). M.F.A., Film and Television Production.

Curricular Emphasis: Computer graphics courses are available to students in film/television production as well as in advertising, graphic arts, visual arts, and interior design.

Facilities/Equipment: Computer center includes DEC Micro VAX II; Macintosh IIci; Macintosh SE; DEC workstation.

Guide POV: Chapman University offers a small, supportive community for the fine arts or media student; diverse curriculum; international locations on inter-term film projects.

CITY COLLEGE OF SAN FRANCISCO
Phelan Ave., San Francisco, CA 94112
(415) 239-3000
City and country two-year institution. Coed, urban location. enrollment: 33,000.

Calendar: Semesters.

Degrees Offered: A.A., A.S.

Curricular Emphasis: Photography—sequential course listings in multi-image production includes training in computer programming; visual design/storyboarding; slide to videotape transfers. Film Production—training in all aspects of film production including film special effects; cel animation techniques.

Facilities/Equipment: Animation stand; optical printer; film and video production and postproduction.

Guide POV: This two-year college offers individuals an opportunity to pursue cel animation studies within the context of an intensive film production curriculum; photography department offers students a rich opportunity to explore multi-image production with attention to video art, installation, and performance art.

COGSWELL COLLEGE

1175 Bordeaux Dr., Sunnyvale, CA 94089
(408) 541-0100
Independent four-year institution. Coed, suburban location. Undergraduate enrollment: 400 students.

Calendar: Trimesters.

Degrees Offered: B.A., Computer and Video Imaging.

Curricular Emphasis: Courses include Graphic Design; Imaging Concepts; 2-D Animation; 3-D Viewing; 3-D Modeling; 3-D Computer Art; 3-D Animation I and II; 3-D Character Animation; Sketching; Drawing for Animation; Scriptwriting; Storyboarding; Authoring; Peripheral Devices; Video Fundamentals; Video Systems; Video Post Production; Computer/Video Production; MIDI Fundatmentals; Audio Recording I and II; Audio Post Production; Introduction to Art; Art History; Algebra; Fractal Geometry; UNIX environment; Game Production and Development; C and C++ Programming.

Facilities/Equipment: Studios and computer graphics labs include Pentium-based workstations with pressure sensitive digitizing tablets; RGB/NTSC monitors; 32 bit image capture boards; 32 bit scanners and VTRS; software includes Adobe Photoshop; Fractal Painter; Lumena Paint; Macromind Director; Autodesk 3-D Studio; AutoCAD; Autodesk Animator Studio; Caligari True Space; Elastic Reality; in addition, there are Power PCs with Photoshop and Director; Silicon Graphics Indy workstations with Alias Power Animator; Alias Eclipse; Xaos Pandemonium and Panfx; complete video production and editing; 24 and 32 track sound studios.

Guide POV: This extremely well-designed program was designed as a response to latest developments in computer graphics technology; graduates, schooled in both technical and artistic aspects of graphics production, will be prepared for a variety of careers in the imaging industry including architectural design and rendering; creating animation for television, advertising and motion pictures; producing multimedia presentations for business and education; developing and producing games; designing industrial prototype visualizations; creating character animations, and pursuing litigation arts (reconstructing crime scenes in courtrooms); the expanding and fluid curriculum is designed to meet applications not yet discovered, such as the establishment of one's own studio.

COMPUTER ARTS INSTITUTE

310 Townsend St., #230, San Francisco, CA 94107
(415) 546-5242
Continuing education courses with variable enrollment.

Curricular Emphasis: Modeling and Animation programs and classes include Computer Ease; 3-D Studio; Animator Pro; Infini-D; Photoshop for the PC; Animation Design and Storyboarding; and Video Game Animation. Macintosh Multimedia classes include Director, Photoshop, and Multimedia Development; Quicktime Video with Premiere. Desktop Publishing classes include Introduction to the Mac; Quark XPress; Pagemaker; Illustrator; Freehand; Fractal Design Painter; Photoshop, and Typographic Design.

Facilities/Equipment: Computer graphics labs include Pentium and 486s, Quadras and Power PCs; students may render animations to tape with rendering workstations.

Guide POV: Stressing new systems and technologies, this lively institute offers classes in computer graphics and animation geared to both artist and executive.

DE ANZA COLLEGE

21250 Stevens Creek, Cupertino, CA 95014
(408) 864-5678
District two-year institution. Coed, suburban location. enrollment: 25,000.

Calendar: Quarters.

Degrees Offered: A.A.

Curricular Emphasis: Film/Television Production—course listings include Introduction to Film Animation; Sound for Animation; Character Animation; History of Animation; Basic Cartooning and Design for Animation; The Animation Storyboard; Animation Production I, II, and III; Professional Animation I, II, and III; History of Independent Video; Introduction to Computer Graphics. Art Department—course listings include Introduction to Computer Graphics; Art and Computer Graphics I and II; Motion Graphics; there is a graphic design option.

Facilities/Equipment: Animation stand; computer graphics lab.

Guide POV: Professional and complete training for filmmakers concentrating on character animation is offered at this two-year college; the computer graphics classes offered through the Art Department stress career training for designers and illustrators.

DIABLO VALLEY COLLEGE

321 Golf Club Rd., Pleasant Hill, CA 94523
(510) 685-1230
District two-year institution. Coed, suburban location. enrollment: 20,000.

Calendar: Semesters.

Degrees Offered: A.A., Communications; Certificate in Television Arts.

Curricular Emphasis: Communications—emphasis on producing special effects for video production.

Facilities/Equipment: Video cameras; computer graphics lab with IBM, 4381, IBM PS/2; Amiga.

Guide POV: Training in computer-generated special effects and music video production is offered to broadcasting students; additional graphics courses are offered through the Computer Science Program.

FOOTHILL COLLEGE
El Monte Rd., Los Altos Hills, CA 94022
(415) 949-7772
City two-year institution. Coed, suburban location. enrollment: 16,000.

Calendar: Quarters.

Degrees Offered: A.A., A.S.

Curricular Emphasis: Film/Television Program—one course in film animation; in addition, sequential courses in computer graphics animation for film and video cover topics such as generating 3-D solids and lighting models; frame-accurate recording; design skills; solid model emulation. Graphic Design Program—courses include Illustration with the Macintosh; Layout and Graphic Design; Production Art; Professional Computer Animation I and II; Film Animation; Advanced Cartooning; Graphics Programming on the Iris Workstation; Anatomy for Artists; Cubicomp Vertigo. Computer and Information Sciences Program—course listings include 3-D Computer Graphics and Solid Modeling; Topics in Computer Graphics Algorithms; Image Processing; Iris 4-D and 3000 Series Workstations.

Facilities/Equipment: Animation stand; film and video cameras; computer graphics lab includes Silicon Graphics Iris 3000 Series and 4-D Series workstations; Tandem; AED frame buffer; Amiga 2000/digiview; Cubicomp; PostScript; Mac SE; Scanner; Data Show; IBM XT; Tecmar; Lumena; PC Paint.

Guide POV: This well-equipped community college provides curricula in both film and computer animation; film production students are offered film animation training as well as sequential studies in computer animation for film/video; there is a separate program for graphic designers emphasizing computer applications in commercial art and film/video production; advanced graphics and animation studies offered to computer science majors.

HUMBOLDT STATE UNIVERSITY
Arcata, CA 95521
(707) 826-3566
State comprehensive institution. Coed, rural location. Undergraduate enrollment: 6,500. Graduate enrollment: 500.

Calendar: Semesters.

Degrees Offered: B.A., M.A., M.F.A.

Curricular Emphasis: Film production includes exploration of documentary, experimental, and animated forms.

Facilities/Equipment: Animation stand; computer graphics laboratory.

Guide POV: Humboldt State University offers filmmakers training in both cel animation and computer graphics with an emphasis on independent production; small classes; interdisciplinary arts program involves theatre, film, and dance.

LOS ANGELES CITY COLLEGE

N. Vermont Ave., Los Angeles, CA 90029
(213) 953-4545
City two-year institution. Coed, urban location. enrollment: 15,000.

Calendar: Semesters.

Degrees Offered: A.A., Radio-Television-Film Department; Production Certificates in Film, Television, Film/Video, and Recording Arts and Sciences.

Curricular Emphasis: Radio-Television-Film Department—character animation may be studied within the context of a comprehensive film production curriculum, with additional courses in directing, writing, and cinematography.

Facilities/Equipment: Animation stand; complete film and video production and postproduction.

Guide POV: Training in character animation is offered to interested students through a broad two-year film production curriculum; includes special projects.

LOS ANGELES VALLEY COLLEGE

Fulton Ave., Van Nuys, CA 91401
(818) 781-1200
City two-year institution. Coed, urban location. enrollment: 21,000.

Calendar: Semesters.

Degrees Offered: A.A., Theatre/Cinema Arts; Occupational Certificate, Motion Picture Production Technician.

Curricular Emphasis: Film writing and production; visual, multimedia approach; extensive screenings; hands-on training; adjunct program in video production; television broadcasting.

Facilities/Equipment: Animation stand; optical printer; SPFX screen; computer graphics lab.

Guide POV: This two-year film program offers practical training "from script to screen," and features studies in both cel and computer animation.

LOYOLA MARYMOUNT UNIVERSITY

Loyola Blvd. at West 80th St., Los Angeles, CA 90045
(310) 338-2700
Private comprehensive institution. Coed, urban location. Undergraduate enrollment: 4,000. Graduate enrollment: 1,000.

Calendar: Semesters.

Degrees Offered: B.A., M.A., Writing for Film and TV; B.A., M.A, Film Production; B.A., M.A., Television Production; B.A., Recording Arts; B.A., Communication Studies.

Curricular Emphasis: Beginning to advanced film projects in character animation.

Facilities/Equipment: Animation studio with Oxberry aerial image; film and television production and postproduction; four sound recording studios.

Guide POV: Full training in character animation is offered to students at this selective private university through a production-oriented Communications

Program; facilities open to all student levels; graduate work culminates in thesis project.

MODESTO JUNIOR COLLEGE

435 College Ave., Modesto, CA 95350
(209) 575-6140
District two-year institution. Coed, urban location. enrollment: 14,000.

Calendar: Semesters.

Degrees Offered: A.S., Computer Graphics Applications; certificate.

Curricular Emphasis: Computer Graphics Applications—courses include 3-D Animation; Multimedia; Desktop Video Graphics; Desktop Video Titling; Illustration; Image Processing; TV Studio Operations; Color and Design; Computer Graphics Portfolio Review; Special Topics in Computer Graphics.

Facilities/Equipment: Computer graphics lab with PC, Mac, and Amiga platforms; Hypermedia; 3-D Studio; Lumena; Coreldraw; Photoshop; Illustrator; Animator Pro and other software; video and digital cameras; WACOMS; video to SVHS.

Guide POV: With a core curriculum culled from the departments of Radio and Television, Art, Architecture, and Engineering, this expanding two-year Computer Graphics program provides well-rounded training for students interested in 2-D or 3-D animation for video as well as desktop publishing and illustration; certificate and degree programs available.

ORANGE COAST COLLEGE

2701 Fairview Rd., Costa Mesa, CA 92628
(714) 432-0202
City two-year institution. Coed, urban location. enrollment: 23,000.

Calendar: Semesters.

Degrees Offered: A.A.

Curricular Emphasis: Film/Video—courses in film animation; the Digital Video course introduces students to digital video as seen in music videos, commercials, and motion pictures; other courses include Computer Graphics Animation; Interactive Multimedia; lab courses.

Facilities/Equipment: Electronic Media lab includes Macintosh software packages.

Guide POV: Professional training in film animation is offered to students through the Film/Video Program; Electronic Media Program offers training for animators, digital video artists, and interactive multimedia artists as well as fine artists.

PLATT COLLEGE

6250 El Cajon Blvd., San Diego, CA 92115
(619) 265-0107
Private vocational institution. Coed, urban location. Trimester calendar. Variable enrollment.

Degrees Offered: Certificate Programs.

Curricular Emphasis: Graphic Design Program—in-depth courses in animation, 3-D imagery, multimedia, digital photography, drawing, painting, and related subjects.

Facilities/Equipment: Computer graphics lab includes Macintosh computers with 19-inch color monitors; laser and color printers; plotters; color and gray scale scanners; video recorders; video scanners; video projection monitor.

Guide POV: Professional career training covering computer graphics applications in both video and print media is offered to students through this intensive 11-month program; students include recent high school graduates as well as professionals returning to school to update skills or pursue career changes; strong placement program.

RANCHO SANTIAGO COLLEGE

Santa Ana, CA 92706

(714) 564-5620

City two-year institution. Coed, urban location. enrollment: 26,000.

Calendar: Semesters.

Degrees Offered: A.A.; Certificate Programs

Curricular Emphasis: Art/Telecommunications—course listings include Introduction to Computer Graphics; Computer Graphics 2-D/3-D Fundamentals; Advanced Modeling and Surfaces; 3-D Motion Concepts; Advanced Animation; Computer Graphics Production.

Facilities/Equipment: Computer graphics lab includes PC-based computers with Autodesk; 3-D Studio Software; video camera; Sony 3/4" videotape recorder.

Guide POV: This two-year college offers career training to students interested in utilizing computer graphics techniques in video animation, special effects, commercial art, and design.

SAN DIEGO CITY COLLEGE

San Diego, CA 92101

(619) 230-2666

City two-year institution. Coed, urban location. enrollment: 12,000.

Calendar: Semesters.

Degrees Offered: A.A., A.S.

Curricular Emphasis: Computer and Information Sciences—course listings include Introduction to Computer Graphics, Computer Graphics on the Macintosh, and Computer Animation on a Macintosh.

Facilities/Equipment: Computer graphics lab includes IBM PS/2s (VGA); color printer; scanner; Dr. Halo; Mac II cx; video cameras; SuperPaint paint and draw program; Video works II.

Guide POV: Computer science majors at this two-year institution may elect computer graphics training to prepare them for careers in video art and animation.

SAN DIEGO STATE UNIVERSITY

5500 Campanile Dr., San Diego, CA 92182-4561

(619) 594-6511

State comprehensive institution. Coed, urban location. Undergraduate enrollment: 25,000. Graduate enrollment: 7,000.

Calendar: Semesters.

Degrees Offered: B.A., Applied Art (emphasis in Graphic Design); M.A., M.F.A., Graphic Design. B.S., Television-Film Production; B.A., M.A., Telecommunications and Film.

Curricular Emphasis: School of Art, Design and Art History—course listings include Advanced Graphic Design—Media; Advanced Graphic Design—Communications Systems; Advanced Graphic Design—Environmental Graphics; Visual Communication Media; Graphic Imagery. Department of Telecommunications and Film—there are courses in character animation; variety of computer graphics classes offered in conjunction with the Art Department.

Facilities/Equipment: Two computer graphics studios with Macintosh systems running Freehand, Illustrator, Pagemaker, Quark, and other software; in addition, telecommunications students make use of an animation stand; film and video production and postproduction, including nonlinear editing; multimedia lab; computer graphics lab.

Guide POV: Art students are offered comprehensive graphic design studies at both undergraduate and graduate levels in preparation for professional careers in design and advertising; majors in telecommunications are offered a diverse program allowing them to pursue projects in both cel animation and computer graphics; graduate telecommunications program offers creative specializations.

SAN FRANCISCO ART INSTITUTE

Chestnut St., San Francisco, CA 94133

(415) 771-7020

Private arts institution. Coed, urban location. Undergraduate enrollment: 578. Graduate enrollment: 250.

Calendar: Semesters.

Degrees Offered: B.F.A., M.F.A., Filmmaking; B.F.A., M.F.A., Performance/Video.

Curricular Emphasis: Filmmaking is taught in a fine arts context, where the expressive intent of the maker is primary; intermedia courses offered combining film with other art disciplines; studio courses in video explore video sculpture; narrative video; teleperformance; installation; computer-based interactive forms based on virtual reality; screen-mediated images; site-sensitive approaches related to architecture, and other approaches; technical workshops.

Facilities/Equipment: Two animation stands, one with tracking camera mount and rotoscope capabilities; two pin-registration optical printers; computer arts facility; complete film and video production and postproduction.

Guide POV: Established in 1871, this is one of the oldest colleges of art in the United States; highly selective, professionally-equipped Fine Arts program for filmmakers and video artists; supportive artist-based community; 24-hour access to facilities; faculty of practicing media artists.

SAN FRANCISCO STATE UNIVERSITY
Holloway Ave., San Francisco, CA 94132
(415) 338-2017
State comprehensive institution. Coed, urban location. Undergraduate enrollment: 25,000. Graduate enrollment: 4,000.

Calendar: Semesters.

Degrees Offered: B.A., M.A., M.F.A.

Curricular Emphasis: Film—Undergraduate and graduate production programs offer a number of electives in character animation. Art Department—Information Arts/Conceptual Design emphasis offers both undergraduate and graduate studies covering such areas as experimental video production; robotics; advanced imaging; conceptual design; interactive cinema; exploration in word and image.

Facilities/Equipment: Animation stand; computer graphics lab includes Macintosh HyperCard system; "C" language software; Mac IIs; Targa; Iris; scanners; sound; complete film and video production and postproduction.

Guide POV: Cel animation is taught through the highly selective Cinema Department which is dedicated to training students in an independent cinema; Art Department offers innovative Information Arts and Conceptual Design Program through which students may explore new technologies and their creative applications.

SAN JOSE STATE UNIVERSITY
San Jose, CA 95192-0135
(408) 924-1000
State comprehensive institution. Coed, small city location. Undergraduate enrollment: 16,100. Graduate enrollment: 6,500.

Calendar: Semesters.

Degrees Offered: B.A., M.F.A., Computers in Fine Art; M.A., Multimedia Computing.

Curricular Emphasis: School of Art and Design—course listings include Introduction to Computer Art; Interactive Multimedia; Graphics Programming and Systems Integration; Computer Animation and Digital Video; Human-Machine Interface; Advanced Projects in Computer Art; Art History and Interactive Multimedia; Advanced Projects in Multimedia; Graduate Seminar in Computers and Electronic Arts.

Facilities/Equipment: Computer workstations include Silicon Graphics Lab; Macintosh Quadra Lab; IBM Lab; Sun Microsystems Server; Intel DVI; variety of software includes Alias; SoftImage; XAOS; Mutigen; Photoshop; Illustrator; Macromind Director; MAX; Supercard; Hypercard; selection of video equipment includes VMI Digital Editing; MII; SVHS; Hi-8; 3/4" Umatic; networking available includes WWW site; ISBN; SJSU Fiber Optic; CSUT1; interactive recording through JVC CD-ROM; Panasonic Laserdisc; Virtual Reality with Sense 8.

Guide POV: An advanced computer center on campus in conjunction with the CADRE Institute (Computers in Art and Design/Research and Education) provides art students with an innovative program featuring both undergraduate and graduate education in computer graphics and interactive media.

SOLANO COMMUNITY COLLEGE
Suisun Valley Rd., Suisun City, CA 94585.
(707) 864-7171
State two-year institution. Coed, suburban location. enrollment: 10,000.

Calendar: Semesters.

Degrees Offered: A.A., Telecommunications.

Curricular Emphasis: Applied Production Program in Film and Video—production courses include character animation; computer art.

Facilities/Equipment: Animation stand; computer graphics lab; film and video production and postproduction.

Guide POV: Offering students a two-year program with class projects to suit a variety of interests, Solano Community College provides film and video production training with special attention to music videos, experimental cinema, and animation.

SOUTHWESTERN COLLEGE
Otay Lakes Rd., Chula Vista, CA 92010
(619) 421-6700
State two-year institution. Coed, suburban location. enrollment: 3,800.

Calendar: Semesters.

Degrees Offered: A.A, Telemedia (Transfer Program); A.S., Telemedia Specialist; A.S., Television Engineering.

Curricular Emphasis: Combines foundation in theory and aesthetics with hands-on practice in film and video production including character animation and computer graphics animation.

Facilities/Equipment: Animation stand; computer graphics lab with paint, video, and animation; complete film and video production and postproduction.

Guide POV: This two-year program offers production training in film and video with an opportunity to explore both artistic and technical aspects of animation; students may choose transfer or career tracks.

STANFORD UNIVERSITY
Stanford, CA. 94305-2050
(415) 723-2300
Private comprehensive institution. Coed, suburban location. Undergraduate enrollment: 6,700. Graduate enrollment: 6,850.

Calendar: Quarters.

Degrees Offered: B.S., M.S., Ph.D., Computer Science.

Curricular Emphasis: Course listings include Human-Computer Interaction; Introduction to Computer Graphics; Computer Graphics: Mathematical Foundations; Computer Graphics: Image Synthesis Techniques; Topics in Computer Graphics; Geometric Algorithms; Computer Systems Modeling; Motion Planning; Advanced Robotic Manipulation; Computer Vision; other areas.

Facilities/Equipment: State-of-the-art computer facilities with variety of systems and software including NEON; DECSYSTEM 5400; Sun-4; NeXT and Symbolics machines; AT&T and HP workstations; MIPS systems; laser printers.

Guide POV: Strong research groups at this most selective institution exist in the areas of analysis of algorithms and theory of computation; artificial intelligence; scientific computing; robotics, and systems; both faculty and students commonly work with investigators at nearby research or industrial institutions; application materials should be sent directly to the Computer Science Department; M.S. program is a terminal professional degree; applicants planning to pursue Ph.D. degree must apply directly to that program; this is one of the highest-ranked Computer Science departments in nation.

THE AMERICAN ANIMATION INSTITUTE
4729 Lankershim Blvd., Los Angeles, CA 91602-1864
(818) 766-0521/762-0060
Private institution. Coed, urban location. Student enrollment: 500.

Calendar: Quarters.

Degrees Offered: None

Curricular Emphasis: Animation studies include basic animation mechanics; introduction to the animation art and industry; in-betweening and assistant animation; animation; background painting and design; layout; character design; storyboarding; life drawing; advanced life drawing, and head drawing.

Facilities/Equipment: 1/2" JVC video time-lapse animation stand; videotape monitors for screenings.

Guide POV: This unique institution was founded in 1980 by the Motion Picture Cartoonists, Local 839 IATSE, a labor union representing the writers, artists, craftspersons and technicians involved in the making of animated cartoons; variety of classes geared to industry professionals; additional apprenticeship-style classes designed for those without professional experience who are seeking their first jobs in screen cartooning; additional training in computer animation available through Hollywood Hands On, available only to active members of IA local unions.

UNIVERSITY OF CALIFORNIA AT BERKELEY
Berkeley, CA 94720
(510) 642-6000
State comprehensive institution. Coed, urban location. Undergraduate enrollment: 21,000. Graduate enrollment: 9,000.

Calendar: Semesters.

Degrees Offered: B.A., Telecommunications; M.A., Journalism. B.S., M.S., Ph.D., Computer Science.

Curricular Emphasis: Video—broadcast journalism with supplementary training in computer graphics/special effects. Computer Science—advanced graphics projects/research.

Facilities/Equipment: Computer graphics lab includes Macintosh computers with graphics interface; VAX; Sun; Tektronix; PS300; Adage; IBM; Lyon Lamb; Bosch; Sony; RCA; complete film and video production and postproduction; Computer Science Research Center.

Guide POV: Journalism majors employ digital effects in video productions; the Computer Science Department here is one of the top-ranked in the country; students pursue advanced research projects.

UNIVERSITY OF CALIFORNIA AT DAVIS

Davis, CA 95616-8610
(916) 752-1011
State comprehensive institution. Coed, urban location. Undergraduate enrollment: 18,000. Graduate enrollment: 5,400.

Calendar: Quarters.

Degrees Offered: B.S., M.S., Ph.D.

Curricular Emphasis: Computer Science—course listings include Computer Graphics; Advanced Raster Graphics; projects.

Facilities/Equipment: Computer Graphics Research Laboratory includes Sequent Symmetry Parallel Processing System; Silicon Graphics IRIS 4D/35 color workstations; Hewlett-Packard HP-Turbo VRX graphics superworkstation; artificial intelligence laboratory.

Guide POV: A comprehensive program in computer science is geared to those most interested in the scientific applications of computer graphics; students are engaged in graphics research in the visualization of complex models, including the modeling of complex scenes, mathematical problems in computer-aided geometric design, visualization techniques, and the design of graphical user/computer interfaces.

UNIVERSITY OF CALIFORNIA AT LOS ANGELES

405 Hilgard Ave., Los Angeles, CA 90024
(310) 853-4321
Research university. Coed, urban location. Undergraduate enrollment: 23,000. Graduate enrollment: 12,000.

Calendar: Quarters.

Degrees Offered: B.A., Film and Television; M.F.A., Animation.

Curricular Emphasis: Animation Workshop—there is an undergraduate emphasis and a graduate major in animation; films from the Workshop range from conceptual to cartoon, from narrative to nonnarrative, from cel to computer animation, from entertainment to experimental, and from the active to the interactive, depending on individual student's choice of style and direction.

Facilities/Equipment: Animation studio, which includes three animation cranes (two 16mm; one 16/35mm); a video pencil test unit; a computer pencil test unit; several microcomputers with both 2-D paint/animation, 3-D object animation, and interactive programs; two 16mm optical printers; complete sound, editing and viewing facilities; complete film and video production and postproduction; extensive animation collection in the UCLA Film and Television Archive and the Workshop's own archives.

Guide POV: All works made in this most selective program are the property of the artists who have created them; the prestigious Animation Workshop offers three undergraduate courses and seven graduate courses, as well as graduate thesis courses; their philosophy stresses individual creative control over all aspects of film; the program receives national and international guest lecturers; there are animation internships.

UNIVERSITY OF CALIFORNIA AT LOS ANGELES EXTENSION
10995 Le Conte Ave., Los Angeles, CA 90026
(310) 206-1422
Continuing education courses with variable enrollment.
Degrees Offered: Visual Arts Department—Certificate in Computer Graphics. Department of Entertainment Studies and Performing Arts—Certificate in Film, Television, Video, and Multimedia, Level I (elective emphasis available in 2-D and 3-D graphics and animation) or Certificate in Film, Television, Video, and Multimedia, Level II (specialization in 2-D and 3-D graphics and animation).
Curricular Emphasis: UCLA Extension, Visual Arts Department—certificate program in computer graphics includes intensive training in animation, interactive multimedia, digital imaging and desktop publishing. UCLA Extension, Department of Entertainment Studies and Performing Arts—curriculum includes lectures, seminars, and hands-on workshops in principles and practice of 2-D and 3-D graphics and animation, with an emphasis on applications for film, television, and multimedia; the courses are part of a comprehensive curriculum in film, television, video, multimedia and music.
Facilities/Equipment: Visual Arts Department—Fully equipped computer graphics lab; CoSA After Effects; Electric Image; Form Z; Macromedia Director; Adobe Photoshop; Illustrator; Premiere; Apple Media Tool; Quark XPress; Aldus PageMaker. Department of Entertainment Studies and Performing Arts—dedicated UCLA Extension/IBM Media Lab with 16 IBM student workstations (486 computers, each with 16-24 MB RAM and 1 GB SCSI External HD networked to file server; Targa+ card and Personal Animation Recorder (PAR) for output to video; Software includes 3-D Studio (with many IPAS routines); Animator Pro; Animation Master; Viewpoint; Topas Professional; Photoshop; Virtus WalkThrough Pro; Virtual Reality; Multimedia Toolbook; Authorware Pro; Director; the Media Lab is an Autodesk Multimedia Authorized Training Center.
Guide POV: Through the excellent Visual Arts program, the university offers an extension program in computer graphics with special attention to computer animation and interactive multimedia; separately, the Department of Entertainment Studies and Performing Arts offers certificates at two levels

with thorough hands-on training in graphics and animation with special attention to applications for film, television, and multimedia; courses taught by leading industry professionals.

UNIVERSITY OF CALIFORNIA AT SAN DIEGO
Gilman Drive, La Jolla, CA 92093
(619) 534-2230
State comprehensive institution. Coed, suburban location. Undergraduate enrollment: 15,000. Graduate enrollment: 3,000.

Calendar: Quarters.

Degrees Offered: B.A., M.F.A., Visual Arts.

Curricular Emphasis: Visual Arts Department—Theoretical/Conceptual program emphasizing avant-garde production including studies in film, video, computer media, environmental and performance art as well as critical theory.

Facilities/Equipment: Animation stand; optical printer; video toaster; computer graphics lab; film and video production and postproduction.

Guide POV: UC San Diego offers full animation and video art studies through the Visual Arts Department with a strong emphasis on avant-garde production.

UNIVERSITY OF CALIFORNIA AT SANTA BARBARA
Santa Barbara, CA 93106—4010
(805) 893-8000
State comprehensive university. Coed, suburban location. Undergraduate enrollment: 15,000.

Calendar: Quarters.

Degrees Offered: B.A., M.F.A., Visual Arts. B.A., Film Studies.

Curricular Emphasis: Art Studio Department—Interdisciplinary program emphasizing collaborative efforts between the arts and humanities including studies in painting, video, narrative, performance, installation art and electronic intermedia as well as critical theory. Film Production Program—narrative; animation; documentary; experimental.

Facilities/Equipment: Computer graphics lab includes Macintosh Quadra and Power PCs; Silicon Graphics Indigo workstations running Wavefront and Alias software; animation stand; 16mm cameras; 16mm editing.

Guide POV: In an innovative move, the lively Art Studio Department is working in collaboration with the College of Engineering on animation projects using Wavefront and Alias software; in addition, undergraduates majoring in Film Studies are introduced to 16mm production and may elect small classes in film animation.

UNIVERSITY OF CALIFORNIA AT SANTA CRUZ
Santa Cruz, CA 95064
(408) 459-0111
State comprehensive university. Coed, suburban location. Undergraduate enrollment: 9,000. Graduate enrollment: 1,000.

Calendar: Quarters.

Degrees Offered: B.S., M.S., Ph.D., Computer and Information Science.

Curricular Emphasis: Computer and Information Science—course listings include Computer Graphics; Computer Animation; Image Processing and Display; Projects.

Facilities/Equipment: Computer graphics lab with 386 PCs (Immagraph); SGI Irises; variety of other systems and software.

Guide POV: The strong computer science curriculum includes advanced undergraduate and graduate projects in computer animation; students receive written narrative evaluation of academic performance.

UNIVERSITY OF SOUTHERN CALIFORNIA
University Park, Los Angeles, CA 90089-2111.
(213) 740-2311
Private comprehensive institution. Coed, urban location. Undergraduate enrollment: 16,000. Graduate enrollment: 12,000.

Calendar: Semesters.

Degrees Offered: B.A., Film/Video Production; M.F.A., Film, Video, and Computer Animation.

Curricular Emphasis: School of Cinema/Television—undergraduates may elect a variety of animation studies; newly created production-intensive Graduate Program emphasizes imagination and originality in the exploration and mastery of animation. The curriculum's progressive and creative approach provides students with the opportunity to create artwork that integrates state-of-the-art computing with high-end film and video technology, including 35mm and 70mm (Omnimax) film recording. The curriculum spans classical character and experimental animation, and encourages projects that explore new forms, including interactive multimedia, performance and installation art, the combination of live action and computer animation, scientific visualization, and virtual reality, among others. The program is augmented by extensive offerings from the world-class Production and Critical Studies Departments. The Computer Animation Laboratory has produced animation for several IMAX films; SCFX, USC's special effects student organization, has been involved in varied production projects.

Facilities/Equipment: Complete Film Animation Studio with two 5300 Oxberry animation stands; one Bowlds-Acme animation stand; Producer's Service 104 optical printer; three single-frame, color, video animation systems; Computer Animation Laboratory includes over 25 Silicon Graphics workstations, including Crimsons, Reality Engines and Indigos; SoftImage; Alias; Wavefront; Renderman; Side Effects Prisms; Parallax and Pixibox software; Apple Macintosh AV; Lab is networked to a 16 processor Silicon Graphics Power Challenge; Solitaire Cine II Film Recorder; music scoring studio; full film, video and television production and postproduction, including AVID editing.

Guide POV: This prestigious School of Cinema-Television, founded in 1929 and the nation's first film school, offers professional undergraduate and graduate education for animators working in a wide spectrum of state-of-the art facilities; the new Graduate Animation Program integrates the creative arts of film and videomaking with the latest technologies of computer animation, multimedia and digital technologies; the innovative program enjoys support from Warner Brothers, Hanna-Barbera Productions, and Silicon Graphics; the department funds selected advanced projects; entering classes in graduate program currently limited to 20 students.

YUBA COLLEGE

2088 North Beale Rd., Marysville, CA 95901
(916) 741-6700
State two-year institution. Coed, suburban location. enrollment: 7,000.

Calendar: Semesters.

Degrees Offered: A.S., Mass Communication; Certificate of Training.

Curricular Emphasis: Video production with a strong emphasis on electronic movie making; state-of-the-art computer effects and editing.

Facilities/Equipment: Animation stand; computer graphics lab; interactive television studio/classroom; video production and postproduction equipment includes A/B roll with Toaster EFX.

Guide POV: This professional two-year program offers a variety of hands-on production opportunities; emphasis on new technologies; computer-generated effects.

Colorado

■■■■■■■■■■■■■■■ ■ ■ ■ ■ ■ ■ ■ ■ ■ ■

AIMS COMMUNITY COLLEGE
P.O. Box 69, Greeley, CO 80632
(303) 330-8008
District two-year institution. Coed, suburban location. enrollment: 15,000.

Calendar: Quarters.

Degrees Offered: A.A., Liberal Arts (students may select emphasis in Communications Media).

Curricular Emphasis: Communications Media—television and radio broadcasting and production including offerings in computer graphics and electronic theory.

Facilities/Equipment: Computer graphics lab; television production and postproduction.

Guide POV: This hands-on program offers technical training in broadcast production including computer-based animation for television.

COLORADO STATE UNIVERSITY
Fort Collins, CO 80523
(303) 491-1101
State comprehensive institution. Coed, suburban location. Undergraduate enrollment: 18,000. Graduate enrollment: 3,000.

Calendar: Semesters.

Degrees Offered: B.S., M.S., Ph.D., Computer Science.

Curricular Emphasis: Computer Science—advanced graphics studies include principles of raster and video graphics techniques; image rendering; ray tracing; image shading; solid modeling; algorithms; other areas.

Facilities/Equipment: Computer-aided design lab with variety of systems and software including equipment donations from IBM, AT&T, and Hewlett-Packard; Macintosh lab donated by Apple Computer; biology students engage in interactive computer simulation; Computer Visualization Laboratory with Silicon Graphics Workstations, Dye Sublimation printer; Sony laser videodisc recorder; Betacam and VHS videotape recorders; software from Alias, Dynamic Graphics, SGI and Wavefront; complete television and video production and postproduction.

Guide POV: Computer graphics instruction is given at this selective state university with special attention to video design, microcomputer systems design, and software/hardware engineering; student co-op program with nearby Hewlett-Packard Company (graphics technology division); additional graphics studies through Technical Journalism Department; Art Department; there is a Semester-At-Sea Program.

COLORADO TECHNICAL COLLEGE
4435 N. Chestnut St., Colorado Springs, CO 80907-3896
(719) 598-0200
Private technical commuter institution. Coed, suburban location. Undergraduate enrollment: 1,200. Graduate enrollment: 375.

Calendar: Quarters.

Degrees Offered: B.S., M.S., D.C.S., Computer Science.

Curricular Emphasis: Computer Science—course listings include Computer Graphics; Neural Networks; Computer Simulation; Software/Human Interface; Software Engineering; other areas.

Facilities/Equipment: Computer center features advanced workstations (80486-based); variety of software.

Guide POV: With an applied technology approach to education, this college provides computer science majors with extensive laboratory exercises and experiences; integrated curriculum blends mathematics, physics, electronics, and applied science with general academic studies; undergraduate focus on software engineering; software/human interface; interactive computer graphics; undergraduate graphics students must develop CAD software system as part of course work; graduate students may concentrate in Software Engineering, Computer Systems Engineering, or Systems Engineering.

METROPOLITAN STATE COLLEGE OF DENVER
1006 Eleventh, Denver, CO 80204
(303) 556-2400
State comprehensive institution. Coed, urban location. Undergraduate enrollment: 17,800.

Calendar: Semesters.

Degrees Offered: B.A., Communications (Multi-Major Broadcasting).

Curricular Emphasis: Television/video production; computer graphics; video art; instructional/industrial.

Facilities/Equipment: Computer graphics lab; video production and postproduction.

Guide POV: Students attending this state college, the largest urban, nonresidential four-year college in the United States, learn all aspects of broadcasting while working on a variety of projects; computer graphics taught in context of video art and computer animation for television; additional instruction in computer graphics through the Art Department.

UNIVERSITY OF COLORADO AT BOULDER
Boulder, CO 80309
(303) 492-1411
State comprehensive institution. Coed, urban location. Undergraduate enrollment: 20,000. Graduate enrollment: 4,000.

Calendar: Semesters.

Degrees Offered: B.F.A., M.F.A., Fine Arts; B.F.A., Film Production, B.S., M.A., Journalism and Mass Communication.

Curricular Emphasis: Film—16mm independent production with training available in cel animation. Television—broadcast training; graphics applications include special effects for video and broadcast television. Fine Arts—special course work in the area of electronic photography at both the undergraduate and graduate levels.

Facilities/Equipment: Animation stands; computer graphics lab; video toaster; optical printer; IBM XT; Colorado Video; complete film and television production and postproduction.

Guide POV: This selective university offers separate quality programs in film and television production; film program is at the vanguard of experimental cinema; film animation projects; special effects for video; digital photography.

UNIVERSITY OF DENVER

2490 S. University Blvd., Denver, CO 80208-0132
(303) 871-2000
Private comprehensive institution. Coed, urban location. Undergraduate enrollment: 3,000. Graduate enrollment: 3,000.

Calendar: Semesters.

Degrees Offered: B.A., B.S., B.F.A.

Curricular Emphasis: Graphic Communications Design Program—course listings include Introduction to the Macintosh; Intermediate Computer Graphics; Advanced Computer Graphics; Illustration and Graphic Design; Creative Team Projects; Symbol and Graphic Communication Design; Portfolio Design. Computer Science Department—course listings include Introduction to Computer Graphics; Advanced Computer Graphics; Special Topics in Graphics.

Facilities/Equipment: Computer graphics lab with variety of systems and software including Adobe Illustrator; Aldus Freehand; Quark XPress; PageMaker; laser and linotronic printers; Microtek scanner; color QMS output devices.

Guide POV: Art students concentrating in graphic communications design utilize the computer as a drawing tool in the creation of a variety of design and illustration projects; emphasis on developing a career portfolio; students majoring in computer science will explore advanced topics such as solid modeling, color theory, shading and illumination models, viewports; human-computer interface issues, and ray tracing.

UNIVERSITY OF SOUTHERN COLORADO

2200 Bonforte Blvd., Pueblo, CO 81001
(719) 549-2835
State comprehensive institution. Coed, urban location. Undergraduate enrollment: 6,000.

Calendar: Semesters.

Degrees Offered: B.A., B.S., Art.

Curricular Emphasis: Art Department—course listings include Graphic

Design I, II, III, IV; Computer Graphic Literacy; Computer Imaging; Animation I, II, III, IV.

Facilities/Equipment: Computer graphics lab includes IBMs with Targa Pentiums; Quark; Photoshop; Macromind; Macs; Imagestudio; Lumena 32; Adobe Illustrator; Adobe Premier; 3-D Studio Panorama; Topaz; Crystal Pro Animator; scanner; video output.

Guide POV: Art students explore computer applications in both design and animation along with traditional methods.

Connecticut

■■■■■■■■■■■■■■■ ■ ■ ■ ■ ■ ■ ■ ■ ■ ■ ■

CONNECTICUT COLLEGE
New London, CT 06320
(203) 439-2200
Private comprehensive institution. Coed, urban location. Undergraduate enrollment: 2,000.

Calendar: Semesters.

Degrees Offered: B.A., Art.

Curricular Emphasis: Art Department—course listings include Graphic Design; Computer Art.

Facilities/Equipment: Computer graphics lab with Mac II; SE; post script printers; Amiga; Photon Cel Animator; Renderman; Studio 8.

Guide POV: Computer animation training is offered to interested students within the context of a fine arts program.

MIDDLESEX COMMUNITY TECHNICAL COLLEGE
Middletown, CT 06457
(203) 343-5800
State two-year institution. Coed, suburban location. enrollment: 3,000.

Calendar: Semesters.

Degrees Offered: A.A.

Curricular Emphasis: Broadcast Communications—television production.

Facilities/Equipment: Computer graphics lab; film and video production and postproduction.

Guide POV: Middlesex Community Technical College offers a practical broadcast production program; technical training in computer-generated effects for television; students may also work in 16mm film.

WESLEYAN UNIVERSITY
Middletown, CT 06457
(203) 347-9411
Private comprehensive institution. Coed, rural location. Undergraduate enrollment: 2,600. Graduate enrollment: 500.

Calendar: Semesters.

Degrees Offered: B.A., Film.

Curricular Emphasis: Students complete both film theory and production courses as part of unified program and are encouraged to take full liberal arts program in addition to film.

Facilities/Equipment: Animation stand; 16mm film production and postproduction.

Guide POV: An interdisciplinary critical studies program is offered in film with courses in production as well as criticism; limited character animation studies available.

YALE UNIVERSITY
New Haven, CT 06520
(203) 432-4771
Private liberal arts institution. Coed, urban location. Undergraduate enrollment: 5,100. Graduate enrollment: 5,400.

Calendar: Semesters.

Degrees Offered: B.F.A., M.F.A., Art.

Curricular Emphasis: Art Department—there is a concentration in graphic design.

Facilities/Equipment: Computer graphics lab with variety of systems and software; film and video equipment.

Guide POV: Founded in 1701, this Ivy League university offers art students 24-hour access to private studios; students may participate in the Yale Summer School Program in Graphic Design, held in Brissago, Switzerland; computer graphics curriculum also offered to computer science and mathematics majors; additional studies in computer science and psychology.

Delaware

■■■■■■■■■■■■■■■■■■■ ■ ■ ■ ■ ■

WESLEY COLLEGE
Dover, DE 19901
(302) 736-2300
Private comprehensive institution. Coed, urban location. Undergraduate enrollment: 850.

Calendar: Semesters.

Degrees Offered: B.A.

Curricular Emphasis: Communication Department—video production; integration of computers, video, audio, and print.

Facilities/Equipment: Complete video production and postproduction including Amiga video graphics.

Guide POV: This growing program provides comprehensive training in media production with an emphasis on the acquisition of technical skills; computer-based animations for video production; attention to special projects.

District of Columbia

■■■■■■■■■■■■■■■■■■ ■ ■ ■ ■ ■ ■ ■ ■

THE AMERICAN UNIVERSITY

4400 Massachusetts Ave. NW, Washington, DC 20016

(202) 885-1000

Private comprehensive institution. Coed, urban location. Undergraduate enrollment: 5,000. Graduate enrollment: 4,000.

Calendar: Semesters.

Degrees Offered: B.F.A., B.A., B.S., M.A., M.S.

Curricular Emphasis: Visual Media/Graduate Film and Video—Character and computer animation projects may be undertaken in production programs; additional courses in computer graphics offered through the Computer Science and Art Departments.

Facilities/Equipment: Animation stand; complete film and video production and postproduction; computer graphics lab.

Guide POV: This professional program provides comprehensive undergraduate and graduate training in film, video, and television production; projects in cel and computer animation; graduate study may be undertaken part-time under certain conditions; strong commitment to independent projects.

CORCORAN SCHOOL OF ART

500 17th St. NW, Washington, DC 20006-4899

(202) 628-9484

Private professional arts institution. Coed, urban location. Undergraduate enrollment: 300.

Calendar: Semesters.

Degrees Offered: B.F.A., Graphic Design; Certificate in Computer Art and Design.

Curricular Emphasis: Computer Graphics—course listings include Macintosh Digital Video; Computer Illustration.

Facilities/Equipment: Computer graphics lab with both black and white and color studios; Macintosh IIsi units with accelerated 24-bit color displays; color scanning; video input equipment; laser printers.

Guide POV: Founded in 1890, this is the only professional school of art and design in the District of Columbia; students pursuing a degree in graphic design may receive instruction in computer graphics techniques for both motion arts and print media; special attention to new digital video techniques; in addition to degree programs, the school offers an extensive open curriculum for those wishing to attend intensive workshops and seminars.

GALLAUDET UNIVERSITY
800 Florida Ave., NE, Washington, DC 20002-3695
(202) 651-5000
Private comprehensive institution. Coed, urban location. Undergraduate enrollment: 2,000.

Calendar: Semesters.

Degrees Offered: B.A., Television, Film and Photography.

Curricular Emphasis: Film and television production; film animation studies available to interested students; other courses include Graphic Design in the Visual Media; Visual Media and the Future; evolving technologies; photography.

Facilities/Equipment: Animation stand; film and video production and post-production; video toaster; computer graphics lab.

Guide POV: Established in 1864, this private college is the only four-year liberal arts university in the world designed exclusively for deaf and hard of hearing students; all instructors teach using sign language; modern facilities; offerings in both film animation and video art.

GEORGE WASHINGTON UNIVERSITY
2121 Eye St., NW, Washington, DC 20052
(202) 994-1000
Private comprehensive institution. Coed, urban location. Undergraduate enrollment: 6,000. Graduate enrollment: 12,000.

Calendar: Semesters.

Degrees Offered: B.A., B.F.A., B.S., M.S., Ph.D.

Curricular Emphasis: Art Department—course listings include Computer Graphics for Artists I, II, and II; Visual Communication. Electrical Engineering and Computer Science—undergraduate and graduate course listings include Interactive Computer Graphics I-III.

Facilities/Equipment: Computer graphics lab includes Macintosh; Laser-Writer; IBM (Artworks); scanners; IBM PS/2 (30 and 50); Circus; Suns; HP 360 SRXs; HP 385 turbo SRX; video and television production and postproduction.

Guide POV: The program in art provides undergraduate students with sequential training in computer graphics; special attention to art and design applications; additional training in creating computer-generated special effects for production students within television broadcasting program; advanced studies in interactive computer graphics offered through the Electrical Engineering and Computer Science Department.

HOWARD UNIVERSITY
2400 6th St. NW, Washington, DC 20059
(202) 806-6100
Private comprehensive institution. Coed, urban location. Undergraduate enrollment: 7,000. Graduate enrollment: 4,000.

Calendar: Semesters.

Degrees Offered: B.A., Radio-Television-Film; M.F.A., Film.

Curricular Emphasis: Film students may study character animation techniques; broadcasting students use computer technology to create special effects for video.

Facilities/Equipment: Animation stand; film and video production and post-production.

Guide POV: Howard University offers students comprehensive production tracks in both film and television; film students may pursue projects in character animation.

Florida

■■■■■■■■■■■■■■■■■■ ■ ■ ■ ■ ■ ■ ■ ■

JACKSONVILLE UNIVERSITY
2800 University Blvd. N., Jacksonville, FL 32211
(904) 744-3950
Private comprehensive institution. Coed, suburban location. Undergraduate enrollment: 2,500.

Calendar: Semesters.

Degrees Offered: B.F.A., Art.

Curricular Emphasis: Art Department—concentration in Computer Art and Design with course listings that include Video Computer Imagery; Computer Design Software; Computer Graphics; Computer Graphics Techniques; Computer-Assisted Design; Graphic Design I and II; Advertising Design I and II; Illustration I and II.

Facilities/Equipment: Computer graphics lab with variety of systems and software.

Guide POV: Computer graphics training is given through a studio arts program which places emphasis on art and design; projects in both print and motion arts media.

MIAMI-DADE COMMUNITY COLLEGE
4800 NW 36 St., Miami, FL 33167
(305) 871-4377
State two-year institution. Coed, urban location. enrollment: 50,000.

Calendar: Semesters.

Degrees Offered: A.S., Film Production Technology; A.S., Radio/Television Broadcasting; A.A., Broadcasting.

Curricular Emphasis: Florida Center of Excellence in Film and Video—Film and video production; computer graphics; character animation; postproduction techniques.

Facilities/Equipment: Animation stand; complete film and video production and postproduction includes on-line control room with digital video effects; computer video graphics and special effects studio; IBM PS/2; Deluxe Paint II.

Guide POV: Enjoying new facilities, this rapidly growing two-year program provides affordable, comprehensive media training in both character and computer animation; certificate and transfer programs.

ORLANDO COLLEGE
5500 Diplomat Circle, Orlando, FL 32810
(407) 628-5870
Private two-year commuter institution. Coed, urban location. enrollment: 2,127.

Calendar: Quarters.

Degrees Offered: A.A.

Curricular Emphasis: Video Arts and Sciences—all aspects of video production with a concentration available in computer animation; courses cover two and three dimensional animation; composition; advanced graphics and state-of-the-art peripherals.

Facilities/Equipment: Complete video production and postproduction; computer graphics lab includes Amiga system.

Guide POV: With an emphasis on video technology and television production, this practical two-year program prepares students for employment in both broadcast and nonbroadcast industries; concentration in computer animation and computer-generated effects for video production.

RINGLING SCHOOL OF ART and DESIGN
Sarasota, FL 34234
(813) 351-4614
Private professional arts institution. Coed, urban location.

Calendar: Semesters.

Degrees Offered: B.F.A., Computer Animation.

Curricular Emphasis: Department of Computer Animation—course listings include Art History; Traditional Animation I and II; Figure Drawing; Creative Geometry; Color and Design; Computer Animation I-IV; Drawing Techniques; Concept Development; Video Production; Storyboarding Techniques; Scripting on UNIX Workstations; Special Topics in Computer Animation; Senior Project; Computer Animation Portfolio.

Facilities/Equipment: Computer classroom facilities include 11 Amiga 2000 and 7 Amiga 1200 computers; lab has video-grabbing device for video input and HP Paintjet color printer for image output; IBM PC lab equipped with 12 IBM PCs and 4 compatibles; the Power Mac lab has 24 seats of the Power 7100/66 computers; this lab is equipped with a flatbed scanner, a slide scanner, video grabbing capabilities, and two laser printers; the Silicon Graphics Indigo Lab houses the high-end computer animation hardware and software including 16 Silicon Graphics Indigo XC24 workstations and digital compositing and painting; variety of software; complete Video Production facility.

Guide POV: This well-equipped program offers a full major in computer animation with special emphasis on creatively working with motion and light within a simulated three-dimensional environment; strong emphasis on acquiring solid skills in traditional conceptual development and the use of drawing as a tool for communication; graduates are employed in areas of television advertising, entertainment and the special effects fields, as well as emerging areas such as medical imaging, courtroom recontructions, scientific and architectural visualizations, development of video games, and so on.

UNIVERSITY OF CENTRAL FLORIDA
4000 Central Florida Blvd., Orlando, FL 23816
(407) 823-2000
State comprehensive institution. Coed, urban location. Undergraduate enrollment: 21,000. Graduate enrollment: 3,000.

Calendar: Semesters.

Degrees Offered: B.A., Communication.

Curricular Emphasis: Motion Picture Division—students may select the animation track with sequential course listings in cel and computer animation; advanced workshops.

Facilities/Equipment: Complete facilities for both cel and computer animation; graphics lab includes PC; Amiga; Mac; SGIs; Alias; film and video equipment.

Guide POV: Complete production training is offered with state-of-the-art facilities in film, animation, television, and video; advanced studies in both cel and computer animation; some production access to major film studio facilities in area.

UNIVERSITY OF FLORIDA
Gainesville, FL 32611
(904) 392-3261
State comprehensive institution. Coed, urban location. Undergraduate enrollment: 30,000. Graduate enrollment: 5,000.

Calendar: Semesters.

Degrees Offered: B.S., M.S., Ph.D., Computer and Information Sciences; B.A., Film Studies; Ph.D., Cultural Studies.

Curricular Emphasis: Computer and Information Sciences—undergraduate and graduate programs offer courses in computer graphics and animation as well as computer simulation; graphics animation courses include modeling, rendering algorithms and animation techniques (keyframe, physically-based); simulation courses stress dynamical system model design and algorithms for serial and parallel execution of models; emphasis on role of simulation models in computer animation. Film Studies—interdisciplinary film major explores topics such as film history and theory; electronic arts; video as architecture; video as theory; visual and cognitive anthropology; social and cognitive psychology; photography; educational media; 16mm film production; varied electives including animation projects provide supplementary focus on media history, theory and criticism.

Facilities/Equipment: SVHS recorder; camera; laser range finder; Silicon Graphics workstations; Sun workstations with graphics cards; parallel machines (nCube2); animation stand; film and video production and post-production.

Guide POV: Students from the Computer and Information Sciences Department obtain positions in advanced research involving computer animation and simulation for employers such as Sega and Disney; in addition, the growing interdisciplinary film program encourages students to work in both film and video, exploring varied genres and pursuing independent projects in cel animation and experimental video.

UNIVERSITY OF MIAMI SCHOOL OF COMMUNICATION
Coral Gables, FL 33124
(305) 284-2265
Private comprehensive institution. Coed, suburban location.

Calendar: Semesters.

Degrees Offered: B.S., Motion Pictures or Video-Film; B.F.A., Communications; M.A., Film Studies; M.F.A., Motion Pictures (tracks in Production and Screenwriting).

Curricular Emphasis: The Motion Picture major offers tracks in producing, writing, business, or film studies; there is a Video-Film major with diverse curriculum; double major in College of Arts and Sciences required; most often selected second major is Theatre Arts; graduate programs in production, screenwriting, and critical studies.

Facilities/Equipment: Animation stand; complete film and video production and postproduction.

Guide POV: Motion Picture majors in this selective program are offered training in 16mm and 8mm film production as well as studies in film theory and history; separate major in Video-Film combines curricula from Motion Pictures and Broadcasting; elective studies in graphics and animated film.

UNIVERSITY OF SOUTH FLORIDA
4202 East Fowler Ave., Tampa, FL 33620-7720
(813) 974-2011
State comprehensive institution. Coed, urban location. Undergraduate enrollment: 32,000. Graduate enrollment: 9,000.

Calendar: Semesters.

Degrees Offered: B.A., M.A., M.F.A.

Curricular Emphasis: Art and Art Education Department—course listings include Introduction to Computer Images; Advanced Computer Images; Computer Animation; Computers for Visual Learning; Directed Study for Graduate Students; Projects.

Facilities/Equipment: Computer graphics lab includes Amigas; video digitizers; video editors; Lumena 8; SG 4D/70G (Alias).

Guide POV: Art students may pursue digital motion graphics at both the undergraduate and graduate levels; attention to experimental projects; computer animation for the creation of art; advanced instruction in cel, programmed and three-dimensional animation techniques.

Georgia

■■■■■■■■■■■■■■ ■ ■ ■ ■ ■ ■ ■ ■ ■

ATLANTA COLLEGE OF ART
1280 Peachtree St. N.E., Atlanta, GA 30309.
(404) 898-1164
Private professional arts institution. Coed, urban location. Undergraduate enrollment: 350.

Calendar: Semesters.

Degrees Offered: B.F.A., Electronic Arts (concentrations in Computer Graphics, Computer Art, and Video).

Curricular Emphasis: Electronic Arts—course listings include Computer Animation; Computer Illustration; Computer Portfolio Preparation; Mac II; Media Internship; Video Production I and II; 3-D Modeling; Experimental Sound I and II; Filmic Narrative; Electronic Cinematography; Non-Narrative Video; Film History.

Facilities/Equipment: Computer art studio with Amiga personal computers and Apple Macintosh systems; variety of software; video.

Guide POV: The electronic arts major at this fine arts college chooses a concentration in computer graphics, computer art, or video; variety of course listings allows students to explore a wide range of disciplines within the computer graphics field, including animation, 3-D modeling, 2-D paintbox systems; digital photography, desktop publishing, computer art, and video art.

AUGUSTA COLLEGE
2500 Walton Way, Augusta, GA 30910
(706) 737-1400
State comprehensive institution. Coed, urban location. Undergraduate enrollment: 4,600. Graduate enrollment: 400.

Calendar: Quarters.

Degrees Offered: B.A., Communications (concentration in Broadcasting/Film).

Curricular Emphasis: Electronic media theory and culture; film-audio-video production; corporate uses of media.

Facilities/Equipment: Complete film and video production and postproduction includes computer graphics palette.

Guide POV: Communication students at this commuter college are offered studies in broadcasting and video production, including computer-based special effects for television.

GEORGIA INSTITUTE OF TECHNOLOGY
Atlanta, GA 30332-0320
(404) 894-2000
State technological institution. Coed, urban location. Undergraduate enrollment: 9,000. Graduate enrollment: 3,500.

Calendar: Quarters.

Degrees Offered: B.S., M.S., Ph.D., Computer Science; B.S., M.S., Ph.D., Industrial and Systems Engineering.

Curricular Emphasis: College of Computing—course listings include Introduction to Computer Graphics; Computer Graphics; Fractal Geometry; Visualization Techniques; Human-Computer Interface; Visualization in Programming; User Interface Systems Design; Advanced Computer Graphics Techniques; Intelligent Robotics and Computer Vision; Projects. Industrial and Systems Engineering—special attention to effective use of interactive computer graphics.

Facilities/Equipment: Graphics, Visualization and Usability Center houses a variety of graphics and multimedia equipment, including high-performance systems from Silicon Graphics, Pixar, Sun, Digital, Apple, and Intel, as well as extensive video and audio facilities for recording and editing; Scientific Visualization Lab houses additional equipment from Digital, Silicon Graphics, and Sun.

Guide POV: Undergraduate and graduate computer science students may train for positions as computer graphics specialists in areas such as software and hardware engineering; systems and software design; special attention to advanced image synthesis, ray tracing, image warping, texture synthesis motion blur, and other advanced graphics topics; solid, diverse curriculum, modern graphics facilities; students may specialize in problem-solving in such areas as visualization in programming and user-interface systems design.

GEORGIA STATE UNIVERSITY
Atlanta, GA 30303-3085
(404) 651-2000
State comprehensive institution. Coed, urban location. Undergraduate enrollment: 23,000. Graduate enrollment: 7,000.

Calendar: Quarters.

Degrees Offered: B.A., Film and Video; M.A., Communication (concentration in Film and Video).

Curricular Emphasis: Film and television production.

Facilities/Equipment: Animation stand; computer graphics.

Guide POV: This state university offers students a full major in film and video with offerings in cel animation and computer-generated effects; expanding graduate program.

SAVANNAH COLLEGE OF ART AND DESIGN
342 Bull St., Savannah, GA 31401-3146
(912) 238-2400
Private comprehensive arts institution. Coed, urban location. Undergraduate enrollment: 1,700. Graduate enrollment: 300.

Calendar: Quarters.

Degrees Offered: B.F.A., M.F.A., Computer Art; Video Production.

Curricular Emphasis: Computer Art Major—computer animation focus with courses offered in electronic painting, 3-D modeling and animation, "C" programming, video production and postproduction, multimedia, and computer art history and aesthetics. Video Major—training in video art and production including music video, narrative, interactive, documentary and sound design.

Facilities/Equipment: Computer Art majors utilize eight computer graphics labs with Mac, Amiga, PC and Silicon Graphics workstations; single-frame controllers; video recording; traditional animation lab; students electing the Video major are equipped with a voice-over studio; video wall and gallery; digital audio system; Tascam MidiStudio; studio and field DAT recorder; video toasters with rendering stations; single-frame controllers; character generators; chromakey studio; Panther Dolly.

Guide POV: This quality-oriented fine arts college offers a full computer graphics program with a concentration in computer animation; undergraduate students work on storyboarding, scripting, and production of two- and three-dimensional computer animations, transferring their work to videotape with audio and special effects; graduate students continue to explore 3-D animation, write storylines, and design interactive programs from their own database of textual and visual information.

SOUTHERN COLLEGE OF TECHNOLOGY
1100 S. Marietta Pkwy., Marietta, GA 30060-2896
(404) 528-7406
State comprehensive institution. Coed, suburban location. Undergraduate enrollment: 3,500. Graduate enrollment: 350.

Calendar: Quarters.

Degrees Offered: B.S., M.S., Computer Science.

Curricular Emphasis: Computer Science Department—curriculum offers concentrations in Computer Graphics, Animation, Visualization, Multimedia, Virtual Reality, and Human Factors; course work covers a survey of display technologies, special architectures for support of graphics systems, algorithms and data structures for manipulation of graphical objects, and consideration of user interface design.

Facilities/Equipment: Multiple computer graphics labs with variety of systems and software that support multimedia.

Guide POV: Computer science students approach the study of the hardware and software of computer graphics systems from the programmer's perspective; there is an animation concentration; master's project for graduate students choosing professional focus; master's thesis for graduate students choosing research focus.

UNIVERSITY OF GEORGIA
Athens, GA 30602
(706) 542-3000
State comprehensive institution. Coed, small town location. Undergraduate enrollment: 22,000. Graduate enrollment: 6,000.

Calendar: Quarters.

Degrees Offered: A.B.J., M.A., M.M.C., Ph.D.

Curricular Emphasis: Audio-film-video production; interested students may pursue projects in character and computer animation.

Facilities/Equipment: Animation stand; computer graphics lab; complete film and video production and postproduction.

Guide POV: Chartered in 1785, this comprehensive land-grant institution offers a highly regarded communications program which focuses on broadcast journalism; computer animation training centers on special effects for video.

Hawaii

■■■■■■■■■■■■■■■■■■■ ■ ■ ■ ■ ■ ■ ■ ■ ■ ■

LEEWARD COMMUNITY COLLEGE
96-045 Ala Ike, Pearl City, HI 96782
(808) 455-0011
State two-year institution. Coed, suburban location. enrollment: 5,500.

Calendar: Semesters.

Degrees Offered: A.S., Television Production; Certificate of Achievement; Certificate of Completion, Vocational/Technical Division.

Curricular Emphasis: Electronic media theory and practical application covering numerous phases of television production, i.e., graphics; audio; lighting; directing; editing; engineering; camera operation; location production.

Facilities/Equipment: Complete television production and postproduction including full audio; computer graphics; digital effects; computerized lighting board; AVID nonlinear editing.

Guide POV: This two-year school offers a recently expanded production-oriented television program; modern techniques in computer graphics for television; practical training prepares students for immediate employment; 77 percent job placement rate in area of interest.

UNIVERSITY OF HAWAII AT MANOA
2530 Dole St., Honolulu, HI 96822
(808) 956-8975
State comprehensive institution. Coed, urban location. Undergraduate enrollment: 12,000. Graduate enrollment: 6,000.

Calendar: Semesters.

Degrees Offered: B.A., M.A., Communication; Ph.D., Communication and Information Services.

Curricular Emphasis: Electronic media theory and culture; audio-video production; media writing; new technologies; multimedia/computer-based production.

Facilities/Equipment: Computer graphics lab; complete television production and postproduction.

Guide POV: This is the major research institution in the University of Hawaii system; communication students learn all aspects of studio and remote production; graduate program focuses on communication research and emerging technologies.

Idaho

■■■■■■■■■■■■■■■■ ■ ■ ■ ■ ■ ■ ■ ■ ■ ■

ALBERTSON COLLEGE OF IDAHO
Caldwell, ID 83605
(208) 459-5011
Private comprehensive institution. Coed, small town location. Undergraduate enrollment: 600.

Calendar: Semesters.

Degrees Offered: B.A., Art; Minor in Computer Graphics.

Curricular Emphasis: The Computer Graphics program is directed by the Department of Art depending on the student's needs and leads to a minor in computer graphics.

Facilities/Equipment: Computer graphics lab with variety of systems and software.

Guide POV: This selective liberal arts college is the state's oldest four-year institution of higher learning; students choosing the minor in computer graphics must complete advanced project; curriculum includes exploration of digital animation techniques; attention to both art and business applications.

BOISE STATE UNIVERSITY
1910 University Dr., Boise, ID 83725
(208) 385-1011
State comprehensive institution. Coed, urban location. Undergraduate enrollment: 12,054. Graduate enrollment: 5,995.

Calendar: Semesters.

Degrees Offered: B.A., M.A.

Curricular Emphasis: Communication Department—electronic media theory and culture; video production.

Facilities/Equipment: Complete video production and postproduction includes video toaster.

Guide POV: This growing department, which has recently instituted an M.A. program, places a strong emphasis on critical understanding of media coupled with practical television production training; graphics instruction for the television special effects artist.

IDAHO STATE UNIVERSITY
741 South 7th Ave., Pocatello, ID 83209
(208) 236-0211
State comprehensive institution. Coed, urban location. Undergraduate enrollment: 6,000. Graduate enrollment: 1,000.

Calendar: Semesters.

Degrees Offered: B.A., Mass Communication (students may select emphasis in Television).

Curricular Emphasis: Mass Communication—television production including news broadcasting, corporate videos, graphic design, and media ethics.

Facilities/Equipment: Complete video production and postproduction includes computer graphics lab.

Guide POV: Idaho State University has recently completed new television studio facilities for its growing program; practical approach; students learn computer-based animation techniques for television broadcasting and corporate advertising.

UNIVERSITY OF IDAHO
Moscow, ID 83843-4199
(208) 885-6111
State comprehensive institution. Coed, rural location. Undergraduate enrollment: 7,000. Graduate enrollment: 2,000.

Calendar: Semesters.

Degrees Offered: B.A., B.S., Communication (students may select emphasis in Visual Communication).

Curricular Emphasis: Communication—television production; film history; advertising.

Facilities/Equipment: Complete video production and postproduction includes computer graphics software.

Guide POV: The School of Communication at this state university offers a full broadcast curriculum including technical training in computer-generated special effects for television.

Illinois

■■■■■■■■■■■■■■■■■■■ ■ ■ ■ ■ ■ ■ ■ ■

COLLEGE OF DuPAGE
22nd St. and Lambert Rd., Glen Ellyn, IL 60137-6599
(708) 858-2800
County two-year institution. Coed, suburban location. enrollment: 34,000.

Calendar: Semesters.

Degrees Offered: A.A.S.

Curricular Emphasis: Communication Arts and Sciences—Television production; multimedia production; 2-D and 3-D computer animation.

Facilities/Equipment: Computer graphics lab includes 2-D and 3-D computer animation software; video production and postproduction.

Guide POV: With an unusually diverse program for a two-year institution, this large college offers a communications program specializing in preparing students for employment in the fields of computer animation, video production, multimedia, and audio production.

COLUMBIA COLLEGE
600 S. Michigan Ave., Chicago, IL 60605-1996
(312) 663-1600
Private comprehensive institution. Coed, urban location. Undergraduate enrollment: 6,666. Graduate enrollment: 342.

Calendar: Semesters.

Degrees Offered: B.A., M.A., M.F.A., Film and Video.

Curricular Emphasis: Film/Video Program—concentration in animation; course listings include Animation I, II, and III; Film Techniques; Animation Storyboard and Concept Development; Animation Camera Seminar; Computer Animation; Drawing for Animation I and II; Stop-Motion Animation Techniques; 3-D Animation, and special projects. Computer Graphics Program—course listings include Computer Graphics and Video; Computer Graphics Experimental Imaging; Computer Graphics 3-D Modeling/Animation; Mac II: Motion Graphics.

Facilities/Equipment: Animation studio with three Oxberry cameras; motorized Mauer camera; Bolex reflex camera; complete film and video production and postproduction; computer graphics lab includes Amiga 1000s and 2000s; Mac IIs (NuVista); IBM AT clones (TARGA 16); Lumena 16; film recorder; camcorder; color printers; Liquid Light Imprint; video digitizer; Crystal 3-D; image capture system; Diaquest frame controller; Digi-View; HyperCard; PixelPaint; variety of other graphics systems and software.

Guide POV: Columbia College offers its students intensive, production-oriented film animation training through the Film/Video department; in addition, a full undergraduate major in computer graphics emphasizes state-of-the-art animation technology.

DePAUL UNIVERSITY

243 S. Wabash, Chicago, IL 60604
(312) 362-8000
Private comprehensive institution. Coed, urban location. Undergraduate
enrollment: 9,200. Graduate enrollment: 6,000.

Calendar: Quarters.

Degrees Offered: B.S., M.S., Ph.D., Computer Science.

Curricular Emphasis: Computer Science and Information Systems—under-
graduate and graduate course listings include Computer Graphics; Advanced
Computer Graphics; Foundations of Visual Computers; Advanced Graphics;
User Interfaces; Visualization; Topics in Computer Graphics; Projects.

Facilities/Equipment: Computer graphics lab with 386s/486s; various SGI
workstations; Harris; scanners; video output; variety of graphics software;
other systems.

Guide POV: Undergraduate and graduate studies in computer graphics are
offered to students with a solid background in mathematics at this commuter
university; advanced topics include visualization; user interfaces; software
design and programming; university goal is to provide computer literacy to
entire community.

LEWIS UNIVERSITY

Romeoville, IL 60441-2298
(815) 838-0500
Private comprehensive institution. Coed, suburban location. Undergraduate
enrollment: 3,650. Graduate enrollment: 800.

Calendar: Semesters.

Degrees Offered: B.A., Radio-TV Broadcasting; B.A., Communications/
Speech; B.A., Journalism.

Curricular Emphasis: Electronic Media Program—curriculum in television
production and graphic animation.

Facilities/Equipment: Complete broadcast production and postproduction
includes computer animation facilities; satellite; cable television; teleconfer-
encing; distance learning.

Guide POV: This competitive private university prepares students for careers
in network, cable, educational, and industrial production; students receive
thorough grounding in creating computer-generated effects.

NORTH CENTRAL COLLEGE

30 N. Brainard St., Naperville, IL 60563
(708) 420-3400
Private liberal arts institution. Coed, suburban location. Undergraduate
enrollment: 2,100.

Calendar: Quarters.

Degrees Offered: B.A., B.S., M.A., M.S.

Curricular Emphasis: Computer Science—undergraduate and graduate graphics curriculum geared to students interested in business and science applications; programming required; graphics algorithms; modeling and simulation; artificial intelligence; projects.

Facilities/Equipment: Computer center includes Sequent parallel computing environment running UNIX; 486-based PC's equipped with color monitors and super-VGA display interfaces.

Guide POV: This growing curriculum in computer graphics is geared to the student interested in graphics programming and design for scientific, business and engineering applications.

NORTHERN ILLINOIS UNIVERSITY
DeKalb, IL 60115-2857
(815) 753-1000
State comprehensive institution. Coed, rural location. Undergraduate enrollment: 20,000. Graduate enrollment: 5,000.

Calendar: Semesters.

Degrees Offered: B.F.A., B.A., M.A., M.F.A., Art.

Curricular Emphasis: Electronic Media—this option within the School of Art emphasizes the application of computer-generated imaging processes in motion graphics, graphic design, and desktop publishing; includes the synthesis of computerized electronic systems with other media such as sound and video; includes training in computer animation, commercial television graphics, and three-dimensional computer graphics. Intermedia Arts—this option within the School of Art emphasizes the creative use of time-based media as an art form, with courses in cinematography and video art.

Facilities/Equipment: Animation stand; computer graphics lab includes variety of animation software; film and video production and postproduction.

Guide POV: The innovative School of Art offers an Electronic Media concentration; curriculum exposes students to a variety of media environments with studies in how electronic media is affecting traditional graphic design, animation, multimedia, and both television and presentation graphics; diverse faculty with backgrounds in animation, photography, cinematography, video, computer graphics, graphic design, and the fine arts.

NORTHWESTERN UNIVERSITY
1801 Hinman St., Evanston, IL 60208
(708) 491-7271
Private comprehensive institution. Coed, suburban location. Undergraduate enrollment: 7,500. Graduate enrollment: 2,500.

Calendar: Quarters.

Degrees Offered: B.S., M.A., Ph.D., Radio/TV/Film; M.F.A., Writing; M.F.A., Production.

Curricular Emphasis: Strong emphasis on a blend of theory and practice; sequential course listings in computer animation.

Facilities/Equipment: Computer graphics facility includes Macintosh-based computer animation; 3-D computer animation (Silicon Graphics/Wavefront

Advanced Visualizer); film and video production and postproduction.

Guide POV: This selective school offers students a program which integrates film and television production training with liberal arts studies; advanced computer animation training for video projects.

SCHOOL OF THE ART INSTITUTE OF CHICAGO

37 S. Wabash Ave., Chicago, IL 60603-3103
(312) 899-5219
Private comprehensive arts institution. Coed, urban location. Undergraduate enrollment: 1,890. Graduate enrollment: 460.

Calendar: Semesters.

Degrees Offered: B.F.A., M.F.A., B.A., M.A.

Curricular Emphasis: Filmmaking—independent film production with several animation courses, including Animation; Drawing for Animation; 2-D Computer Animation. Art and Technology—course listings include Experimental Computer Imaging; Advanced Computer Imaging; Computer Graphics Programming; 2-D and 3-D Computer Animation; Interactive Media; Kinetics; Holography. Video—students explore image manipulation; multichannel installations; experimental narrative, and documentary forms while developing personal style.

Facilities/Equipment: Oxberry animation stand; Oxberry 1500 optical printer; video synthesis systems; sound studio; complete film and video production and postproduction includes color special effects generator; character generator; specially designed equipment to support electronic experimentation; computer graphics lab includes Macintosh II computers; Amiga 2000 computers; IBM and compatible computers with Lumena software; Silicon Graphics personal Iris computers with Alias software; various animation software; video digitizers; color scanners; color printers; film recorders; video recording equipment; keyboard and MIDI interfaces; holography studios; electronics workshop for building computer-controlled kinetic sculptures and interactive installations.

Guide POV: The School of the Art Institute is a studio fine arts institution offering comprehensive studies in cel animation, documentary and experimental film/video production; in addition, there are quality studies in computer programming for animation, image processing, and for the development of synthetic realities and virtual environments; encouragement of multidisciplinary arts interaction; exploration of new technologies; visiting video artists; innovative interdisciplinary Time Arts Program promotes studies in art and technology and blends studies in computer-aided art and design, video, sound, lasers, filmmaking, electronics/kinetics, and performance.

SOUTHERN ILLINOIS UNIVERSITY AT CARBONDALE

Carbondale, IL 62901
(618) 453-2121
State comprehensive institution. Coed, rural location. Undergraduate enrollment: 20,000. Graduate enrollment: 4,000.

Calendar: Semesters.

Degrees Offered: B.A., M.F.A., Cinema and Photography; B.A., Radio and Television; M.A., Telecommunications.

Curricular Emphasis: Department of Cinema and Photography—film and photography production. Department of Radio-Television—corporate video; television production; new technologies; meteorology.

Facilities/Equipment: Animation stand; computer graphics lab; film and video production and postproduction.

Guide POV: Southern Illinois University offers separate production majors for those choosing to work in film or television; both departments are well-equipped and provide comprehensive training; studies in cel animation and computer-generated special effects for video.

UNIVERSITY OF CHICAGO
Chicago, IL 60637
(312) 702-1234
Private comprehensive institution. Coed, urban location. Undergraduate enrollment: 3,550. Graduate enrollment: 8,200.

Calendar: Semesters.

Degrees Offered: B.A., M.S., Ph.D., Computer Science.

Curricular Emphasis: Computer Science—variety of course listings at all levels for students with serious interest in computer graphics research.

Facilities/Equipment: Computer graphics facility includes two Sun microcomputers; Silicon Graphics 4-D/240 minicomputer supplemented with eight Silicon Graphics Indy Workstations and a Silicon Graphics PowerChallenge XL Super Computer; variety of other systems and software.

Guide POV: Students in this highly selective program conduct advanced computer graphics research.

UNIVERSITY OF ILLINOIS AT CHICAGO
750 S. Halstead, Chicago, IL 60607
(312) 996-7000
State comprehensive institution. Coed, urban location. Undergraduate enrollment: 25,000. Graduate enrollment: 8,000.

Calendar: Semesters.

Degrees Offered: B.F.A., M.F.A., Art (concentrations in Film/Animation/Video, Electronic Visualization, Graphic Design, Photography, Studio Arts); B.S., M.S., Ph.D., Computer Engineering.

Curricular Emphasis: Photography, Film, and Electronic Media—Animated, experimental and narrative projects may incorporate cel and computer animation techniques; graphic design program stresses graphics programming, interactive software design and advanced film/video animation. Electrical Engineering and Computer Science Department—the Electronic Visualization Laboratory conducts graduate research with courses that include Computer Graphics I and II; Computer Animation; Computer Vision I and II; Human-Computer Interaction; Projects.

Facilities/Equipment: Film and video production and postproduction includes switcher/special effects generator; Oxberry animation stand; computer animation facility; Electronic Visualization Lab; computer graphics facility includes AT&T 6300s (Targa); Mac IIs; AT&T Pixel machines; Iris 3130; Hewlett-Packard; Vista; video output; CRAY access; Alias; variety of other systems and software.

Guide POV: Students in the selective, lively fine arts program explore the social, cultural, and ideological possibilities of film and electronic media including cel animation, electronic visualization and computer graphics; concentration in graphic design utilizes contemporary technology in film, video, print, and digital computers; multimedia projects; diverse curriculum; in addition, the highly-ranked, well-equipped Electrical Engineering and Computer Science Department conducts advanced graduate research in computer animation, computer vision, and related areas of interest to the graphics specialist.

UNIVERSITY OF ILLINOIS AT URBANA-CHAMPAIGN
Urbana, IL 61801
(217) 333-0302
State comprehensive institution. Coed, rural location. Undergraduate enrollment: 26,000. Graduate enrollment: 8,800.

Calendar: Semesters.

Degrees Offered: B.S., M.S., M.C.S., Ph.D., Computer Science; B.S., M.S., Journalism; B.A., Art (students may select emphasis in Cinematography-Production).

Curricular Emphasis: Computer Science—students may specialize in advanced computer graphics research and design; department houses Artificial Intelligence and Graphics Laboratory. Film—studies in cinematography through Art Department. Television—broadcast journalism sequence.

Facilities/Equipment: Animation stand; computerized optical printing and SFX lab; video transfers; switcher/special effects generator; Amiga desktop video system; state-of-the-art computer facilities includes NeXT; Encore Multimaxes; Intel Hypercubes; many sophisticated graphics workstations including IBM R/S 6000; Hewlett-Packard; Silicon Graphics; film recorder; Versatec; HP plotters; color printer; Thinking Machine CMO-2; supercomputers; film and video production and postproduction.

Guide POV: This state university has one of the top-ranked computer science departments in the country; advanced research in areas of artificial intelligence, visual programming environments, scientific visualization, real-time computing systems, etc; the Art Department offers comprehensive studies in the craft of cinematography including cel animation; the Journalism Department offers a television program that emphasizes public affairs journalism and includes training for the television/video special effects artist.

WESTERN ILLINOIS UNIVERSITY

Macomb, IL 61455

(309) 295-1414

State comprehensive institution. Coed, rural location. Undergraduate enrollment: 10,000. Graduate enrollment: 2,300.

Calendar: Semesters.

Degrees Offered: Interdisciplinary Minor in Film.

Curricular Emphasis: College of Arts and Sciences, Education, and Fine Arts—independent film production; animation.

Facilities/Equipment: Animation stand; film and video production and post-production.

Guide POV: The lively interdisciplinary film program at this university emphasizes criticism, alternative cinema, and animation production.

Indiana

■■■■■■■■■■■■■■■■■■■■■ ■ ■ ■ ■ ■ ■ ■ ■

ANDERSON UNIVERSITY
1100 East 5th St., Anderson, IN 46012
(317) 649-9071
Private comprehensive institution. Coed, urban location. Undergraduate enrollment: 1,800.

Calendar: Semesters.

Degrees Offered: B.S., M.S., Computer Science; B.A., Mass Communication (students may select emphasis in Broadcasting).

Curricular Emphasis: Computer Science Deparment—training in computer animation includes advanced studies in raster graphics and video graphics techniques; image rendering and shading techniques. Radio, Television and Film Department—Covenant Productions, the university teleproduction facility, produces family and religious centered programming for a national market.

Facilities/Equipment: Complete video and television production and postproduction including Grass Valley switcher; Chyron Superscribe character generator; 24-channel audio board; Pinnacle Prizm; computer graphics lab.

Guide POV: This private college, affiliated with the Church of God, offers a professional television production program that stresses religious programming; university-run art and animation company affiliated with student co-op program.

BALL STATE UNIVERSITY
Muncie, IN 47306
(317) 289-1241
State comprehensive institution. Coed, small city location. Undergraduate enrollment: 18,000. Graduate enrollment: 2,000.

Calendar: Semesters.

Degrees Offered: B.A., Telecommunications.

Curricular Emphasis: Broadcast and nonbroadcast video graphics; media writing; television production; Super-8 film production; instructional video.

Facilities/Equipment: Computer graphics lab with variety of workstations; complete television and video production and postproduction.

Guide POV: Students majoring in telecommunications choose from a variety of production-oriented courses in television, film, and corporate video; modern expanded production facilities with computer graphics animation lab; additional course work through Computer Science Department stresses software development.

INDIANA UNIVERSITY

Bloomington, IN 47405

(812) 855-4848

State comprehensive institution. Coed, small city location. Undergraduate enrollment: 25,000. Graduate enrollment: 7,500.

Calendar: Semesters.

Degrees Offered: B.A., Comparative Literature (students may select emphasis in Film); Ph.D. Minor in Film Studies; B.A., Telecommunications; M.S., Media Management; M.A., Ph.D., Mass Communications.

Curricular Emphasis: Film students may elect basic training in cel animation; telecommunications students may train in aspects of computer animation for video and television; electronic communications research.

Facilities/Equipment: Animation stand; film and video production and post-production; video translators; interactive media equipment; computer-assisted laser disk video; computer graphics lab.

Guide POV: The Film Studies Program offered through the Comparative Literature Department focuses on film history, theory, and criticism while providing students with 16mm production experience, including cel animation; separate concentration in Electronic Media Production prepares students for careers in broadcast television or corporate video production and includes training in digital effects.

INDIANA UNIVERSITY AT INDIANAPOLIS

Indianapolis, IN 46202

(317) 274-5555

State comprehensive institution. Coed, urban location. Undergraduate enrollment: 26,000.

Calendar: Semesters.

Degrees Offered: B.A., Telecommunications.

Curricular Emphasis: Media production including training in video, audio, computer graphics, sync slide tape.

Facilities/Equipment: Complete video production and postproduction; computer graphics lab includes TARGA system.

Guide POV: This telecommunications major emphases new technologies; hands-on video production training; instruction for the television special effects artist.

PURDUE UNIVERSITY

West Lafayette, IN 47907

(317) 494-4600

State comprehensive institution. Coed, suburban location. Undergraduate enrollment: 30,000. Graduate enrollment: 6,000.

Calendar: Semesters.

Degrees Offered: B.F.A., B.A., B.S.

Curricular Emphasis: Creative Arts—course listings in Art and Design include Computer Graphics; special projects.

Facilities/Equipment: Complete video production and postproduction; computer graphics lab includes IBM PC/XT clones; Mac SEs and Plus Zenith 286; plotters; videoworks; Suns; IBM PC/AT clones.

Guide POV: Computer graphics training with an emphasis on design and illustration is offered through the Creative Arts Program; in addition, the Communication Department offers graphics training for broadcast technicians.

PURDUE UNIVERSITY CALUMET
Hammond, IN 46323-2094
(219) 989-2993
State comprehensive institution. Coed, urban location. Undergraduate enrollment: 8,500. Graduate enrollment: 1,000.

Calendar: Semesters.

Degrees Offered: B.A., Radio-Television; M.A., Telecommunications; B.S., Information Systems and Computer Programming.

Curricular Emphasis: Communication and Creative Arts Department—broadcast production; broadcast management; computer graphics for television/video; telecommunications. Information Systems and Computer Programming—course listings include Computer Graphics; Projects.

Facilities/Equipment: Complete television and video production and postproduction; computer graphics lab.

Guide POV: This commuter university offers the computer science major studies and projects in computer graphics; in addition, television production students create computer-generated effects for programming.

ROSE-HULMAN INSTITUTE OF TECHNOLOGY
Terre Haute, IN 47803-3999
(812) 877-1511
Private professional institution. Suburban location. Undergraduate enrollment: 1,300. Graduate enrollment: 95.

Calendar: Quarters.

Degrees Offered: B.S., Computer Science.

Curricular Emphasis: Computer Science Department—course listings include Computer Graphics; Advanced Computer Graphics; Fractals; Projects.

Facilities/Equipment: Computer graphics lab with variety of systems and software including Suns; Silicon Graphics; Indigo 2 Workstations; color NeXT workstations; color printers and scanner.

Guide POV: This private university offers specialized computer graphics training for the student with a strong background in mathematics and physics.

UNIVERSITY OF NOTRE DAME

Notre Dame, IN 46556

(219) 631-5000

Private comprehensive institution. Coed, urban location. Undergraduate enrollment: 7,000. Graduate enrollment: 3,000.

Calendar: Semesters.

Degrees Offered: B.A., B.F.A., Art. B.S., Computer Science and Engineering. B.A., Communication and Theatre.

Curricular Emphasis: Art, Art History and Design Department—concentrations in photography and design, among other areas; course listings include Digital Imagemaking; 3-D Digital Design; Digital Studios I and II; Digital Photography; Computer Science and Engineering Department—course listings include Computer Graphics; Computer System Design; Computer Simulation; Computer Hardware Design; Microcomputers; Sustems Programming; other areas.

Facilities/Equipment: Computer graphics labs with variety of systems and software; complete film, video and television production and postproduction.

Guide POV: Founded in 1842, this private university offers the art major a concentratiuon in graphic, product, and digital design; digital studies focus on mastering new technologies in order to serve and liberate creative process and help define new vidual vocabulary; in addition, the computer science major may pursue advanced studies in computer graphics, computer simulation, and computer systems design; finally, the Communication and Theatre Program blends critical media studies with intensive production activity; concentration in film/video; exploration of both traditional and experimental forms.

UNIVERSITY OF SOUTHERN INDIANA

8600 University Blvd., Evansville IN 47712

(812) 465-7079

State four-year comprehensive institution. Coed, suburban location. Undergraduate enrollment: 5,200.

Calendar: Semesters.

Degrees Offered: B.A., B.S., Art (emphasis in Graphic Design); B.A., B.S., Communications.

Curricular Emphasis: Art Department—sequential basic training in graphic design. Communications Department—students with an emphasis in advertising may elect courses in graphic design in conjunction with the Art Department.

Facilities/Equipment: Computer graphics lab with Macintosh computers; color monitors; variety of software; complete film and television production and postproduction.

Guide POV: An expanding graphics program at this affordable state university is available to majors in both art and communications.

Iowa

■■■■■■■■■■■■■■■■ ■ ■ ■ ■ ■ ■ ■ ■

IOWA STATE UNIVERSITY

Ames, IA 50011-2090

(515) 294-4111

State comprehensive institution. Coed, rural location. Undergraduate enrollment: 21,500. Graduate enrollment: 4,000.

Calendar: Semesters.

Degrees Offered: B.F.A., B.A., B.S.

Curricular Emphasis: Journalism and Mass Communication—electronic media studies; broadcast journalism; basic cel and computer animation. Art and Design—graphic design option stresses print as well as audio-visual media.

Facilities/Equipment: Animation stand; computer graphics lab; complete film and television production and postproduction.

Guide POV: The production-oriented Communication Department offers intensive television broadcasting experience along with formal media studies; basic cel animation studies offered as well as computer graphics animation for television; in addition, there is a program in graphic design offered through the School of Art and Design.

MOUNT MERCY COLLEGE

1330 Elmhurst Dr. NE, Cedar Rapids, IA 52402-4798

(319) 363-8213

Private comprehensive institution. Coed, urban location. Undergraduate enrollment: 1,000.

Calendar: Semesters.

Degrees Offered: B.A., Art.

Curricular Emphasis: Art Department—curriculum in computer graphics blends aesthetics with technical instruction.

Facilities/Equipment: Computer graphics lab includes 386s; Apple Macintosh; scanners.

Guide POV: The Art Department offers specialized training in microcomputer graphics with an emphasis on design and illustration applications.

TEIKYO MARYCREST UNIVERSITY

1607 W. 12th St., Davenport, IA 52804

(319) 326-9532

Private comprehensive institution. Coed, small city location. Undergraduate enrollment: 800.

Calendar: Semesters.

Degrees Offered: B.A.

Curricular Emphasis: Department of Art and Computer Graphics—course listings include 2-D Animation; Readings in Computer Graphics; Art and Computers-Introduction; Computer Paint Systems; Principles in 3-D Animation; Advanced Issues in 3-D Animation; Multimedia I, II, III; Seminar in Computer Graphics; Senior Thesis in Computer Graphics; Network Principles; UNIX; Digital Photography; Seminar and Special Projects; in addition, students attend several major conferences per year including SIGGRAPH, Software USA (Chicago), and Virtual Reality.

Facilities/Equipment: Computer graphics lab hardware includes DX2 486-66s; SGI Indigo; laser and color ink jet output; 24 bit video and scanner input; software includes 3-D Studio; Animator Pro; Topas; RIO; Personal Animation Recorder; VREAM; TIPS; lab open 24 hours per day.

Guide POV: This well-rated, innovative program, the first to offer an integrated undergraduate computer graphics degree, trains students in both print and motion graphics for careers in animation studios, video production houses, and television studios, as well as in advertising and publishing; incorporation of 3-D animation; paint systems; computer-aided design (CAD); presentation graphics, and desktop publishing.

UNIVERSITY OF IOWA

Iowa City, IA 52242

(319) 335-3500

State comprehensive institution. Coed, urban location. Undergraduate enrollment: 19,110. Graduate enrollment: 8,935.

Calendar: Semesters.

Degrees Offered: B.A., Broadcasting and Film; M.A., Film Studies, Media/Broadcast Studies, Production Studies; Ph.D., Film Studies, Broadcasting Studies.

Curricular Emphasis: Comprehensive film and television criticism and production including animation and video art.

Facilities/Equipment: Animation stand; complete film and video production and postproduction; computer graphics lab.

Guide POV: Founded in 1847, this public university offers a comprehensive film and electronic media curriculum that includes animation projects.

UNIVERSITY OF NORTHERN IOWA

Cedar Falls, IA 50614-0139

(319) 273-2311

State comprehensive institution. Coed, small city location. Undergraduate enrollment: 11,500. Graduate enrollment: 2,000.

Calendar: Semesters.

Degrees Offered: B.A., Broadcasting.

Curricular Emphasis: Electronic media theory and culture; television production.

Facilities/Equipment: Complete television production and postproduction; computer graphics lab includes three Amiga stations.

Guide POV: Communication students may undertake computer graphics training within the context of a full telecommunications major; computer graphics training geared to designing titles and news graphics for television.

Kansas

■■■■■■■■■■■■■■■■■■ ■ ■ ■ ■ ■ ■ ■ ■ ■

FORT HAYS STATE UNIVERSITY
600 Park St., Hays, KS 67601-4099
(913) 628-4000
State comprehensive institution. Coed, small town location.

Calendar: Semesters.

Degrees Offered: B.A., M.S., Communication. B.F.A., M.F.A., Art.

Curricular Emphasis: Mass Communication Department—television production, including graphics techniques for video and television; there are two courses in cinematography. Art Department—a course entitled Computer-Assisted Graphics Design explores the use of the computer as an artistic tool.

Facilities/Equipment: Television production and postproduction includes Amiga computer graphics; Chyron VP-1 Titles; interactive television facilities.

Guide POV: This state university offers hands-on broadcast and nonbroadcast training; students produce for a variety of network and cable outlets; emphasis on new technologies.

SOUTHWESTERN COLLEGE
100 College St., Winfield, KS 67156-2443
(316) 221-4150
Private comprehensive institution. Coed, small city location. Undergraduate enrollment: 550. Graduate enrollment: 43.

Calendar: Semesters.

Degrees Offered: B.A., Mass Communications and Film Studies.

Curricular Emphasis: Video production (short fiction/films); video art; television studio and field work; corporate video production; critical studies in film (analysis and criticism).

Facilities/Equipment: Complete video and television production and postproduction includes graphics lab.

Guide POV: This small college offers an innovative media program presenting students with the opportunity to explore the possibilities of dramatic storytelling in video as well as to train intensively in traditional broadcasting techniques.

UNIVERSITY OF KANSAS
Lawrence, KS 66045
(913) 864-2700
State comprehensive institution. Coed, suburban location. Undergraduate enrollment: 26,000. Graduate enrollment: 4,000.

Calendar: Semesters.

Degrees Offered: Film—B.A., B.G.S., Film; B.A., B.G.S., Theatre and Film; M.A., Film; Ph.D., Theatre and Film. Television—B.S., M.S., Journalism.

Curricular Emphasis: Department of Theatre and Film—Basic to advanced 16mm production; film animation; VHS video production. School of Journalism—Broadcast news production and management; computer graphics for broadcasting.

Facilities/Equipment: Oldfather Studios houses animation, film and video production and postproduction equipment; broadcast students have access to full television and video production and postproduction equipment including switcher/special effects generators.

Guide POV: This public university offers separate, comprehensive degree programs in film and television; nonbroadcast/independent video production offered through Department of Theatre and Film; film students may undertake various animation projects; broadcast students study computer animation techniques for television; additional training in computer graphics through the Art Department.

Kentucky

■■■■■■■■■■■■■■■■■■■■ ■ ■ ■ ■ ■ ■ ■

ASBURY COLLEGE
Lexington Ave., Wilmore, KY 40390-1198
(606) 858-3511
Private comprehensive institution. Coed, rural location. Undergraduate enrollment: 1,100.

Calendar: Semesters.

Degrees Offered: B.A., Broadcast Communications (students may select emphasis in Radio/Television/Film).

Curricular Emphasis: Media management; performance; radio and television production; film studies.

Facilities/Equipment: Basic film equipment and complete television production and postproduction.

Guide POV: Asbury College is a private liberal arts that emphasizes Christian orthodoxy; small media program offers sequential television production studies with additional training in cel and computer animation techniques.

UNIVERSITY OF KENTUCKY
Funkhouser Building, Lexington, KY 40506-0054
(606) 257-9000
State comprehensive institution. Coed, suburban location. Undergraduate enrollment: 15,500.

Calendar: Semesters.

Degrees Offered: B.A., B.S., M.S., Ph.D., Computer Science.

Curricular Emphasis: Course listings include Computer Graphics; Artificial Intelligence; Algorithm Design; Geometric Modeling; Computer Vision; Image Processing; Advanced Graph Algorithms; Systems Software; other topics.

Facilities/Equipment: Modern computer graphics facilities with variety of systems and software.

Guide POV: This selective program trains computer scientists from the undergraduate to doctorate level; advanced research in computer graphics; vision; artificial intelligence.

UNIVERSITY OF LOUISVILLE
Louisville, KY 40292
(502) 588-5555
State comprehensive institution. Coed, suburban location. Undergraduate enrollment: 12,500. Graduate enrollment: 3,500.

Calendar: Semesters.

Degrees Offered: B.S., M.S., Engineering Mathematics and Computer Science; M.S., Applied Mathematics; Ph.D., Computer Science and Engineering.

Curricular Emphasis: Engineering Mathematics and Computer Science Department—course listings include Computer Graphics; Image Processing and Pattern Recognition; Computer Vision; Stochastic Processes; Advanced Simulation; Advanced Experimental Design in Engineering.

Facilities/Equipment: Modern computer graphics facilities with variety of systems and software.

Guide POV: This program offers a highly diverse curriculum with special attention to graphics hardware and interactive engineering graphics techniques; topics include graphic object representation and transformation; three-dimensional graphics; long-term advanced projects.

WESTERN KENTUCKY UNIVERSITY
1 Big Red Way, Bowling Green, KY 42101
(502) 745-3296
State comprehensive institution. Coed, rural location. Undergraduate enrollment: 15,000.

Calendar: Semesters.

Degrees Offered: B.A., Broadcasting, Mass Communication; M.A., Communications.

Curricular Emphasis: Film, video, radio and television production including computer graphics and electronic art; critical studies; script writing; broadcast and nonbroadcast production; broadcast news.

Facilities/Equipment: Animation stand; 16mm film cameras; two television studios; 12 remote production packs; four edit bays; 12 Amigas; three Video Toasters, one with Video Flyer; FM radio station with two production rooms and news room.

Guide POV: Featuring a wide range of course listings in film, video, and audio production, this department offers professional degree studies that include film and computer animation, film production for television, broadcast news, video producing, directing, and postproduction; professional facilities and equipment exclusively for student use.

Louisiana
■■■■■■■■■■■■■■■■■■■ ■ ■ ■ ■ ■ ■

LOUISIANA STATE UNIVERSITY
Baton Rouge, LA 70803
(504) 388-3202
State comprehensive multicampus institution. Coed, urban location. Undergraduate enrollment: 17,200.

Calendar: Semesters.

Degrees Offered: B.F.A., M.F.A., Art.

Curricular Emphasis: Art Department—course listings include Computer Art I and II; Three-Dimensional Design; Advanced Computer Art I and II; Graduate Seminar: Three-Dimensional Art.

Facilities/Equipment: Computer graphics lab with variety of systems and software.

Guide POV: This well-regarded research university offers art students an opportunity to pursue advanced studies in computer art; in addition, undergraduate and graduate studies in computer graphics are offered through both the Computer Science and the Mechanical Engineering Departments, with an emphasis on interactive computer graphics and computer-aided geometric modeling.

LOUISIANA TECH UNIVERSITY
Ruston, LA 71272
(318) 257-0211
State comprehensive institution. Coed, small town location. Undergraduate enrollment: 6,500. Graduate enrollment: 1,900.

Calendar: Quarters

Degrees Offered: B.S., Computer Science.

Curricular Emphasis: Computer Science Department—course listings include Computer Graphics; Advanced Topics in Computer Graphics; Artificial Intelligence I and II; Applied Computing Project; Systems Design; Special Problems; other areas.

Facilities/Equipment: Computer graphics lab with variety of systems and software.

Guide POV: The computer science curriculum concentrates on algorithm design, programming techniques and state-of-the-art concepts in computer systems; advanced topics in computer graphics include reflection models, shading techniques, ray tracing, texture and animation.

NICHOLLS STATE UNIVERSITY
906 E. First St., Thibodaux, LA 70310
(504) 446-8111
State comprehensive institution. Coed, rural location. Undergraduate enrollment: 7,000.

Calendar: Semesters.

Degrees Offered: B.F.A., Art. B.A., Mass Communication.

Curricular Emphasis: Art Department—courses include Graphic Design I, II, III, and IV, which treat various problems in computer graphics. Mass Communication Department—training in television/video production.

Facilities/Equipment: Complete television production and postproduction including computer graphics; 16mm editing equipment and projectors; computer graphics lab for art students with variety of software.

Guide POV: Nicholls State University offers art students thorough computer graphics training with an emphasis on design; development of portfolio; broadcast students learn computer graphics design for television.

NORTHEAST LOUISIANA UNIVERSITY
Monroe, LA 71209
(318) 342-1419
State comprehensive institution. Coed, small city location. Undergraduate enrollment: 11,500. Graduate enrollment: 700.

Calendar: Semesters.

Degrees Offered: B.A., Radio/TV/Film (with emphasis in radio, television, and film production, management, or broadcast news); M.A., Communications (students may select emphasis in Radio/TV/Film).

Curricular Emphasis: Blend of theory and training in radio, television and film production; specializations in management, production, and broadcast news; video and film advertising assignments accepted from outside clients.

Facilities/Equipment: Complete audio, video and film production and postproduction including Video Toaster.

Guide POV: Northeast Louisiana University offers comprehensive training in radio, television, and film production; students choose area of specialization; training in computer graphics centers on video art as well as television special effects and titling.

XAVIER UNIVERSITY OF LOUISIANA
7325 Palmetto St., New Orleans, LA 70125
(504) 486-7411
Private comprehensive institution. Coed, urban location. Undergraduate enrollment: 2,700. Graduate enrollment: 500.

Calendar: Semesters.

Degrees Offered: B.A., Mass Communications.

Curricular Emphasis: Electronic media theory and culture; television/video production; video art.

Facilities/Equipment: Video and television production and postproduction includes computer graphics lab.

Guide POV: This small private university offers television and video production training within a liberal arts curriculum; projects in television production and video art; students work on a variety of productions that air locally.

Maine

■■■■■■■■■■■■■■■■■■■ ■ ■ ■ ■ ■ ■ ■ ■ ■

NEW ENGLAND SCHOOL OF BROADCASTING
One College Circle, Bangor, ME 04401
(207) 947-6083
Private two-year institution. Coed, suburban location. enrollment: 125.

Calendar: Semesters.

Degrees Offered: A.S., Broadcast Communications; certificates.

Curricular Emphasis: Television production.

Facilities/Equipment: Television production and postproduction including special effects generator.

Guide POV: Located on the campus of Husson College, this two-year institution was established in 1981 to train students for technical positions in the field of broadcasting, including computer-generated designs and special effects.

UNIVERSITY OF MAINE
Orono, ME 04469
(207) 581-1110
State comprehensive institution. Coed, small town location. Undergraduate enrollment: 11,000. Graduate—2,000.

Calendar: Semesters.

Degrees Offered: B.A., B.S., Computer Science.

Curricular Emphasis: Computer Science Department—course listings include Interactive Computer Graphics I and II; Advanced Computer Graphics; Projects.

Facilities/Equipment: Computer graphics lab includes IBM RTs; Suns; plotter; other systems and software.

Guide POV: Undergraduates at this state university pursue special projects in the area of interactive computer graphics through a broadly-designed, solid Computer Science curriculum.

Maryland

ANNE ARUNDEL COMMUNITY COLLEGE
101 College Pkwy., Arnold, MD 21012
(410) 647-7100
County two-year institution. Coed, suburban location. enrollment: 7,000.

Calendar: Semesters.

Degrees Offered: A.A., Communication Arts Technology; Certificate in Video Production.

Curricular Emphasis: Technical aspects of media production for cel and computer animation artists.

Facilities/Equipment: Animation stand; basic film and video production and postproduction.

Guide POV: This two-year college offers a varied curriculum with practical technical degrees in animation, graphics, production, and management.

FREDERICK COMMUNITY COLLEGE
7932 Opossumtown Pike, Frederick, MD 21702
(301) 846-2400
County two-year institution. Coed, suburban location. enrollment: 12,000.

Calendar: Semesters.

Degrees Offered: A.A., Communications.

Curricular Emphasis: Communications—course listings include Computer Graphics and Design; Communications Graphics I and II; Video Production; Intermediate Video Production; Publications Design.

Facilities/Equipment: Computer graphics lab with Macs; Pagemaker; Superpaint; Mac 3-D; video production and postproduction including time code editing.

Guide POV: This two-year college offers students an opportunity to solve design application problems using word processing, drawing, painting, and desktop publishing software packages; students produce graphic media for video, printed media, and slides; video production projects.

GOUCHER COLLEGE
1021 Dulaney Valley Rd., Baltimore, MD 21204-2794
(410) 337-6000
Private liberal arts institution. Coed, suburban location. Undergraduate enrollment: 1,100.

Calendar: Semesters.

Degrees Offered: B.A., Communication; B.A., Mathematics and Computer Science.

Curricular Emphasis: Communication Department—audio-video production includes limited computer video projects.

Facilities/Equipment: Computer video laboratory; video and television production and postproduction.

Guide POV: Formerly a women's college but coeducational since 1986, this private institution includes in its curriculum training in video and television production through its communication major; Mathematics and Computer Science Department also offers instruction on mathematical elements as they relate to computer graphics; cross-registration available at Johns Hopkins and other area colleges.

HOOD COLLEGE
Frederick, MD 21701
(301) 696-3606
Private comprehensive institution. Coed, small city location. Undergraduate enrollment: 1,000. Graduate enrollment: 900.

Calendar: Semesters.

Degrees Offered: B.A., Communication Arts.

Curricular Emphasis: Communication Arts—course listings include Graphics I and II; Computer Art.

Facilities/Equipment: Complete video 3/4" studio and location; computer graphics lab.

Guide POV: Hood College offers its students an individualized course of studies in film and video production; projects include video art, fiction, documentary, experimental, and news; additional courses in computer graphics through the Art and Computer Science departments.

JOHNS HOPKINS UNIVERSITY
3400 N. Charles St., Baltimore, MD 21218
(410) 516-8000
Private comprehensive institution. Coed, urban location. Undergraduate enrollment: 3,000. Graduate enrollment: 1,500.

Calendar: Semesters.

Degrees Offered: B.A., B.S., M.S.E., Ph.D.

Curricular Emphasis: Computer Science—course listings include Computer Graphics; Computer Vision; Computational Geometry; Advanced Computer Graphics; graduate seminar in computer graphics covers such subjects as animation techniques, color theory, graphics languages, graphics hardware, fractals, ray-tracing, anti-aliasing, modeling, hidden-surface removal, and shading models.

Facilities/Equipment: Computer center includes state-of-the-art hardware and software, including graphics.

Guide POV: This most selective university offers a computer science program stressing computer graphics in terms of engineering and programming; strong emphasis on new technologies; current research conducted in computer vision, computational geometry, computer graphics, robotics, artificial intelligence, and other areas; in addition, the art program offers a course in cartooning; study abroad at Johns Hopkins in Bologna, Italy.

MARYLAND INSTITUTE COLLEGE OF ART
1300 W. Mount Royal Ave., Baltimore, MD 21217-9986
(410) 669-9200
Private professional arts college. Coed, urban location. Undergraduate enrollment: 850. Graduate enrollment: 80.

Calendar: Semesters.

Degrees Offered: B.F.A., M.F.A.

Curricular Emphasis: Visual Communication—course listings include Advanced Computer Graphics; Hypermedia Computer; Imaging for Television; Drawing for Animation I and II; Illustration/Solid Modeling.

Facilities/Equipment: Computer Center includes Macintosh Quadra 660A/V; Macintosh IIci; Macintosh IIsi; LaCie Silverscanner II color scanner; Epson ES-1200C color scanner with transparency adapter; Howtek Scanmaster color scanner; Syquest removable cartridge drives; Canon CJ-10 color copier/printer/scanner; Epson Color Stylus color printer; Laserwriter II NT black and white laser printer; Hewlett-Packard laser-jet 4MP black and white laser printer; software includes Adobe Premiere; Adobe Photoshop; Adobe Illustrator; Aldus Freehand; Aldus PageMaker; Macromedia Director; Fractal Design Painter; Quark XPress; Virtus Walkthru Pro.

Guide POV: This is a selective arts college that offers advanced training emphasizing the use of the computer as an artistic tool; graduates may pursue careers in television, film, advertising, digital imaging and with games companies; student assignments are for commercial, nonprofit, and public service clients.

UNIVERSITY OF MARYLAND AT COLLEGE PARK
College Park, MD 20742
(301) 405-1000
State comprehensive institution. Coed, suburban location. Undergraduate enrollment: 22,000. Graduate enrollment: 9,000.

Calendar: Semesters.

Degrees Offered: B.S., M.S., Ph.D., Computer Science.

Curricular Emphasis: Course listings include Image Processing; Special Problems in Computer Science; Software Design and Development; other topics.

Facilities/Equipment: Computer graphics lab with variety of systems and software.

Guide POV: Computer science students at all levels may investigate new topics in computer graphics with special attention to systems and software design.

Massachusetts
■■■■■■■■■■■■■■■■■■■■■■■■ ■ ■ ■ ■ ■

BOSTON UNIVERSITY
640 Commonwealth Ave., Boston, MA 02215
(617) 353-2000
Private comprehensive institution. Coed, urban location. Undergraduate enrollment: 16,000. Graduate enrollment: 11,000.

Calendar: Semesters.

Degrees Offered: B.S., Broadcasting, B.S., Film; M.S., Broadcasting; Film Studies; Film Production; Broadcast Administration.

Curricular Emphasis: Comprehensive training in all aspects of film, video, and television production; film emphasis on independent productions; advanced projects in film animation.

Facilities/Equipment: Animation stand; complete film and video production and postproduction; graphics special effects.

Guide POV: There are separate, quality tracks for film and television majors; film department is "director" oriented and encourages the development of independent narrative productions; sequential television program is "producer" oriented.

DEAN COLLEGE
99 Main St., Franklin, MA 02038
(508) 528-9100
Private two-year institution. Coed, suburban location. enrollment: 1,000.

Calendar: Semesters.

Degrees Offered: A.A., Communication Arts.

Curricular Emphasis: Audio and video production; media writing; journalism.

Facilities/Equipment: Complete 1/2" television studio; complete 1/2" location; postproduction video includes Amiga graphics; Chyron titles; two 1/2" editing suites.

Guide POV: Sequential audio and video production studies are offered at this private college; practical training for technical support positions includes training in computer-generated special effects for television.

EMERSON COLLEGE
100 Beacon St., Boston, MA 02116
(617) 578-8500
Private comprehensive institution. Coed, urban location. Undergraduate enrollment: 2,100. Graduate enrollment: 400.

Calendar: Semesters.

Degrees Offered: B.A., B.S., Mass Communication (concentration in Film or Television); B.F.A., Film; M.A., Video.

Curricular Emphasis: Independent and commercial film and television production includes Animation I, which covers such methods as cutouts, clay, sand, pixillation, and basic cel animation; Animation Workshop, in which the student produces a major animation project from conception through fine cut with synchronized sound tracks; computer graphics for television special effects.

Facilities/Equipment: Film and Video students may utilize a computer graphics lab; AVID Media Composer 400S system; Quantel 7000 Digital Paintbox; animation stand; optical printer; complete film and video production and postproduction. Center for Computer Technologies and Communication also houses variety of computer systems and software including SuperPaint, Cricket Draw, Pagemaker, and Adobe Illustrator graphics packages.

Guide POV: Specializing in communications and the performing arts, Emerson College has concentrations in both film and television production; there are active student film and video production societies; students may pursue specialized, advanced studies in cel animation; additional computer graphics studies through Computer Applications and Mathematics Department.

FITCHBURG STATE COLLEGE
Pearl St., Fitchburg, MA 01420
(508) 345-2151
State comprehensive institution. Coed, small city location. Undergraduate enrollment: 4,000. Graduate enrollment: 800.

Calendar: Semesters.

Degrees Offered: B.S., Television; Film; Graphics; Technical Communication; Photography; Interactive Media.

Curricular Emphasis: Communications/Media Program—Comprehensive training in media arts with specializations that include computer graphics; interactive communications; course listings include Graphic Design I, II, and II; Electronic Graphic Design; Advanced Electronic Graphic Design; projects in digital typography, illustration systems; television graphics; computer layout and pagination; package design and presentation graphics.

Facilities/Equipment: Animation stand; computer graphics multi-image suite; workstations; interactive suites; complete film and video production and postproduction.

Guide POV: Communication majors at Fitchburg State College enjoy an innovative program with modern facilities; specializations in graphics, interactive communications, technical communications, television, and film; strong job placement program.

FRAMINGHAM STATE COLLEGE
100 State St., Framingham, MA 01701
(508) 620-1220
State comprehensive institution. Coed, suburban location. Undergraduate enrollment: 3,500.

Calendar: Semesters.

Degrees Offered: B.A., Communication Arts.

Curricular Emphasis: Option in Mediated Graphics Communication includes courses such as Mediated Graphics Design; Computerized Graphics Processing and Production.

Facilities/Equipment: Video 3/4" studio; complete 3/4" and 1/2" location; computer graphics lab.

Guide POV: Located 20 miles west of Boston, this state college offers a degree program in television production that combines theoretical studies with practical application; technical specialization provides training in the use of computer-based video graphics.

GREENFIELD COMMUNITY COLLEGE
College Dr., Greenfield, MA 01301
(413) 774-3131
State two-year institution. Coed, rural location. enrollment: 3,000.

Calendar: Semesters.

Degrees Offered: A.S., Art (Media Emphasis).

Curricular Emphasis: Television studio and field production; electronic studio production training; graphic design.

Facilities/Equipment: Television/video production and postproduction; computer graphics lab.

Guide POV: Specializing in preparing students for entry-level technical support positions in television and video, this small media program involves students in all aspects of production, including potential integrations of graphic, photographic, and video media; additional graphics courses through the Engineering and Data Processing programs.

HAMPSHIRE COLLEGE
Amherst, MA 01002
(413) 549-4600
Private comprehensive institution. Coed, small town location. Undergraduate enrollment: 1,100.

Calendar: Semesters.

Degrees Offered: B.A., Film/Photography/Video/Computer Graphics.

Curricular Emphasis: Experimental, documentary, and narrative filmmaking and video production; photography; digital multimedia; computer graphics; training available in both cel and computer animation.

Facilities/Equipment: Animation stand; optical printer; image processing workstation; film and video production and postproduction; Macintosh AV graphics; CD-ROM production.

Guide POV: Students attending this selective liberal arts college may also attend film and video classes at Amherst College, Mt. Holyoke College, Smith College, and the University of Massachusetts; individualized program of study stressing close working relationships with faculty; students may complete their programs in fewer than four years.

HARVARD UNIVERSITY
Cambridge, MA 02138
(617) 495-1000
Private comprehensive institution. Coed, urban location. Undergraduate enrollment: 7,000. Graduate enrollment: 12,000.

Calendar: Semesters.

Degrees Offered: B.S., S.M., Ph.D., Computer Science. B.A., concentration in Visual and Environmental Studies.

Curricular Emphasis: Computer Science—curriculum is geared to the student who will be working in the pure sciences; areas of interest include systems; computer and information science and technology; materials and mechanics; applied physics and devices, and the Earth and its environment. Visual and Environmental Studies—documentary production; film animation.

Facilities/Equipment: Animation stand; complete 16mm production; small format video; Center for Research in Computing Technology houses a Silicon Graphics workstation for graphics research; variety of graphics software; Pierce Hall Laboratory houses facilities for research in computer vision and robotics; VLSI design and simulation.

Guide POV: The Computer Science and Electrical, Computer, and Systems Engineering Department at Harvard University stresses scientific applications of graphics and other computer science research; in addition, there is an undergraduate visual arts program emphasizing nonfiction film and video making; film animation training available to interested students.

MASSACHUSETTS COLLEGE OF ART
621 Huntington Ave., Boston, MA 02115
(617) 232-1555
Public comprehensive arts institution. Coed, urban location. Undergraduate enrollment: 1,000. Graduate enrollment: 90.

Calendar: Semesters.

Degrees Offered: B.F.A., M.F.A., Fine Arts (with concentrations in Film, Photography, and Studio for Interrelated Media, including video).

Curricular Emphasis: Media and Performing Arts Department—Film students are offered courses in Super-8 and 16mm film production, including experimental animation; Studio for Interrelated Media students focus on expanded use of 3/4" format production, including computer animation, while exploring interdisciplinary work in artistic media such as light, projection, movement, xerography, audio synthesizer, photography, filmmaking, or tools of their own design; separate critical studies program in film criticism.

Facilities/Equipment: Animation stand; computer graphics center includes Apple IIGS, Macintosh, IBM PCs and clones; Amiga microcomputers; Lisas; complete Super-8 and 16mm production and postproduction; video (genlock).

Guide POV: Founded in 1873, this was the first school of professional art education in the United States; concentrations in film or interrelated media (including video); students encouraged to explore use of new technologies; multidimensional performance; film and computer animation.

MASSACHUSETTS INSTITUTE OF TECHNOLOGY

77 Massachusetts Ave., Cambridge, MA 02139

(617) 253-1000

Private comprehensive institution. Coed, urban location. Undergraduate enrollment: 6,000. Graduate enrollment: 6,000.

Calendar: Semesters.

Degrees Offered: B.S., Interdisciplinary Major (students may select emphasis in Media Arts and Sciences); M.S., Visual Studies; Ph.D., Media Arts and Sciences.

Curricular Emphasis: Media Arts and Sciences—this new, multidisciplinary program explores the invention, study, and creative use of new information technologies; current research in the Computer Graphics and Animation Group focuses on issues of dynamic, kinematic, and goal-directed graphical simulation and includes the development of, and interaction with, virtual environments; some related areas of inquiry include Computer Graphics and Design (Visible Language Workshop); Workshop in Elastic Movie Time (Interactive Multimedia); Video Production; Digital Video; Cinematic Storytelling; Image Representations for Vision; Vision and Modeling; Holography and 3-D Imaging; Synthetic Holography; Advanced Human Interface; Advanced Design of Dynamic and Intelligent Information Graphics; Graphic Imaging Media; advanced research in variety of multimedia projects, production and editing tools, and video networking.

Facilities/Equipment: Media Lab houses state-of-the-art video center with new and experimental video workstations; interactive video; video finger; visible language workshop; MacGlib video library; elastic tools, etc., as well as various new equipment under development.

Guide POV: Students participating in this most innovative newly-created program will explore the study, invention, and creative use of new information technologies; advanced research includes work in spatial imaging; interactive cinema; computer graphics and animation; digital video; synthetic holography; elastic media; vision and modeling; synthesis of graphics with artificial intelligence; television of the future; advanced human interface; most selective admissions; all graduate students of the Media Lab receive research assistantships.

MONTSERRAT COLLEGE OF ART

23 Essex St., Beverly, MA 01915

(508) 922-4268

Private fine arts institution. Coed, small city location. Undergraduate enrollment: 300.

Calendar: Semesters.

Degrees Offered: B.F.A., Fine Arts (with concentrations in Illustration; Graphic Design; Photography; others).

Curricular Emphasis: Illustration—course listings include Computer and Cel Animation; Mixed Media Illustration; Natural Science Illustration; Advertising Illustration; Computer Imaging; Children's Book Illustration. Graphic

Design—course listings include Computer Design; Graphic Design I-IV; Photo Design; Expressive Design; Typography; Internships.

Facilities/Equipment: Computer graphics lab with Macintosh computers; color monitors; color and b/w laser printers; CD-ROM graphics systems and software include Adobe Photoshop, Adobe Illustrator, and Quark Xpress; video equipment includes camcorders; monitors; recorders; editors; audio and film equipment.

Guide POV: Illustration majors attending this fine arts college explore computer and cel animation, concentrating on techniques such as digitizing and manipulating drawings, painting and text generation; graphic design majors pursue long-term projects utilizing computer techniques to produce finished work; photography majors may also work in digital photo techniques, experimental film or video; throughout, the college atmosphere promotes the use of technology as a tool to develop personal expression.

MOUNT WACHUSETT COMMUNITY COLLEGE

444 Green St., Gardner, MA 01440-1000
(508) 632-6600
State two-year institution. Coed, suburban location. enrollment: 2,000.

Calendar: Semesters.

Degrees Offered: A.S., Broadcasting and Telecommunications.

Curricular Emphasis: Hands-on television production; broadcast writing; electronic media operations and management; photography; audio multitrack recording.

Facilities/Equipment: Two full-color television studios; two complete 3/4" studios and location; multisource video editing suite with computer graphics; edit decision list storage; digital video effects.

Guide POV: This two-year school offers career broadcast training with an emphasis on new technologies; digital graphics for television.

NEW ENGLAND SCHOOL OF ART AND DESIGN

28 Newbury St., Boston, MA 02116-3276
(617) 536-0383
Private comprehensive arts institution. Coed, urban location. Undergraduate enrollment: 300.

Calendar: Semesters.

Degrees Offered: B.F.A., Graphic Design.

Curricular Emphasis: Graphic Design Program—course listings include 3-D Computer Animation; Computer Presentation Graphics I and II; TV Broadcast Production Techniques; Computer Graphics Portfolio; 3-D Computer Modeling; Object-Oriented Computer Graphics; Electronic Design.

Facilities/Equipment: Three computer graphics labs (two IBM-based and one Macintosh-based); NU-VISTA graphics adapter allows for video image-grab and displays up to 16 million colors; SuperPaint; PixelPaint; Swivel 3-D; MacroMind Director; scanner; film and video equipment.

Guide POV: This is a small, well-equipped professional school of visual communications; enrollment in computer graphics courses is limited to one student per computer; flexible program trains student for employment in video production houses, architecture and engineering firms, television stations, design studios, advertising agencies, and the corporate field; cross-registration with Suffolk University.

SCHOOL OF THE MUSEUM OF FINE ARTS

The Fenway, Boston, MA 02115
(617) 267-6100
Private professional arts institution. Coed, urban location. Undergraduate enrollment: 620. Graduate enrollment: 50.

Calendar: Semesters.

Degrees Offered: B.F.A., M.F.A., Film, Video, Animation/Film; B.F.A. with B.A. or B.S., Combined Five-Year Degree Program; M.A.T.

Curricular Emphasis: Fine arts program with full training in cel animation, computer art and animation, film and video production; combined five-year program leads to the B.F.A and either the B.A. or B.S.

Facilities/Equipment: Animation stand; complete film and video production and postproduction; chromakey; special effects generator; digital visual effects unit; Amiga computer graphics with genlock for character generation; film to video transfer.

Guide POV: A department of the Museum of Fine Arts, this private institution awards both undergraduate and graduate degrees in the visual arts; full undergraduate film animation program; graduate programs offered in affiliation with Tufts University.

SIMMONS COLLEGE

300 The Fenway, Boston, MA 02115.
(617) 738-2000
Private comprehensive institution. Undergraduate women's and graduate coed, urban location. Undergraduate enrollment: 1,209. Graduate enrollment: 1,600.

Calendar: Semesters.

Degrees Offered: B.S., Mathematics/Physics/Computer Science (concentration in Computer Science).

Curricular Emphasis: Mathematics/Physics/Computer Science—course listings include Computer Graphics; Computer Systems; Computer Organization and Architecture; Artificial Intelligence; other areas.

Facilities/Equipment: Computer graphics lab with variety of systems and software.

Guide POV: Topics explored include modeling and image formation, viewports, windowing, segmentation, geometrical transformation and image manipulation, translations, scaling, rotations, zooming, hardware considerations, display technologies, interactive devices, vector and raster scan technologies, color, and animation techniques; projects involving graphics applications in various fields.

TUFTS UNIVERSITY
Medford, MA 02155
(617) 628-5000
Private comprehensive institution. Coed, urban location. Undergraduate enrollment: 4,500. Graduate enrollment: 3,200.

Calendar: Semesters.

Degrees Offered: B.S., M.S., Ph.D., Computer Science.

Curricular Emphasis: Computer Science—advanced research in computer graphics applications; computer vision; artificial intelligence; other areas.

Facilities/Equipment: Computer graphics lab with variety of systems and software.

Guide POV: This solid program in computer science offers students an opportunity to engage in long-term graphics projects for a variety of scientific, educational, and artistic applications.

UNIVERSITY OF LOWELL
Lowell, MA 01854
(508) 934-4000
State comprehensive institution. Coed, urban location. Undergraduate enrollment: 8,000. Graduate enrollment: 3,000.

Calendar: Semesters.

Degrees Offered: B.S., M.S., Ph.D., Computer Science.

Curricular Emphasis: Computer Science Department—undergraduate and graduate course listings include Computer Graphics I and II; Graduate Computer Graphics I and II; Topics in Computer Graphics; Scientific Data Visualization; Computer Vision; Projects.

Facilities/Equipment: Computer graphics lab with variety of systems and software including Sun workstations; DEC; Apollo; DG; Stellar; Ardent; Pixar.

Guide POV: Computer science majors may engage in research involving graphics design and applications; special attention at graduate level to field of computer vision; student co-op program with nearby Mercury Computer Systems.

UNIVERSITY OF MASSACHUSETTS AT AMHERST
S. College, Amherst, MA 01003
(413) 545-0111
State comprehensive institution. Coed, rural location. Undergraduate enrollment: 17,000. Graduate enrollment: 6,000.

Calendar: Semesters.

Degrees Offered: Certificate in Film Studies.

Curricular Emphasis: Interdisciplinary Humanities, Fine Arts, and Social and Behavioral Sciences Program offers courses in film history, screenwriting, and film and television production, including character animation.

Facilities/Equipment: Animation stand;16mm film cameras; editing equipment; complete video 1/2" location.

Guide POV: This interdepartmental and intercollegial certificate program, instituted in 1991, provides an integrated course of studies in film and video as contemporary art forms; on-campus coordination of film/video equipment and facilities; students benefit from 5-College film studies exchange.

UNIVERSITY OF MASSACHUSETTS AT BOSTON
Harbor Campus, Boston, MA 02125.
(617) 287-5000
State comprehensive institution. Coed, urban location. Undergraduate enrollment: 9,000. Graduate enrollment: 3,000.

Calendar: Semesters.

Degrees Offered: B.A., Art (Film and Video Concentration).

Curricular Emphasis: Film/Video studies and training with an emphasis on independent/experimental production.

Facilities/Equipment: Panasonic 1/2" video cameras; Sony Hi-8mm cameras; Super-8 cameras (Elmo, Minolta, and Bauer, among others); postproduction includes limited computer graphics.

Guide POV: Art Department majors choosing courses within the Film and Video Concentration will be introduced to a variety of possible personal approaches to the film and video mediums.

WILLIAMS COLLEGE
Williamstown, MA 01267
(413) 597-3131
Private comprehensive institution. Coed, small town location. Undergraduate enrollment: 2,000.

Calendar: Semesters.

Degrees Offered: B.S., Computer Science.

Curricular Emphasis: Computer Science—course listings include Art and Science of Computer Graphics; Computer Graphics; Projects.

Facilities/Equipment: Computer graphics lab with Macintosh; Sparcs; variety of software.

Guide POV: Computer science majors may explore graphics projects from both an aesthetic and technical standpoint; small classes; variety of projects.

WORCESTER STATE COLLEGE
486 Chandler St., Worcester, MA 01602
(508) 793-8000
State comprehensive institution. Coed, urban location. Undergraduate enrollment: 5,075. Graduate enrollment: 725.

Calendar: Semesters.

Degrees Offered: B.A., Communications (students may select emphasis in Communication Media or Theatre).

Curricular Emphasis: Film, video, and television production including film and computer animation; electronic media theory and culture; critical studies in film; media writing.

Facilities/Equipment: Computer animation equipment; complete 3/4" television studio; complete 3/4" and 1/2" location.

Guide POV: This state college, located 40 miles west of Boston, offers students full training in both film and television production; exploration of experimental, news, animation, narrative, and documentary forms.

Michigan

■■■■■■■■■■■■■■■■■■■■■■■ ■ ■ ■ ■ ■ ■

COLLEGE OF ART AND DESIGN

Center for Creative Studies, 245 E. Kirby, Detroit, MI 48202
(313) 872-3118
Private professional arts institution. Coed, urban location. Undergraduate enrollment: 1,000.

Calendar: Semesters.

Degrees Offered: B.F.A.

Curricular Emphasis: Fine Arts Major—electives in video and 8mm film production with an emphasis on experimental, documentary, and animation; mixed-media installations. Graphic Communication, Art Direction Major—topics include computer graphics in design/illustration; video special effects; computer animation; computer graphics and video production techniques in advertising (two semesters).

Facilities/Equipment: Super-8 film production and postproduction; complete 3/4" television studio; complete 3/4" and 1/2" video location and editing; computer graphics lab includes PC-based workstations featuring video image capture; two-dimensional scanning; PaintBox capabilities; Coreldraw and TIPS software; three-dimensional modeling; color printers; drum plotter; extensive software library; translation capabilities; high-end Silicon Graphics IRIS workstations; Alias software provides full modeling, rendering, and animation capabilities.

Guide POV: An expanding computer graphics curriculum is offered through the Graphic Design, Industrial Design, and Fine Arts Departments at this quality arts college; Art Direction majors concentrate on computer graphics and video production techniques in terms of advertising and design; Fine Arts majors explore experimental video production and 8mm film.

EASTERN MICHIGAN UNIVERSITY

Ypsilanti, MI 48197
(313) 487-1849
State comprehensive institution. Coed, urban location. Undergraduate enrollment: 20,000. Graduate enrollment: 5,000.

Calendar: Semesters.

Degrees Offered: B.A., B.S.

Curricular Emphasis: Telecommunications and Film—electronic media studies include radio, television, cable, and film; program provides balance between theory and production; corporate video projects.

Facilities/Equipment: Animation stand; complete film and video production and postproduction; computer graphics.

Guide POV: The flexible liberal arts program at this public university prepares students for graduate study or for entry-level positions in production and management; courses in both cel and computer animation; in addition, both undergraduate and graduate computer graphics training is available through Computer Science Department.

GRAND VALLEY STATE UNIVERSITY
Allendale, MI 49401
(616) 895-6611
State comprehensive institution. Coed, suburban location. Undergraduate enrollment: 10,000. Graduate enrollment: 3,000.

Calendar: Semesters.

Degrees Offered: B.A., B.S., Film and Video Production; B.A., B.S., Broadcasting; M.S., Communication.

Curricular Emphasis: Film/Video Production Program—there is an emphasis in film animation; additional course work in film history and aesthetics; 16mm production techniques; screenwriting; cinematography; directing; lighting; postproduction; developing technologies; advanced workshops. Television/Video—computer image making; video art; critical studies; video production techniques; news/documentary; business and educational media; broadcast operations.

Facilities/Equipment: Animation stand; J-K optical printer; complete film and video production and postproduction includes graphics lab using Macintosh II; CRT; plotter.

Guide POV: Featuring a small program, this state university offers studies in aesthetics as well as professional production training in film, video, and television; sequential studies in both film animation and 2-D/3-D computer image-making.

LANSING COMMUNITY COLLEGE
500 N. Washington Square, Lansing, MI 48901-9963
(517) 483-1957
State/city two-year institution. Coed, urban location. enrollment: 22,000.

Calendar: Semesters.

Degrees Offered: A.A.S., Applied Science in Computer Animation, Radio/TV/Media, Film or Photographic Technology.

Curricular Emphasis: Media/Art—16mm production techniques; dramatic; documentary; cel animation; two- and three-dimensional computer animation; electronic design; experimental; postproduction; developing technologies; advanced workshops. Television/Video—video production techniques; news and documentary; instructional and industrial; computer graphics; multi-image; FOCUS workshop on advancing technologies.

Facilities/Equipment: Animation stand; complete film and video production and postproduction; computer graphics lab includes Dell Pentium and 486; TOPAS; Fractal Design Painter; Adobe Photoshop; Lumena; Sony BVU 950; Sony VHS; Quadra 800 and 650; Adobe Photoshop; PageMaker; Quark XPress; MacroMedia Director; FreeHand; Adobe Illustrator; Fractal Design Painter; Adobe Premiere; Sony VHS; Laserwriter IIg; Mitsubishi Dye-Sublimation Printer; Tektronix Phaser IIIpxi; DataProducts Typhoon Laser Printer.

Guide POV: With an unusually diverse program for a two-year college, this school provides course listings that cover student interests ranging from new video technologies and multi-image workshops to experimental filmmaking; sequential training in character animation; computer animation projects; writing integrated at every level of program; solid concentration in computer graphics with enrollment of 250 students.

MUSKEGON COMMUNITY COLLEGE
S. Quarterline Rd., Muskegon, MI 49442
(616) 773-9131
County two-year institution. Coed, urban location. enrollment: 6,000.

Calendar: Semesters.

Degrees Offered: A.A., Media.

Curricular Emphasis: Media—film course work concentrates on theoretical studies, use of educational media, animation, documentary and instructional production; television course work centers on television and video production emphasizing broadcast journalism and computer graphics.

Facilities/Equipment: Animation stand; complete Super-8; complete S-VHS studio and location; Amiga graphics.

Guide POV: Preparing students for entry-level career positions in film, video, and television, this two-year program focuses on studio and field training; course work in both cel animation and computer-based animation for video production and television broadcasting.

NORTHERN MICHIGAN UNIVERSITY
Marquette, MI 49885
(906) 227-1000
State comprehensive institution. Coed, urban location. Undergraduate enrollment: 7,500. Graduate enrollment: 1,000.

Calendar: Semesters.

Degrees Offered: B.A., B.S., B.F.A., M.A., M.A.E.

Curricular Emphasis: Art and Design—critical studies; media writing; audio-film-video production; film animation; video art; video production for corporate clients.

Facilities/Equipment: Animation stand; complete film and video production and postproduction including computer graphics.

Guide POV: Offering a wide variety of course listings, this state university provides training in both film and television production with studies in cel and computer animation; small classes; individualized instruction.

SPRING ARBOR COLLEGE
Spring Arbor, MI 49283
(517) 750-1200
Private comprehensive institution. Coed, small town location. Undergraduate enrollment: 700.

Calendar: Semesters.

Degrees Offered: B.A., Art.

Curricular Emphasis: Art Department—course listings include Computer-Assisted Graphic Design I, II, and III.

Facilities/Equipment: Computer graphics lab.

Guide POV: Through the Art Department, students in graphic design assemble a career portfolio while solving problems in two- and three-dimensional modeling, animation and movement on the computer; attention to both artistic and commercial applications; practical emphasis on advertising art.

UNIVERSITY OF MICHIGAN
Ann Arbor, MI 48109
(313) 764-1817
State comprehensive institution. Coed, suburban location. Undergraduate enrollment: 24,000. Graduate enrollment: 14,000.

Calendar: Semesters.

Degrees Offered: B.A., Film and Video Studies.

Curricular Emphasis: Film history and theory with component in film and video production; separate communication degree that includes courses in film, television, and radio offered through Communications Department.

Facilities/Equipment: Complete film and video production and postproduction; computer animation facilities include Apollo network; Intelligent Light.

Guide POV: This Film and Video Studies Program offers a multidisciplinary curriculum covering the history and aesthetics of film and video; emphasis on film and video art, computer animation, narrative, documentary, and experimental forms; separate broadcast listings through Communications Department; additional course in computer animation through Computer Science Department.

WAYNE STATE UNIVERSITY
Detroit, MI 48202.
(313) 577-2424
State comprehensive institution. Coed, urban location. Undergraduate enrollment: 20,000. Graduate enrollment: 10,000.

Calendar: Semesters.

Degrees Offered: B.F.A., Art.

Curricular Emphasis: Art Department—course listings include Computer Art; Projects.

Facilities/Equipment: Computer graphics lab with Amiga; Macintosh; variety of software; complete film, video, and television production and postproduction.

Guide POV: Art students receive instruction in computer art and animation with attention to the development of creative potential; individual projects; additional course work in creating graphics for television and corporate video offered through the Radio, Television, and Film Department.

WESTERN MICHIGAN UNIVERSITY

Kalamazoo, MI 49008

(616) 387-1000

State comprehensive institution. Coed, suburban location. Undergraduate enrollment: 27,000. Graduate enrollment: 6,500.

Calendar: Semesters.

Department of Communication

Degrees Offered: B.F.A., B.A., B.S.

Curricular Emphasis: Art Department—course listings include Computer Imaging; advanced training in computer art.

Facilities/Equipment: Complete film, video and television production and postproduction including switcher/special effects generators; modern computer-aided art lab with Macintosh; video output; variety of software; Design Center.

Guide POV: This public university offers art majors an opportunity to explore advanced creative uses of computer imaging techniques; students benefit from well-equipped studio spaces and modern computer-aided art laboratory; there are over 500 majors in this popular department, but classes are kept small; attention to creation of individual portfolio.

Minnesota

■■■■■■■■■■■■■■■■■■■ ■ ■ ■ ■ ■ ■ ■ ■

HENNEPIN TECHNICAL COLLEGE
9200 Flying Cloud Dr., Eden Prairie, MN 55347
(612) 944-2222
9000 Brooklyn Blvd., Brooklyn Park, MN
(612) 425-3800
State two-year institution. Coed, suburban location. enrollment: 13,000.

Calendar: Quarters.

Degrees Offered: A.A.S.

Curricular Emphasis: Audiovisual Media Production—course listings include Computers in Media Production; Introduction to Paint Computer Graphics; Introduction to 3-D Computer Graphics; Video Production and Postproduction; Computer Colored Artwork Illustration; Image Processing 3-D Modeling for Video; Computer Desktop Video Production; additional option in Presentation Computer Graphics.

Facilities/Equipment: Video equipment; computer graphics lab with variety of software.

Guide POV: For students interested in the use of video and computer graphics for careers in video production, marketing, illustration, or corporate presentation, this two-year program offers an interesting array of specialized courses; in addition, there is a separate Television Production Technician Program that trains for all aspects of broadcasting, including effects.

INTERMEDIA ARTS OF MINNESOTA
425 Ontario St. S.E., Minneapolis, MN 55414
(612) 627-4444
Private nonprofit media arts center affiliated with the Department of Studio Arts, University of Minnesota. Coed, urban location. Undergraduate enrollment: 300.

Calendar: Quarters.

Degrees Offered: B.A. and B.F.A. programs in Video, Computer, and Audio Arts accredited through the Studio Arts Department of the University of Minnesota.

Curricular Emphasis: Studio Arts Department—computer animation; video production; material produced for screening series; video installations; performance artists.

Facilities/Equipment: Computer graphics lab (all computer animation output to video); computer graphics and animation equipment includes NewTek video toasters; MIDI sound station; Ikegami 3/4" and Sony Hi-8 production equipment; 3/4" to 3/4" and Hi-8 to 3/4" editing stations.

Guide POV: Intermedia Arts is a nonprofit institution offering beginning to advanced studies in video technology; currently the only regional media arts center in the upper Midwest that specializes in video and computer animation; degree program through affiliation with University of Minnesota.

MINNEAPOLIS COLLEGE OF ART AND DESIGN

2501 Stevens Ave. S., Minneapolis, MN 55404
(612) 874-6223
Private comprehensive arts institution. Coed, urban location. Undergraduate enrollment: 550.

Calendar: Semesters.

Degrees Offered: B.F.A., M.F.A., Visual Studies.

Curricular Emphasis: Program in film, video, and photography; interactive media studies; sequential training in both cel and computer animation; course listings include Film I, II, III, and IV; Video I, II, III, and IV; Computer Graphics I and II; Advanced Computer Applications.

Facilities/Equipment: Animation stands and rotoscope tables; Oxberry animation stand; six computer labs encompassing Macintosh, Macintosh Power PC, DOS-PC, and Silicon Graphics workstations; animation and graphic software including MacroMedia Director; HyperCard; Photoshop; Painter; Premiere; Infini-D; Morph; StrataVision 3-D; Ray Dream Designer; Dimensions; Swivel 3-D Pro; form Z; TOPAS and 3-D Studio; high-end software including Wavefront Advanced Visualizer; 3-Design; Kinemation; Dynamation; Video Composer; and ASDG's Elastic Reality; complete Super-8 and 16mm; complete 3/4" and Hi-8 studio and location; Internet access and network applications including Fetch, Telnet, Netscape, Mosaic, and TurboGopher.

Guide POV: Undergraduates attending this well-equipped fine arts school are encouraged to work in film, video, photography, and interactive media; film students may pursue advanced projects in animation; computer projects center on multimedia scripting; 3-D rendering of objects; advanced color image manipulation; animation; importing sound and exporting to video; students may pursue one-semester studies at various art institutes in the United States as well as in Canada, Italy and Japan; one-semester New York Studio Program.

MINNEAPOLIS COMMUNITY COLLEGE

1501 Hennepin Ave., Minneapolis, MN 55403-1779
(612) 341-7000
State two-year institution. Coed, urban location. enrollment: 3,500.

Calendar: Quarters.

Degrees Offered: A.S., Video Production; A.S., Filmmaking.

Curricular Emphasis: Video Production Program—course listings include Video Production I, II, and III; Computer Graphics and Animation; Studio Television Production I and II; Experimental and Documentary Film and Video; Advanced Postproduction; Financial Management for Film and Video Makers; MIDI (digital) Recording; American Film Institute Workshops; separate concentration in filmmaking.

Facilities/Equipment: Complete film and video production and postproduction; computer graphics lab with microcomputer and video output; MIDI studio equipment.

Guide POV: Students enrolled in this Video Production Program receive practical instruction in diverse aspects of video technology for entry-level production positions or transfer to a four-year institution.

MINNEAPOLIS TECHNICAL COLLEGE
1415 Hennepin Ave., Minneapolis, MN 55403
(612) 370-9400
State two-year institution. Coed, urban location. enrollment: 2,000.

Calendar: Quarters.

Degrees Offered: A.A.S., Media Production Certificate.

Curricular Emphasis: Computer Graphics and Animation—courses include Desktop Video I: 2-D Paint; Desktop Video II: 2-D Animation; Desktop Video III: 3-D Modeling; Desktop Video IV: 3-D Animation; Desktop Video Editing; Graduate Portfolio Lab; Advanced Software Exploration; Video Production I and II; Scripting and Storyboarding.

Facilities/Equipment: Video 3/4" studio and location; 3/4" A/B roll editing; NewTek/Amiga video toaster workstation; IBM/TARGA 2-D and 3-D graphics workstations.

Guide POV: A professionally-equipped two-year technical college, this institution offers career training to prospective video animators and technicians; solid, varied curriculum in desktop video motion graphics; emphasis on new technologies; focus on personal development as well as career training and placement.

SCHOOL OF COMMUNICATION ARTS IN MINNEAPOLIS
American Center for Computer Imaging
2526 27th Ave. S., Minneapolis, MN 55406
(612) 721-5357
Private two-year institution. Coed, urban location. enrollment: 400.

Calendar: Semesters.

Degrees Offered: Certificates in Computer Art and Animation; Video Production and Technology; Professional Video Production.

Curricular Emphasis: Video Art—video animation (Macintosh, 486 PCs and Silicon Graphics).

Facilities/Equipment: 155 video workstations for computer graphics and animation; Silicon Graphics Indigos; Betacam postproduction; development work on program in advanced animation design utilizes new Multimedia software/hardware.

Guide POV: This two-year private institution places special emphasis on video graphics and animation; students are offered accelerated instruction with every class held in a computer studio; full-time development staff monitors new technology; Animation School reflects philosophy that curriculum must reflect latest tools and techniques of industry; graduates employed as computer animators, video graphic artists, and computer illustrators; practical emphasis; sister-school in Raleigh, NC.

ST. CLOUD STATE UNIVERSITY
St. Cloud, MN 56301

(612) 255-0121

State comprehensive institution. Coed, suburban location. Undergraduate enrollment: 17,000. Graduate enrollment: 1,500.

Calendar: Quarters.

Degrees Offered: B.S., M.S., Mass Communication. B.A., Art/Fine Arts with emphasis in Graphic Design.

Curricular Emphasis: Mass Communications—television/video production training includes designing graphic effects for television and video.

Facilities/Equipment: Television 1" and 3/4" studio; complete 3/4" and 1/2" location; postproduction includes computer graphics lab with AVID; sound and static storage and manipulation; art students utilize lab geared to digital designing; there is digital photography hardware and software.

Guide POV: Through a selective Department of Mass Communications, students at this state college acquire professional production and postproduction experience that includes training in video graphics design; in addition, photojournalism students create digital photography; art majors in graphic design focus on advertising and design applications.

ST. OLAF COLLEGE
Northfield, MN 55057

(507) 646-2222

Private comprehensive institution. Coed, small town location. Undergraduate enrollment: 3,000.

Calendar: Semesters.

Degrees Offered: B.A., Art (students may select emphasis in Film/Video).

Curricular Emphasis: Art Department—video and film animation production within a liberal arts curriculum; special interest in current motion graphics techniques; video art.

Facilities/Equipment: Film animation studio includes animation stand; optical printer; complete film and video production and postproduction; computer graphics lab includes Amiga and Macintosh computers; animation sequences are recorded into a 3/4" video recorder with frame accuracy and immediate playback potential.

Guide POV: Founded a century ago by Lutheran immigrants from Norway and named after that country's patron saint, this liberal arts college offers its art majors sequential training in motion graphics using the newest video technology and animation techniques; attention to individual projects.

UNIVERSITY OF MINNESOTA AT DULUTH
10 University Dr., Duluth, MN 55812

(218) 726-8000

State comprehensive institution. Coed, urban location. Undergraduate enrollment: 6,000. Graduate enrollment: 300.

Calendar: Quarters.

Degrees Offered: B.F.A., Art.

Curricular Emphasis: Art Department—course listings include Graphic Design; Computer Animation Design; intermedia studies; projects.

Facilities/Equipment: Computer graphics lab with variety of systems and software; video equipment.

Guide POV: Art students are exposed to principles of computer-based color graphics; opportunity to emphasize animation for broadcast film and video applications; additional undergraduate and graduate course work through Computer Science Department explores graphics from the perspectives of user interface design, raster scan and vector displays, 3-D transformations and viewing, projections, clipping, hierarchical object modeling, hidden edge and surface removal, ray-tracing, shading and use of color.

UNIVERSITY OF MINNESOTA AT TWIN CITIES
Minneapolis, MN 55455
(612) 625-5000
State comprehensive institution. Coed, urban location. Undergraduate enrollment: 38,000. Graduate enrollment: 11,000.

Calendar: Quarters.

Degrees Offered: B.S., M.S., Ph.D.

Curricular Emphasis: Computer Science—undergraduate course listings include Computer Graphics I and II and treat topics such as curves and surfaces; 3-D clipping; hidden line and hidden surface removal; realistic image generation; advance display system architectures; modeling of 3-D graphics programming; advanced and graduate research in computer-aided design for VLSI; robotics; computer vision; other subjects.

Facilities/Equipment: Computer graphics facilities include variety of workstations and software; includes MacIIs; Hewlett-Packards; Suns; NeXT cubes; laser printers.

Guide POV: This campus of the University of Minnesota system enjoys a state-of-the-art computer facility; emphasis on scientific and engineering applications of graphics research.

Mississippi

■■■■■■■■■■■■■■■■■■■ ■ ■ ■ ■ ■ ■

UNIVERSITY OF MISSISSIPPI
University, MS 38677
(601) 232-7211
State comprehensive institution. Coed, small town location. Undergraduate enrollment: 8,500. Graduate enrollment: 2,000.

Calendar: Semesters.

Degrees Offered: B.A., B.S., M.S., Ph.D., Computer and Information Science.

Curricular Emphasis: Computer and Information Science Program—course listings include Computer Graphics; Software Engineering; Computer Simulation; Software Design and Development.

Facilities/Equipment: Computer lab with variety of advanced hardware and software.

Guide POV: Students may explore principles of graphics fundamentals, elementary figures, shading, geometric transformations, graphics program design, and interactive techniques.

UNIVERSITY OF SOUTHERN MISSISSIPPI
Southern Station, Hattiesburg, MS 39406-5011
(601) 266-7011
State comprehensive institution. Coed, suburban location. Undergraduate enrollment: 10,000. Graduate enrollment: 2,000.

Calendar: Semesters.

Degrees Offered: B.A., B.S., Radio, Television, and Film.

Curricular Emphasis: The Film Production emphasis offers preparation for all phases of professional film production, including animation; the Radio and Television Production emphasis is designed to prepare producers and directors for broadcasting, cable television, and corporate production positions.

Facilities/Equipment: Animation stand; complete film and video production and postproduction includes switcher/special effects; electronic graphics.

Guide POV: Comprehensive undergraduate studies in both film and television production are offered; independent projects in cel animation; computer graphics training geared to designing titles and news graphics for live television, film production and promotions; students choose area of emphasis along with a minor concentration.

Missouri

■■■■■■■■■■■■■■■■■■■ ■ ■ ■ ■ ■ ■

DRURY COLLEGE
900 N. Benton Ave., Springfield, MO 65802
(417) 865-8731
Private comprehensive institution. Coed, urban location. Undergraduate enrollment: 3,000. Graduate enrollment: 300.

Calendar: Semesters.

Degrees Offered: B.A., Communication.

Curricular Emphasis: Radio and television broadcasting track includes Graphic Design I and II; Lab in Television Production; separate tracks in Sports Communication and other related fields.

Facilities/Equipment: Television/video production and postproduction includes switcher/special effects generators; computer graphics lab.

Guide POV: Communication majors at this private college may choose the radio/television broadcast track, which includes training in graphic design for television; cross-registration with Landowne College in London.

ST. LOUIS COMMUNITY COLLEGE AT MERAMEC
11333 Big Bend Blvd., Kirkwood, MO 63122-5799
(314) 984-7500
State two-year institution. Coed, suburban location. enrollment: 15,000.

Calendar: Semesters.

Degrees Offered: A.A., Art, Certificates in Computer Imaging and Desktop Publishing. A.A., Communications.

Curricular Emphasis: Art Department—variety of listings include Advanced Computer Animation; Storyboarding. Communications—course listings include Television Production; Advanced Video Production; Super-8 Film-making.

Facilities/Equipment: Art Department features an Electronics Imaging Studio equipped with Power Macs, scanners, digitizers and hi-resolution black and white and color printers; software base includes Quark XPress, Pagemaker; Photoshop; Illustrator; Alias Sketch and others; Communication Department is equipped with animation stand; Super-8 film production and postproduction; 3/4" television studio and 1/2" location; video postproduction includes special effects; graphics lab with Apples; Printshop; Fantavision; DazzleDraw.

Guide POV: The Graphic Design program available to art majors provides training in advanced computer animation; in addition, communications students are offered an opportunity to explore character animation and special effects graphics for television and video production.

UNIVERSITY OF MISSOURI AT COLUMBIA

Columbia, MO 65211

(314) 882-2121

State comprehensive institution. Coed, urban location. Undergraduate enrollment: 18,000. Graduate enrollment: 6,000.

Calendar: Semesters.

Degrees Offered: B.A., M.A., Ph.D.

Curricular Emphasis: Electrical and Computer Engineering Department—undergraduate and graduate course listings include Digital Image Processing; Computer Vision; Interactive Computer Graphics; Projects. Communication Department—television production and postproduction techniques; Student Video Festival.

Facilities/Equipment: Computer graphics lab includes VAX; Apollo; Vicom; ME3220; Lexidata; Tek 4105; video digitizer; complete video and television production and postproduction.

Guide POV: Established in 1893, this is the largest of the four institutions in the University of Missouri system; advanced topics such as interactive computer graphics and computer vision are pursued at the undergraduate and graduate levels through the Electrical and Computer Engineering Department; Communication Department provides undergraduates with television production training that includes basic graphic design for broadcasting; graduate program is theory-oriented.

WASHINGTON UNIVERSITY

Lindell and Skinker Campus, St. Louis, MO 63130-4862

(314) 935-5000

Private comprehensive institution. Coed, suburban location. Undergraduate enrollment: 5,000. Graduate enrollment: 5,000.

Calendar: Semesters.

Degrees Offered: B.S., M.S., Computer Science.

Curricular Emphasis: Course listings include Computer Graphics; Advanced Algorithms; Computation Structures; Software Engineering.

Facilities/Equipment: Computer graphics lab includes Sun, DEC, VAX, and NeXT computers and workstations; numerous minicomputers; variety of state-of-the-art graphics and image-processing equipment.

Guide POV: Students in this selective program may explore such topics in graphics as computer animation, perspective, designing interactive graphics systems, building standard graphics packages, hidden surface, shading and other areas.

WEBSTER UNIVERSITY

470 E. Lockwood, St. Louis, MO 63119

(314) 968-6900

Private comprehensive institution. Coed, suburban location. Undergraduate enrollment: 2,000. Graduate enrollment: 1,500.

Calendar: Semesters.

Degrees Offered: B.A., M.A., Media Communications (emphasis on Video/Film).

Curricular Emphasis: Course listings include Video Production I and II; Filmmaking I and II; Advanced Video Production; Applied Aesthetics; Proseminar in Film/Video Production; Interactive Video; combined B.A./M.A. Accelerated Program option; visiting film and video artists; interdisciplinary film production projects.

Facilities/Equipment: Animation stand; complete film and video production and postproduction; video editing in digital 3-D format; computer graphics lab.

Guide POV: Students in this program are given advanced training in both film and video production; cel animation and computer graphics training available; limit of 15 students in production classes; additional campuses in England, Switzerland, Austria, and the Netherlands.

Montana

■■■■■■■■■■■■■■■■ ■ ■ ■ ■ ■ ■ ■ ■

MONTANA STATE UNIVERSITY
Bozeman, MT 59717
(406) 994-0211
State comprehensive institution. Coed, rural location. Undergraduate enrollment: 9,000. Graduate enrollment: 1,000.

Calendar: Semesters.

Degrees Offered: B.S., M.S., Computer Science; B.A., Media and Theatre Arts (concentration in Motion Picture/Video Production).

Curricular Emphasis: Computer Science—advanced courses in graphics and scientific visualization, image analysis, simulation, software engineering, artificial intelligence, pattern recognition and algorithm design, among others. Media and Theatre Arts—learning through experience all aspects of motion picture and video production; electives in animation; Yellowstone Media Arts Summer Workshops in motion picture/video production.

Facilities/Equipment: Animation stand; complete film, video and television production and postproduction; high-performance computer graphics, animation, and image processing systems.

Guide POV: A well-equipped Computer Science Department encourages students to pursue advanced projects; topics include advanced graphics computational models; visualization in scientific computing; animation techniques; architectures; chaotic models; in addition, the lively Media and Theatre Arts Department offers thorough instruction in film and video production, including animation for interested students.

UNIVERSITY OF MONTANA
Missoula, MT 59812
(406) 243-0211
State comprehensive institution. Coed, urban location. Undergraduate enrollment: 8,300. Graduate enrollment: 1,700.

Calendar: Semesters.

Degrees Offered: B.S., M.S., Computer Science.

Curricular Emphasis: Computer Science—course listings include Computer Graphics; Advanced Computer Graphics; special topics.

Facilities/Equipment: Computer graphics facilities include DEC; IBM; Sun; Iris; Apollo workstations; number of PCs and Macintoshes; specialized facilities.

Guide POV: This well-equipped Computer Science Department offers advanced research in areas such as graphics, simulation, artificial intelligence, and parallel processing, among others; graduate program includes special emphasis on software development methodology; additional graphics/cartography course listings through Geography Department.

Nebraska

■■■■■■■■■■■■■■■■■■■ ■ ■ ■ ■ ■ ■

COLLEGE OF SAINT MARY
1901 S. 72nd St., Omaha, NE 68124
(402) 399-2400
Private comprehensive institution. Coed, urban location. Undergraduate enrollment: 600.

Calendar: Semesters.

Degrees Offered: B.A., Computer Graphics.

Curricular Emphasis: Computer Graphics—there is a full major with six courses in the core curriculum including a senior thesis that involves the completion of a number of hard copy works in graphic design or personal expression.

Facilities/Equipment: Computer graphics lab includes variety of systems and software.

Guide POV: The College of Saint Mary offers students a newly-designed full major in computer graphics with comprehensive training for both print and motion arts media; philosophy of department is interdisciplinary, combining the study of art, color, line, shape, spatial relationships, and creative choice with computer science and business.

HASTINGS COLLEGE
7th and Turner Sts., Hastings, NE 68901
(402) 463-2402
Private comprehensive institution. Coed, small town location. Undergraduate enrollment: 950.

Calendar: Semesters.

Degrees Offered: B.A., Communication Arts (students may select emphasis in Broadcasting).

Curricular Emphasis: Television and radio production; broadcast journalism.

Facilities/Equipment: Two full-color television studios; three editing bays; computer postproduction suite; complete 3/4" and S-VHS location including seven ENG units; Grass Valley Switcher; teleprompter; computer graphics; A/B/C roll and cuts only editing.

Guide POV: Computer graphics training is presented in the context of a full broadcast and liberal arts curriculum; program offers well-equipped, small production classes.

UNIVERSITY OF NEBRASKA AT KEARNEY
905 W. 25th St., Kearney, NE 68849
(308) 865-8353
State comprehensive institution. Coed, small town location. Undergraduate enrollment: 8,000. Graduate enrollment: 1,750.

Calendar: Semesters.

Degrees Offered: B.F.A., Art.

Curricular Emphasis: Art Department—there is a graphic design option with course listings that include 3-D Design; Animated Graphics for Television or Video; Advanced Graphic Design.

Facilities/Equipment: Computer graphics lab with variety of systems and software; animation stand; video production and postproduction.

Guide POV: The University of Nebraska at Kearney offers art majors an option in graphic design with instruction in both print and motion arts media; in addition, film animation projects may be undertaken by individuals majoring in English as part of a seminar-based film studies curriculum.

UNIVERSITY OF NEBRASKA AT OMAHA
South 60th and Dodge St., Omaha, NE 68132
(402) 554-2800
State comprehensive institution. Coed, urban location. Undergraduate enrollment: 16,000. Graduate enrollment: 2,500.

Calendar: Semesters.

Degrees Offered: B.A., B.S.

Curricular Emphasis: Mathematics and Computer Science Department—course listings include Computer Graphics; Topics in Modeling; areas covered include Markov chains; Markov processes (including birth and death processes); chaotic systems; fractal geometries; other topics.

Facilities/Equipment: Computer graphics lab includes variety of graphics systems and software; complete television production and postproduction includes Grass Valley Switcher Chyron.

Guide POV: This commuter university offers the advanced computer science major an opportunity to develop skills in graphics design and research.

Nevada

■ ■■■■■■■■■■■■■■■■■■ ■ ■ ■ ■ ■ ■ ■

UNIVERSITY OF NEVADA AT LAS VEGAS
4505 S. Marland Pkwy., Las Vegas, NV 89154-5015
(702) 895-3011
State comprehensive institution. Coed, urban location. Undergraduate enrollment: 20,000. Graduate enrollment: 1,500.

Calendar: Semesters.

Degrees Offered: B.S., M.S., Ph.D., Computer Science; B.A., Communication Studies (students may select emphasis in Television).

Curricular Emphasis: Computer Science—course listings include Introduction to Computer Graphics; Computer Graphics; Advanced Computer Graphics; advanced projects.

Facilities/Equipment: Computer graphics lab includes 386s (VGA); SGI 4Ds; Suns.

Guide POV: This Computer Science Department, while concentrating on a variety of concepts and systems, offers both undergraduate and graduate training in computer graphics programming and research; additional training in computer graphics for broadcast media through the Communication Studies Program.

UNIVERSITY OF NEVADA AT RENO
Reno, NV 89557
(702) 784-1110
State comprehensive institution. Coed, urban location. Undergraduate enrollment: 11,000. Graduate enrollment: 2,000.

Calendar: Semesters.

Degrees Offered: B.A., Art.

Curricular Emphasis: Film/Video—Electronic media and film theory, aesthetics and history; video art; video installations/exhibitions.

Facilities/Equipment: Television and video production and postproduction; computer graphics lab.

Guide POV: This campus of the University of Nevada system features a small Art Department offering students a critical survey of film and video along with production work emphasizing both broadcast and nonbroadcast video as a means of creative expression; exploration of new media; course listings in broadcast production offered through Journalism Department.

New Hampshire

■■■■■■■■■■■■■■■■■■■■■■ ■ ■ ■ ■ ■

DARTMOUTH COLLEGE
Hanover, NH 03755-3599.
(603) 646-1110
Private comprehensive institution. Coed, small town location. Undergraduate enrollment: 4,500. Graduate enrollment: 300.

Calendar: Ten-week terms, coinciding with seasons.

Degrees Offered: B.A., Film Studies (with emphasis in theory, history, and criticism, production, or screenwriting).

Curricular Emphasis: Film Studies—theory/aesthetics, history, and criticism; screenwriting; film and video production including projects in cel animation.

Facilities/Equipment: Animation stand; complete Super-8 and 16mm; television/video complete 1/2" studio and location.

Guide POV: This small program combines critical studies with production experience in 8mm, 16mm, VHS and Super VHS formats; individual projects in cel animation.

KEENE STATE COLLEGE
229 Main St., Keene, NH 03431-4183
(603) 352-1909
State comprehensive institution. Coed, rural location. Undergraduate enrollment: 4,300. Graduate enrollment: 400.

Calendar: Semesters.

Degrees Offered: B.A., Theatre Arts, Speech and Film.

Curricular Emphasis: Film/Video—there are separate tracks in production and history/theory with attention to experimental, documentary, independent, and animated forms as well as the classical Hollywood narrative.

Facilities/Equipment: Animation stand; 35mm and 70mm projection with Dolby Surround Sound; editing suite; sound transfer facility; screening rooms; film library; television studio; audio studio; control room; complete Super-8 and 16mm equipment; Nagra and Sennheiser sound; Moviola 16mm Flatbed editor; film to video transfer; complete 3/4" and 1/2" location.

Guide POV: Quality training is offered in independent film and video production.

UNIVERSITY OF NEW HAMPSHIRE
Durham, NH 03824-3556
(603) 862-1234
State comprehensive institution. Coed, semirural location. Undergraduate enrollment: 9,300. Graduate enrollment: 1,200.

Calendar: Semesters.

Degrees Offered: B.S., M.S., Ph.D.

Curricular Emphasis: Computer Science Department—research studies blend theoretical and applied aspects of computer science; major areas of inquiry include computer graphics; artificial intelligence; parallel computing; programming environments; database systems.

Facilities/Equipment: Computer centers with Sun network; VAXstation; DEC-station; Silicon Graphics high-performance workstations; NCUBE 64-node hypercube parallel computer; Prime machines; Macintosh and IBM-compatible microcomputer clusters.

Guide POV: This small graduate program features solid training for scientists wishing to pursue advanced studies in computer graphics; current research is focused on the development of systems and methodology for multidimensional scientific visualization, and the evaluation of parallel graphics and visualization algorithms.

New Jersey

■■■■■■■■■■■■■■■■■■■■ ■ ■ ■ ■ ■ ■ ■

COUNTY COLLEGE OF MORRIS

Center Grove Rd., Randolph, NJ 07869-2086
(201) 328-5000
County two-year institution. Coed, suburban location. enrollment: 10,000.

Calendar: Semesters.

Degrees Offered: A.A.

Curricular Emphasis: Media Studies—television production curriculum includes advanced computer graphics for television with training in all aspects of digital video production technology such as special effects; 3-D modeling; animation; electronic postproduction.

Facilities/Equipment: Computer animation facilities and equipment includes video still store devices; video switchers; digital video effects units; character generators; paint systems; high-resolution 3-D animation systems.

Guide POV: Students seeking computer graphics training for careers in the television industry are offered a well-equipped, two-year program providing thorough, practical experience.

ESSEX COUNTY COLLEGE

303 University Ave., Newark, NJ 07102
(201) 877-3000
State two-year institution. Coed, urban location. enrollment: 8,000.

Calendar: Semesters.

Degrees Offered: A.A.S., Television Production.

Curricular Emphasis: Television and video production includes computer graphics training.

Facilities/Equipment: Complete 1" and 3/4" television studio; complete 3/4" and 1/2" location including graphics and special effects; Grass Valley Switcher; computerized editing.

Guide POV: Production students at this community college receive practical training using modern television facilities, with attention to special effects graphics for television and video production.

FAIRLEIGH DICKINSON UNIVERSITY

1000 River Rd., Teaneck, NJ 07666-1914
(201) 692-2000
Private comprehensive institution. Coed, suburban and urban locations.

Calendar: Semesters.

Degrees Offered: B.A., Art; B.A., Communications.

Curricular Emphasis: Art Department— graphic design concentration with course listings that include Computer Graphics; Graphic Design and Production. Communications—comprehensive film and television production.

Facilities/Equipment: Computer graphics lab with various software; complete film, video, and television production and postproduction.

Guide POV: Art majors are offered a goal-oriented program designed for those seeking careers as computer graphics production artists, illustrators, designers, and advertising artists; Communication Department offers comprehensive training in film/television production including graphics; adult degree program; study abroad at campus in England.

JERSEY CITY STATE COLLEGE
2039 Kennedy Blvd., Jersey City, NJ 07305
(201) 200-2000
State comprehensive institution. Coed, urban location. Undergraduate enrollment: 5,500. Graduate enrollment: 1,200.

Calendar: Semesters.

Degrees Offered: B.A., Media Arts.

Curricular Emphasis: Film animation; narrative production; experimental; computer graphics; news/documentary; video art. **Facilities/Equipment:** Animation stand; complete 16mm production; 4-camera color studio; digital effects editing suite; computer graphics suite.

Guide POV: Hands-on film and video production training is offered at this fully equipped school with courses in traditional narrative and news production as well as film animation, computer graphics, and video art.

KEAN COLLEGE OF NEW JERSEY
Union, NJ 07083
(908) 527-2000
Public comprehensive institution. Coed, suburban location. Undergraduate enrollment: 8,000.

Calendar: Semesters.

Degrees Offered: B.A., B.F.A., Fine Arts.

Curricular Emphasis: Fine Arts Studio and Art Education—the Visual Communications curriculum includes Computer Graphics I and II; Computer Graphics for Visual Communications; Desktop Publishing; Computer Animation; Independent Study.

Facilities/Equipment: Computer graphics lab with Power Macintosh 8100/100 AV; scanners; laser printers; color printer; graphic tablets.

Guide POV: Fine Arts Studio majors may elect several computer graphics courses as part of their major; Visual Communications students are required to take several courses specific to their field; other students may elect such courses as part of course work in humanities.

MERCER COUNTY COMMUNITY COLLEGE
1200 Old Trenton Rd., Trenton, NJ 08690-0182
(609) 586-4800
County two-year institution. Coed, suburban and urban locations. enrollment: 8,500.

Calendar: Semesters.

Degrees Offered: A.A.S., Computer Graphics; A.A.S., Television.

Curricular Emphasis: The Computer Graphics major prepares students to produce still and moving graphics in full color using 2-D, 3-D, animation and multimedia authoring and related software and to operate all graphics input and output devices including scanners, printers, film recorders, video cameras, bit pads, and tape decks. The Television major provides training in audio-video production; computer graphics for television and video; video art; program material produced for college county-wide cable television network.

Facilities/Equipment: Computer graphics center includes Macintosh and PC hardware and software; computer animation editing to 3/4" video cassette; microbased turnkey system; 2-D, 3-D, animation and multimedia software; complete video and television production and postproduction including Chyron ACG; computerized prompter; Ampex Switcher; five-meter TV satellite earth station.

Guide POV: This community college possesses the largest multiuse educational television and radio facility in New Jersey; the major in computer graphics offers a solid curriculum through which students explore media-based applications of current graphics and animation technology.

MONTCLAIR STATE COLLEGE
Normal Valley Rd., Upper Montclair, NJ 07043
(201) 655-4000
State comprehensive institution. Coed, suburban location. Undergraduate enrollment: 11,000. Graduate enrollment: 3,000.

Calendar: Semesters.

Degrees Offered: B.A., with an interdisciplinary film minor (Film Studies and Filmmaking).

Curricular Emphasis: Center for Film Studies—theory, aesthetics, history, and criticism; 8mm and 16mm film production including animated, experimental, narrative, and documentary forms.

Facilities/Equipment: Animation stand; complete Super-8 and 16mm production and postproduction.

Guide POV: This state college, located 15 miles west of New York City, offers undergraduates choosing the film minor the possibility of producing individual projects in film animation while training in a variety of genres.

NEW JERSEY INSTITUTE OF TECHNOLOGY
323 Martin Luther King Blvd., Newark, NJ 07191-8087
(201) 596-3000
State comprehensive institution. Coed, urban location. Undergraduate enrollment: 3,200. Graduate enrollment: 2,500.

Calendar: Semesters.

Degrees Offered: B.S., M.S., Computer and Information Science.

Curricular Emphasis: Computer and Information Science—course listings include Computer Programming and Graphics Problems; Minicomputer Systems; Computer-Augmented Design; Introduction to Artificial Intelligence; Programming for Interactive Computer Graphics; Human-Computer Interfaces; Systems Simulation; other areas.

Facilities/Equipment: Computer graphics lab with variety of systems and software.

Guide POV: Students attending this competitive public technological university may focus attention on interactive graphics oriented toward computer-aided design systems; interactive languages; simulation languages; validation of models; artificial intelligence; other areas; undergraduate and graduate projects.

PRINCETON UNIVERSITY
Princeton, NJ 08544
(609) 258-3000
Private comprehensive institution. Coed, small town location. Undergraduate enrollment: 4,900. Graduate enrollment: 1,800.

Calendar: Semesters.

Degrees Offered: B.S., M.S., Ph.D., Computer Science.

Curricular Emphasis: Computer Science—variety of undergraduate and graduate course listings for the student interested in computer graphics.

Facilities/Equipment: State-of-the-art computer center includes specialized IRIS and Sun workstations.

Guide POV: Established in 1746, this Ivy League university offers students advanced training in computer graphics and animation with special attention to geometric modeling; computer-aided design.

RARITAN VALLEY COMMUNITY COLLEGE
State Highway 28 and Lamington Rd., North Branch, NJ 08876
(908) 526-1200
County two-year institution. Coed, suburban location. enrollment: 6,000.

Calendar: Semesters.

Degrees Offered: A.A., Studio Arts; Communications; Commercial Art with Computers.

Curricular Emphasis: Studio Arts Department—curriculum includes course listings in film and video production and computer graphics, with additional offerings in drawing, design, photography, and ceramics; course listings include Computer Art I, II, and III; 2-D Design with Computers; 3-D Design; Computer Graphics I and II; Film Production I and II; Video Production I and II; Illustration; Cartooning.

Facilities/Equipment: Complete computer graphics/animation studio with variety of systems and software including state-of-the-art low, medium and high resolution equipment; VECTRIX and Apple programming; film production and postproduction; television studio equipment; complete 1/2" video location.

Guide POV: The Studio Art major at this two-year college offers an interesting fine and motion arts curriculum with special attention to projects in computer graphics and animation; topics include techniques for incorporating menu-driven paint systems, computer-video interfacing, high-resolution graphics, point systems, video digitizing, single-frame animation, computer/video recording, three-dimensional imaging (still and motion); video art; animated cartoon projects.

ROWAN COLLEGE OF NEW JERSEY
Glassboro, NJ 08028
(609) 863-5000
State comprehensive institution. Coed, suburban location. Undergraduate enrollment: 7,000.

Calendar: Semesters.

Degrees Offered: B.A., B.F.A., Art.

Curricular Emphasis: Art Department—course listings include Computer Art Techniques I and II; Graphic Design I-VII; Motion Graphics I and II; Puppetry I-VIII; Illustration I-VII; Electronic Publishing.

Facilities/Equipment: Computer graphics studio includes Infini-D, Cinemation, Macintosh TOPAS, Macromind Director; video output.

Guide POV: The art student is offered a solid, intensive curriculum that provides computer art instruction for a variety of applications, both commercial and artistic; attention to student portfolio; animation projects are captured on both disk and tape; there is a special concentration in puppetry.

RUTGERS UNIVERSITY AT CAMDEN
311 North Fifth, Camden, NJ 08102
(609) 225-6243
Public multicampus comprehensive institution. Coed, urban location. Undergraduate enrollment: 2,500.

Calendar: Semesters.

Degrees Offered: B.A., Art.

Curricular Emphasis: Art Department—course listings include Computer Animation I and II; Computer Art I and II; Desktop Publishing; Computer Graphics Internship; Graphic Design Internship.

Facilities/Equipment: Computer graphics center includes Amiga 2000; Sun 3/60; OSU/agE; Sony 3/4" video; Genigraphics; video digitizer; SGI Indy RPC 4600 24 bit system with Indy video output to 3/4" tape; Alias Power Animator V5.11 Power Mac 7100/668/2; Power Mac 7100 8/250C; WACOM Mac Tablets; Mac HPIIcs color scanner; QMS Colorscript printer; Polaroid slide maker; slide scanner.

Guide POV: Students are offered a variety of options in art; two of these consist of well-rounded graphic design options that provide advanced training in three-dimensional computer animation techniques, computer graphics and illustration, and graphic design with video interaction, as well as sequential instruction in the traditional art mediums; in addition, computer graphics instruction is offered through the Computer Science Department to those students with a strong background in mathematics and physics; options in computing sciences and information systems; part-time and evening studies available for working adults, although some requirements in art can be completed only through daytime attendance.

SETON HALL UNIVERSITY
South Orange, NJ 07079-2691
(201) 761-9474
Private comprehensive institution. Coed, suburban location. Undergraduate enrollment: 4,400. Graduate enrollment: 2,400.

Calendar: Semesters.

Degrees Offered: B.A., B.S.

Curricular Emphasis: Communication Graphics—course listings include Introduction to Computer Graphics; Advanced Computer Graphics and Animation; Digital Photography; Computer Design in Advertising Art; Presentation and Information Graphics; Advanced Electronic Design and Desktop Publishing; in addition, there is a four-course studio television production sequence and courses in still photography.

Facilities/Equipment: Eight-station DOS-and-Windows-based computer graphics and animation laboratory features Paint, 3-D animation, and image processing software, including Photoshop, Coreldraw and Autodesk 3-D Studio; Primara color printer; PCR film recorder; frame controller; Targa; separate 16-station Macintosh desktop publishing laboratory with laserwriter and Linotronic 300; Quark; Pagemaker; Aldus Persuasion; in addition, there are complete film and television production and postproduction facilities.

Guide POV: This well-equipped university offers students advanced undergraduate training in computer graphics and animation for careers in video production, advertising, publishing, and design.

THE JOE KUBERT SCHOOL OF CARTOON AND GRAPHIC ART, INC.
37 Myrtle Ave., Dover, NJ 07801
(201) 361-1327
Private institution. Coed, suburban location. Student enrollment: 200.

Calendar: Quarters.

Degrees Offered: Both one year (requiring 36 credit hours) and two year (requiring 72 credit hours) certificates of completion are offered. Diplomas may be awarded after completion of the three-year curriculum (108 credit hours).

Curricular Emphasis: Studies involve the use and capabilities of the Oxberry camera stand, computers, animation discs, rotoscoping, taping, timing, editing, and various aspects of animation techniques.

Facilities/Equipment: Animation boards and pegged discs are supplied to all students; in addition to the Oxberry stand and camera, state-of-the-art computer hardware and software are available; pencil testing equipment, claymation, and stop-motion facilities.

Guide POV: This state-approved institution offers a three year course in cartoon graphics; studies focus on methods and materials used in the animation profession; technical studies and the business of cartoon art are also examined.

TRENTON STATE COLLEGE

Trenton, NJ 08650-4700
(609) 771-1855
State comprehensive institution. Coed, suburban location. Undergraduate enrollment: 5,000. Graduate enrollment: 1,000.

Calendar: Semesters.

Degrees Offered: B.A., B.F.A, Art.

Curricular Emphasis: Art/Computer Graphics—course listings include Computer Graphics Art and Design I, II and III; Computer Animation I and II; Introduction to Computer Graphics in Art and Design; topics and projects.

Facilities/Equipment: Computer graphics lab includes Targa; 386s; Macintosh; video output; video digitizer; variety of graphics and animation software.

Guide POV: Trenton State College offers professional, practical training for graphic designers and computer artists; students work on variety of computer art and animation projects; emphasis on both design and motion arts applications.

WILLIAM PATERSON COLLEGE

300 Pompton Rd., Wayne, NJ 07470
(201) 595-2000
State comprehensive institution. Coed, suburban location. Undergraduate enrollment: 12,000. Graduate enrollment: 1,600.

Calendar: Semesters.

Degrees Offered: B.A., B.F.A., M.A., Computer Animation.

Curricular Emphasis: Art Department—undergraduate course listings include Computer Paint and 2-D Art; Electronic Publishing; 3-D Computer Graphics; Advanced 2-D Computer Art Paint; Advanced Electronic Publishing; Advanced 3-D Computer Graphics; Computer Animation. Master's Program in Computer Animation—course listings include Computer Modeling; Advanced Computer Modeling; Computer Animation; Advanced Computer Animation; Computer Art and Design; Advanced Computer Art and Design; Graduate Project; Graduate Thesis.

Facilities/Equipment: Undergraduate computer graphics lab includes three 4-D and three 3130 Silicon Graphics workstations; Macintosh; ninePCs; Graduate computer graphics lab includes two Personal Iris and three Indigo 2XL Silicon Graphics workstations; software includes Alias and Wavefront, among others; 3/4" editing facility for sound and video; in addition, complete film, video and television production and postproduction on campus.

Guide POV: Sequential course listings in all aspects of computer graphics and animation are offered through the Art Department, including a full graduate program in computer animation; additional courses in broadcast production offered through Communication Department.

New Mexico

■■■■■■■■■■■■■■■■■■■■■ ■ ■ ■ ■ ■ ■ ■ ■

NEW MEXICO HIGHLANDS UNIVERSITY
Las Vegas, NM 87701
(505) 425-7511
State comprehensive institution. Coed, small city location. Undergraduate enrollment: 2,000.

Calendar: Semesters.

Degrees Offered: B.A.

Curricular Emphasis: Graphic Design—course listings include Electronic Imaging I and II; Electronic Photography; Graphic Design I, II, and III.

Facilities/Equipment: Electronic Imaging Studio includes 286 and 386s (Targa); Mac SE; color printer; Matrix film recorder and video equipment; Lumena.

Guide POV: This four-year professional program emphasizes career training in all aspects of graphic design within a liberal arts curriculum; animation projects.

NEW MEXICO STATE UNIVERSITY
Las Cruces, NM 88003-0001
(505) 646-0111
State comprehensive institution. Coed, suburban location. Undergraduate enrollment: 15,000. Graduate enrollment: 2,000.

Calendar: Semesters.

Degrees Offered: B.A.

Curricular Emphasis: Studio and field production training includes creating digital techniques for special effects and titles; program material produced for PBS station KRWG-TV, housed on campus, which reaches a population of 300,000 in New Mexico and Texas.

Facilities/Equipment: Complete television studio and location; audio bay; control room; editing suites; computer graphics suite.

Guide POV: This state university offers students complete mass communication studies with a strong emphasis on broadcast journalism; production students create computer-generated effects for television; there are also sequences in print, public relations and advertising.

UNIVERSITY OF NEW MEXICO AT ALBUQUERQUE
Albuquerque, NM 87131
(505) 277-3312
State comprehensive institution. Coed, urban location. Undergraduate enrollment: 24,000. Graduate enrollment: 2,000.

Calendar: Semesters.

Degrees Offered: B.S., M.S., Ph.D., Computer Science/Engineering.

Curricular Emphasis: Computer Science Department—course listings include Computer Vision; Image Processing by Digital Computer; Computer Graphics I and II; Simulation; Undergraduate/Graduate Projects.

Facilities/Equipment: Computer and Information Resources and Technology center with Macs; IBM; printers; software.

Guide POV: This public university offers both undergraduates and graduates an opportunity to explore a variety of new trends in computer science; strong emphasis on the use of computer graphics to solve engineering problems; use of modern vector and raster devices; description and manipulation of two- and three-dimensional objects; hidden surface removal; other areas include computer vision; simulation; university also offers Evening and Weekend Degree Programs to accommodate working students.

UNIVERSITY OF NEW MEXICO AT GALLUP
200 College Dr., Gallup, NM 87301
(505) 863-7500
State two-year institution. Coed, small town location. enrollment: 3,000.

Calendar: Semesters.

Degrees Offered: A.A., Fine Arts; A.A.S., Graphics Technology.

Curricular Emphasis: Fine Arts—news/documentary video production; computer graphics effects for studio technicians. Graphics Technology—print media graphics curriculum with training that includes still video and image enhancement.

Facilities/Equipment: Super-8 and 16mm projectors; complete 1/2" video location; 3/4" editing equipment; computer graphics equipment; students also have access to area broadcast facilities.

Guide POV: Students at this community college study film/video theory and basic production as part of an arts curriculum; basic training in digital special effects for broadcasting; separate program in graphics technology emphasizes print media.

New York

■■■■■■■■■■■■■■■■■■■■■ ■ ■ ■ ■ ■ ■ ■

ADELPHI UNIVERSITY
South Ave., Garden City, NY 11530
(516) 877-3000
Private comprehensive institution. Coed, suburban location. Undergraduate enrollment: 7,000. Graduate enrollment: 2,500.

Calendar: Semesters.

Degrees Offered: B.A.

Curricular Emphasis: Film and video production and aesthetics; annual student film and video festival; videos produced for sponsored projects.

Facilities/Equipment: Animation stand; complete film and video production and postproduction; computer graphics.

Guide POV: Sequential production training in both film and video is offered here with a strong emphasis on aesthetics; opportunity to engage in film animation projects; video art.

BARD COLLEGE
Annandale-on-Hudson, NY 12504
(914) 758-6822
Private comprehensive institution. Coed, rural location. Undergraduate enrollment: 920. Graduate enrollment: 60.

Calendar: Semesters.

Degrees Offered: B.A., Film; M.F.A., Film and Video.

Curricular Emphasis: 16mm film production and editing; screenwriting; aesthetics; animated, experimental, and documentary forms; video art.

Facilities/Equipment: Complete 16mm production and postproduction; film-to-video transfer; 1/2" video; JVC and S-VHS cameras and editing units; animation stand; JK optical printer; Amiga computer graphics; time coder/reader.

Guide POV: Bard College offers a quality program emphasizing aesthetics, experimental film production, and postproduction techniques; faculty of media artists; small graduate program extends studies in graphic film techniques with attention to animation, rephotography, rotoscoping, drawing on film, and other methods.

BOROUGH OF MANHATTAN COMMUNITY COLLEGE
199 Chambers St., New York, NY 10007
(212) 346-8000
City two-year institution. Coed, urban location. enrollment: 12,000.

Calendar: Semesters.

Degrees Offered: A.A.S., Corporate and Cable Communications.

Curricular Emphasis: Corporate and Cable Communications Program—

Two-year curriculum prepares students for entry-level videotape production and operations/management positions in corporate communications departments, audiovisual production companies, industrial videotape production centers, and the cable television industry.

Facilities/Equipment: Broadcast quality television studio with satellite uplinking/downlinking connectivity; 1" and 3/4" postproduction capability with computer graphics, including multimedia production.

Guide POV: This community college offers a program featuring training in video production with a nonbroadcast emphasis and includes technical instruction in video graphics.

CAYUGA COMMUNITY COLLEGE
Franklin St., Auburn, NY 13021
(315) 255-1743
State two-year institution. Coed, suburban location. enrollment: 2,000.

Calendar: Semesters.

Degrees Offered: A.A.S., Design/Drafting; Radio/TV Broadcasting; Broadcasting Technology.

Curricular Emphasis: Design/Drafting—training in computer graphics and animation. Telecommunications—hands-on broadcast production, including special effects.

Facilities/Equipment: Computer graphics lab with IBM XTs and ATs; complete video and television production and postproduction includes videotoaster workstation.

Guide POV: This community college offers computer animation studies for design/drafting students as well as a production-oriented two-year program in telecommunications; travel-study course in London offers comprehensive view of broadcasting industry in Great Britain.

CITY UNIVERSITY OF NEW YORK—BROOKLYN COLLEGE
2900 Bedford Ave., Brooklyn, NY 11210-2889
(718) 951-5000
State comprehensive institution. Coed, urban location. Undergraduate enrollment: 14,000. Graduate enrollment: 3,000.

Calendar: Semesters.

Degrees Offered: B.A., with a concentration in Film Production and Film Studies; Certificate in Film Production.

Curricular Emphasis: Film Department—theory, criticism, history; fiction and nonfiction production; animation; directing; cinematography; screenwriting; sound.

Facilities/Equipment: Animation stand; complete Super-8 and 16mm production and postproduction.

Guide POV: This university offers a comprehensive program in film production and criticism; diverse curriculum covers all aspects of filmmaking, including animation.

CITY UNIVERSITY OF NEW YORK—CITY COLLEGE
Convent Ave. at W. 138th St., New York, NY 10031
(212) 650-7000
State comprehensive institution. Coed, urban location. Undergraduate enrollment: 14,000.

Calendar: Semesters.

Degrees Offered: B.F.A., Art, B.A., Communications (concentration in Film and Video Production); B.F.A., M.F.A., Film and Video Production.

Curricular Emphasis: Art Department—course listings include Computer Graphics Workshop: Design on the Macintosh I; Computer Graphics Workshop: Color Paint Systems; Computer Graphics Workshop: Design on the Macintosh II; Graphic Design Portfolio; Media Integration. Communications, Film, and Video Department—advanced film and video production; television studio and location production; film and video festivals; program material produced for local PBS affiliates, for Arts and Entertainment network, and for cable outlets.

Facilities/Equipment: Macintosh (plus, IIcx) video graphics lab; 24 bit color; Laserwriters; page and video with scanner software; output to Imagewriter II and Laserprinter; IBM PCs; film, video and nonlinear postproduction suites; complete film/video production and postproduction includes digital nonlinear postproduction for film and video; complete 3/4" studio includes switcher, character generator, digital effects.

Guide POV: There are a variety of courses in computer graphics techniques available to art majors, with an emphasis on design; communications majors are instructed in media production skills; expanding video and graphics facilities.

CITY UNIVERSITY OF NEW YORK—COLLEGE OF STATEN ISLAND
2800 Victory Blvd., NY 10314
(718) 982-2520
State comprehensive institution. Coed, urban location. Undergraduate enrollment: 16,000. Graduate enrollment: 1,000.

Calendar: Semesters.

Degrees Offered: B.S., Communications.

Curricular Emphasis: Course listings in film/video production with an expanding program in media graphics.

Facilities/Equipment: New graphics design studio; complete film and video production and postproduction.

Guide POV: Communications majors learn the basics of film and video production while exploring techniques in both moving image and print graphics.

CITY UNIVERSITY OF NEW YORK—HUNTER COLLEGE
695 Park Ave., New York, NY 10021
(212) 772-4000
Public liberal arts college. Coed, urban location. Undergraduate enrollment: 10,000. Graduate enrollment: 5,000.

Calendar: Semesters.

Degrees Offered: B.A., Film Production.

Curricular Emphasis: Film and video production emphasizing narrative, documentary, experimental and animated forms.

Facilities/Equipment: Animation stand; complete 16mm production and postproduction; video production, and postproduction.

Guide POV: Students who select the production major work in both film and video while refining screenwriting techniques; substantial work in fiction; animated projects.

CITY UNIVERSITY OF NEW YORK—YORK COLLEGE
94-20 Guy R. Brewer Blvd., Jamaica, NY 11451
(718) 262-2000
State comprehensive institution. Coed, urban location. Undergraduate enrollment: 5,000.

Calendar: Semesters.

Degrees Offered: B.A., Fine Arts.

Curricular Emphasis: Fine Arts—basic video production; video art; sequential training in computer graphics as a design instrument.

Facilities/Equipment: Complete 1" studio; computer graphics lab with Macintosh; SuperPaint; Pro3-D; PageMaker; Super-8 editing equipment.

Guide POV: Production training in film, video, and computer graphics is offered within a fine arts context; experimental approaches explore cinematic and video approaches to image, light, sound, time, and motion; additional graphics training for designers.

COLLEGE OF SAINT ROSE
432 Western Ave., Albany, NY 12203
(518) 454-5265
Private comprehensive institution. Coed, urban location. Undergraduate enrollment: 2,655. Graduate enrollment: 1,200.

Calendar: Semesters.

Degrees Offered: B.A., Public Communications.

Curricular Emphasis: Radio/TV production; journalism.

Facilities/Equipment: Complete 3/4" industrial studio and 1/2" location; IBM Targa graphics system; 10-station Macintosh lab with PowerMac 6100s; broadcast grade audio production.

Guide POV: A comprehensive communication major is available emphasizing both print and broadcast mediums and featuring practical training in computer-based effects for television.

COLUMBIA UNIVERSITY
New York, NY 10027
(212) 854-1754
Private comprehensive institution. Coed, urban location. Undergraduate

enrollment: 5,600. Graduate enrollment: 13,000.

Calendar: Semesters.

Degrees Offered: B.S., Academic Computing.

Curricular Emphasis: Academic Computing—course listings include Computer Graphics and Applications; Experimental Imaging; 2-D/3-D Imaging (Targa); 2-D/3-D Imaging (Mac); 2-D/3-D Imaging Studio; Computer Graphics and Video I and II; Computer Imaging Seminar; 3-D Modeling and Animation I, II, and III; Professional Applications in 2-D Computer Graphics; Graphics for Cable; Multimedia Preproduction and Design; Mac II: Motion Graphics; Advanced HyperCard and Multimedia; special projects in computer graphics arts.

Facilities/Equipment: More than a dozen computer laboratories with Macintosh, Commodore Amigas, IBM type personal computers; Targa; SGI; advanced graphics workstations; variety of software includes Deluxe Paint IV; Disney Animation Studio; DCTV Cinemorph; PixelPaint; MacVision; Photoshop; Swivel 3-D; MacroMind Director; Crystalgraphics TOPAS 3-D; TimeArts Lumena; Ron Scott's QFX Image Processing software; Video Toaster; Ami Link Editing; InVision; Broadcast Titler 2; AT&T TIPS (Truevision Image Processing software); variety of experimental systems in development; laser and color printers; projects created on music keyboards, high-resolution monitors and advanced systems, then mixed and edited on video and audio tape.

Guide POV: The Department of Academic Computing is an innovative program tailored for the new discipline of computer motion graphics; state-of-the-art facilities; special focus on computer imaging, virtual worlds, animation and visualization techniques; other courses examine computer interaction and multimedia; in addition, there is a graduate film production program as well as broadcast training through the Department of Journalism.

GENESEE COMMUNITY COLLEGE

College Rd., Batavia, NY 14020-9704
(716) 343-0055
State and county two-year institution. Coed, small town location. enrollment: 3,500.

Calendar: Semesters.

Degrees Offered: A.S., Communications and Media Arts (with a concentration in Radio/TV).

Curricular Emphasis: Television/video production including sequential course listings in graphic design.

Facilities/Equipment: Complete 3/4" full color studio and 1/2" location including DXC-327 Sony Chip Cameras; computerized graphics; video toaster.

Guide POV: Intensive television and radio production training is offered to students at this two-year community college; core requirements in journalism, graphic design, black and white photography, and mass media.

HOFSTRA UNIVERSITY
1000 Fulton Ave., Hempstead, NY 11550-1090
(516) 463-6600
Private comprehensive institution. Coed, suburban location. Undergraduate enrollment: 7,000. Graduate enrollment: 5,500.

Calendar: Semesters.

Degrees Offered: B.A., B.S., M.S., Computer Science.

Curricular Emphasis: Computer Science—a diverse curriculum includes advanced training in computer graphics; computer modeling; robotics.

Facilities/Equipment: Several computer laboratories house a variety of systems including Macintosh IIcx computers; IBM and MS-DOS compatible computers, with new 386-based color systems; Silicon Graphics Iris 3-D graphics workstation; high-end PCs and other computers.

Guide POV: Computer Science students with a background in calculus, programming and data structures study graphics technology in terms of interactive graphics, hardware and software, data structures, mathematical manipulation of graphical objects, the user interface, and the fundamental implementation of algorithms.

ITHACA COLLEGE
Ithaca, NY 14850
(607) 274-3011
Private comprehensive institution. Coed, rural location. Undergraduate enrollment: 6,000. Graduate enrollment: 150.

Calendar: Semesters.

Degrees Offered: B.S., B.A., B.F.A., Communications.

Curricular Emphasis: Corporate Communication—this program trains students in the production, use and management of nonbroadcast formats such as slide/tape; multi-image; video; graphics/print; computer-based media; interactive video; photography. Cinema and Photography—curriculum stresses both theory and practical experience with a strong emphasis on professional internships. Film, Photography, and Visual Arts—innovative program provides an intensive course of study in artistic media production; students work in film, photography, video, and art; film and computer-based animated projects.

Facilities/Equipment: Film animation suites; computer animation labs; multi-image lab; interactive media lab; separate computer-equipped labs support studies in graphics, new technology and media research; multitrack sound studios; full motion picture, video and television facilities; photography complex.

Guide POV: The School of Communications at this private college has invested in state-of-the-art facilities to support all areas of computer-based technology and research in media; students may pursue advanced film and computer animation projects; separate specializations in corporate communications, cinema and photography, and film, photography and visual arts.

LONG ISLAND UNIVERSITY AT BROOKLYN

One University Plaza, Brooklyn, NY 11201
(718) 488-1000
Private comprehensive institution. Coed, urban location. Undergraduate enrollment: 5,000. Graduate enrollment: 4,000.

Calendar: Semesters.

Degrees Offered: B.A., Media Arts.

Curricular Emphasis: Television production; computer graphics photography.

Facilities/Equipment: Computer graphics studio; complete 3/4" three-camera studio; multiformat A/B roll editing suites; 16mm film production lab.

Guide POV: Part of the Long Island University system, this university offers a media arts program designed for students seeking training in television and audio production, computer graphics, multimedia, scriptwriting and mass communications; projects in computer-based animation for video production, corporate advertising, and television broadcasting.

LONG ISLAND UNIVERSITY—C.W. POST CAMPUS

Brookville, NY 11548
(516) 299-2000
Private four-year comprehensive institution. Coed, suburban location. Undergraduate enrollment: 5,000. Graduate enrollment: 3,000.

Calendar: Semesters.

Degrees Offered: B.F.A., Fine Arts/Mixed Program/Computer Graphics.

Curricular Emphasis: Course listings include Animation and Computer Graphics Workshop; Intermediate Animation and Computer Graphics Workshop; Advanced Animation and Computer Graphics Workshop; Desktop Video/Animation; Presentation Graphics; complete training in television production and postproduction.

Facilities/Equipment: Macintosh computer graphics lab with current animation hardware and software; complete film, video, and television production and postproduction.

Guide POV: Undergraduates may major in animation and computer graphics, participating in intensive, sequential studies that require a variety of personal and small group projects; diverse training available in both film and video production.

MARIST COLLEGE

North Rd., Poughkeepsie, NY 12601
(914) 575-3000
Private comprehensive institution. Coed, suburban location. Undergraduate enrollment: 3,000. Graduate enrollment: 100.

Calendar: Semesters.

Degrees Offered: B.S., M.S., Computer Science.

Curricular Emphasis: Computer Science—course listings in computer graphics including Computer Art; Computer Animation; the Graphics Research

Group, composed of interested students and faculty members, work on diverse projects such as fractals, ray tracing, physically-based modeling, chaotic dynamical systems, and animation.

Facilities/Equipment: Computer facilities with IBM RISC 6000/C10 systems; IBM-PC/486s; Hewlett Packard ScanJet IIC color flatbed scanner; optical character Hewlett Packard DeskJet 500C color inkjet printer; software includes Harvard Graphics; Deluxe Paint.

Guide POV: This private college offers advanced graphics studies to the interested computer science major; special attention to newest technologies and experimental research; in addition, the Communication Arts Department offers basic production training in film and video.

NEW SCHOOL FOR SOCIAL RESEARCH
66W. 12th St., New York, NY 10011
(212) 229-5600
Independent comprehensive institution emphasizing adult education. Coed, urban location. Undergraduate enrollment: 6,000. Graduate enrollment: 2,000.

Calendar: Semesters.

Degrees Offered: Undergraduate—B.A., Humanities (emphasis in Film); Certificate in Film Production; M.A., Media Studies (production sequence).

Curricular Emphasis: Graduate Media Studies—communication theory with emphasis on media concepts and practice through production leading to an M.A. degree with advanced course listings in audio, video and film production.

Facilities/Equipment: Animation stand; computer graphics production facilities; complete film and video production and postproduction.

Guide POV: Conceived as an alternative school for working adults, the New School offers a variety of options for students interested in the media arts; an individually-tailored graduate program offers studies in communication theory as well as production work in both 16mm film and video, including film and computer-based motion graphics; many communication courses may be chosen as part of a flexible curriculum leading to a B.A. degree in Humanities and Social Science; Certificate Program in Film Production; accelerated B.A./M.A. option.

NEW YORK INSTITUTE OF TECHNOLOGY
Wheatly Rd., Old Westbury Campus, Old Westbury, NY 11568
(516) 686-7516
Private comprehensive institution. Coed, suburban location. Undergraduate enrollment: 8,000. Graduate enrollment: 4,000.

Calendar: Semesters.

Degrees Offered: B.F.A., Fine Arts (areas include fine arts, design graphics and interior design); B.S., Advertising; B.A., Communication Arts (with emphasis in Film/Television); M.A., Communication Arts (with emphases in Computer Graphics, Filmmaking, and Video).

Curricular Emphasis: Fine Arts Department—design graphics option trains students in all visual communications media including television, film, print and photography; course listings includes Computer Graphics in Art and Design; Computer Video I and II; Animation Production I, II, III, and IV (projects in both film and computer graphics animation); Animation Internship; senior projects and thesis in computer graphics; separate computer graphics/photographics option includes training in both two and three-dimensional design. Communication Arts Department—film and television production; computer graphics technology; graduate specializations include computer graphics or graphic arts and media production (including film animation). Advertising Department—curriculum emphasizes new digital technologies.

Facilities/Equipment: Animation stand; modern computer graphics/animation labs with variety of hardware and software including Images II; complete film, video and television production and postproduction.

Guide POV: Comprehensive training in both film and computer graphics animation is offered to students majoring in both fine and communication arts at this private technical institute; in addition, there is a graduate program in communication arts providing advanced training to both film and computer graphics animators; a separate advertising department emphasizes techniques in computing and digital technologies.

NEW YORK UNIVERSITY
Tisch School of the Arts, 721 Broadway, New York, NY 10003
(212) 998-1820
Private comprehensive institution. Coed, urban location. Undergraduate enrollment: 2,200. Graduate enrollment: 800.

Calendar: Semesters.

Degrees Offered: B.F.A., Film (concentration in animation); B.F.A., Television; M.F.A., Animation; M.P.S., Interactive Telecommunications.

Curricular Emphasis: Department of Film and Television —undergraduates are offered a variety of courses in both cel and computer graphics animation including Animation Story Visualization; History of Animation; Drawing and Design for Animation; Animation Action Analysis; Animation Camera Technology; Stop-Motion Animation; Cel Animation; Advanced 2-D Computer Imaging; Introduction to 2-D/3-D Computer Graphics; graduate department in cinema provides separate animation track; animation and video festivals. Interactive Telecommunications Program—this curriculum explores new communications technologies made possible by the convergence of computers with video, graphics, and publishing; course listings include Video for New Media; Computer Graphics: Design for the Screen; Animation on the Macintosh; Experimental Multimedia Workshop; Interactive Video; Interactive Media for Marketing; variety of others.

Facilities/Equipment: Film animation studio; computer graphics lab includes high-performance, real-time color graphics workstation; Amiga; Macintosh; variety of software includes Videoworks; Director; pen plotters; laser printers; complete film and video production and postproduction; complete 35mm available for graduate and some undergraduate projects; complete television studios and location equipment; MIDI studio; Alternate Media Center, containing interactive and graphics labs, conducts advanced research centering on problem-solving with an emphasis on nonbroadcast telecommunications.

Guide POV: Most selective, the Tisch School of the Arts offers a variety of quality programs geared to animators and to those working in emerging technologies; Department of Film and Television provides undergraduates with comprehensive training in media production combined with studies in the liberal arts; advanced training in both cel and computer graphics animation; West Coast Alumni Group job bank matches listings and graduates; Graduate Film Program provides self-contained Animation Department; there is a separate, innovative Interactive Telecommunications Program providing graduate training in emerging computer technologies, exploring their applications in various media such as video, graphics, and publishing; course listings cover entertainment, business, telecommunications, marketing, research, and public service fields with courses in computer graphics and animation.

PARSONS SCHOOL OF DESIGN

66 Fifth Ave., New York, NY 10011
(212) 229-8950
Private professional arts institution and a division of the New School for Social Research. Coed, urban location. Undergraduate enrollment: 2,300. Graduate enrollment: 140. Continuing Education enrollment: 1,975.

Calendar: Semesters.

Degrees Offered: B.F.A., B.B.A., B.A./B.F.A., M.F.A., M.Arch., M.A., A.A.S.

Curricular Emphasis: Whether students concentrate in one field or pursue a multimedia investigation of the fine arts, they receive thorough guidance and access to professional equipment; students receive a solid introduction to computer graphics (2-D, 3-D, and animation) during the freshman foundation year, followed by intermediate courses on industry standard platforms and the pursuit of advanced independent research; seniors may intern with professional design firms in New York; Continuing Education courses are offered to students with focused interests such as Desktop Publishing and AutoCAD.

Facilities/Equipment: Foundation Computing Laboratory; Parsons Computing Center which includes a 200-station Macintosh facility with sophisticated input and output capabilities; advanced satellite labs such as the Center for Agile Computing (modeling, rendering, animation platforms by Alias, Wavefront, SoftImage and Athena); Fashion Design Computing Laboratory (CDI, InfoDesign, AVL); Experimental Multimedia Workshop (including multiple dedicated World-Wide-Web sites); facilities are networked via a high-speed, fiber-optic WAN; Direct Internet access occurs through dedicated T1 connection.

Guide POV: Providing an experience-based education for students intending to pursue careers in design, the faculty at Parsons, composed of industry professionals, emphasizes real world themes and applications; the ambitious computing curriculum is directed at fostering experimentation and spans its nine undergraduate majors; the school challenges its students not only to master

•••

the technology relevant to their chosen fields, but also to use a variety of cutting-edge equipment and platforms, some of which are so new they are unique to these facilities.

PRATT INSTITUTE
200 Willoughby Ave., Brooklyn, NY 11205
(718) 636-3600
Private comprehensive institution. Coed, urban location. Undergraduate enrollment: 3,000. Graduate enrollment: 750.

Calendar: Semesters.

Degrees Offered: B.F.A., M.F.A., Computer Graphics; B.F.A., Media Arts.

Curricular Emphasis: Department of Computer Graphics and Interactive Multimedia—undergraduate course listings include Introduction to Computer Graphics I and II; Introduction to Computer Graphics Programming I and II; Graphic Design With a Computer I and II; 3-D Modeling with Computer Graphics I; Introduction to 3-D Computer Modeling and Animation; 3-D Computer Animation I and II; Interactive Media I; Computer-Aided Design and Drafting I and II; Computer Graphics Portfolio; Illustration with Computer Graphics; Computer Graphics in Context. Graduate Program in Computer Graphics includes options in computer animation, interactive systems/multimedia, experimental media, and electronic pre-press; advanced computer animation workshops. Media Arts Department—students work in both film and video with undergraduate course listings that include Animation; Film and Television Graphics; Computer Animation and Graphics for Film and Television; Postproduction Computer Animation and Graphics; Video Graphics for the Artist and Designer; Advanced Postproduction.

Facilities/Equipment: Computer graphics resources include 35 Apple Macintosh and Quadra computers with graphics boards and color monitors; large selection of graphics software including interactive multimedia, draw, animation, and electronic pre-press programs; 10 Silicon Graphics workstations running the Alias and SoftImage three-dimensional modeling and animation software; one Quantel Graphic Paintbox; fifteen PC-compatible computers with Targa graphics boards, graphics tablets and assorted input and output peripherals running the Tips paint and image processing program; one Sony 3/4" Video Editing System with A/B roll and special effects capabilities; large array of input and output peripherals including video recorders, film recorders, printers and scanners; additional computer resources available through other Pratt programs include a DEC VAX 6210 minicomputer, three Skok CAD systems, 10 Sun Sparc stations, and dozens of additional PC and Macintosh systems.

Guide POV: This highly ranked, markedly well-equipped arts school offers 24-hour access to facilities; program in Computer Graphics prepares students for careers in computer animation and video production as well as in design, publishing, software development, and electronic and interactive databases; full master's program in computer graphics with advanced thesis projects; in addition, the Media Arts Department provides undergraduate studies in both cel and computer animation with special attention to computer animation and graphics techniques for film and television; this curriculum combines photography, film, video, and animation studies into one academic area in which students elect a specific field of concentration while garnering experience in all facets of department's program of studies.

RENSSELAER POLYTECHNIC INSTITUTE

Troy, NY 12180-3590

(518) 276-6000

Private comprehensive institution. Coed, urban location. Undergraduate enrollment: 4,500. Graduate enrollment: 3,000.

Calendar: Semesters.

Degrees Offered: B.F.A., M.F.A., Electronic Arts; B.S., M.S. Ph.D., Computer and Systems Engineering.

Curricular Emphasis: Electronic Arts—this is a program for the musical and/or visual artist specializing in computer-based and electronic-based technology, with advanced studies in video art, computer imaging and animation, and computer music. Computer and Systems Engineering—undergraduate to advanced research studies in computer graphics; computer image processing and pattern recognition; artificial intelligence and robotics; computer systems; other areas.

Facilities/Equipment: Rensselaer Design Research Center is supported by more than 40 companies and government agencies, with funding directed to research studies in areas such as high performance graphics systems, geometric modeling, design, and visualization; newest systems from Apple, AT&T, Digital Equipment Corporation, Hewlett-Packard, IBM, Sun, and Silicon Graphics; state-of-the-art computer animation systems and software; video equipment; MIDI studio.

Guide POV: Founded in 1824, Rensselaer Polytechnic Institute provides advanced computer graphics and animation studies with markedly comprehensive, state-of-the art facilities; separate quality programs tailored to the student interested in either fine arts or computer engineering.

ROCHESTER INSTITUTE OF TECHNOLOGY

One Lamb Dr., Rochester, NY 14623-0887

(716) 475-2411

Private comprehensive institution. Coed, suburban location. Undergraduate enrollment: 11,000. Graduate enrollment: 1,500.

Calendar: Quarters.

Degrees Offered: A.A.S., B.F.A., Film and Video; M.F.A., Computer Animation; M.F.A./M.S.T., Computer Graphics Design; B.S., M.S., Ph.D., Imaging Arts; M.S., Graphic Arts Systems.

Curricular Emphasis: Film and Video Department—areas of study include film and video animation; writing; directing; producing; graduate major in computer animation combines technical and aesthetic practices with the learning of relevant programming techniques. Imaging Science—undergraduate and graduate degree programs explore field of solid state imaging including high-definition television and computer animation, as well as other areas involving the detecting, creating, displaying and perceiving of images, such as holography, electronic printing, and remote sensing; strong background in chemistry, physics, and calculus required.

Facilities/Equipment: Center for Imaging Arts houses animation stands; computer graphics generators; micro-computer animation room with Mac II microcomputers and high-resolution TOPAZ 3-D animation systems; complete Super-8 and 16mm film production and postproduction; complete 3/4" and 1/2" video location; editing including Grass Valley 110 component switch; Amiga toaster; computer and cel animation.

Guide POV: Students enrolled in the lively media program work in both film and video and must produce animation, narrative fiction, and documentary projects before choosing a concentration in either animation, writing, directing, or production; 24-hour equipment checkout; required senior thesis project; required crew assignments; there is a graduate major in computer animation; separate degree program in imaging science is currently the nation's only Ph.D. program in this emerging technology; advanced studies in high-definition television and computer animation, holographic imaging, robotics, digital image processing, electrophotography, satellite imaging systems, optics, laser systems and related fields; related studies include advanced certificate program available in interactive media design through the American Video Institute where students explore graphic design in terms of interactive media, videodisc systems, image-bank management, advanced video techniques, optical disc storage, moving imagery, and communication theory.

SAINT JOHN'S UNIVERSITY
Grand Central and Utopia Pkwys., Jamaica, NY 11439
(718) 990-6161
Private comprehensive institution. Coed, urban location. Undergraduate enrollment: 16,000. Graduate enrollment: 5,000.

Calendar: Semesters.

Degrees Offered: B.F.A., Graphic Design. B.S., Communication Arts.

Curricular Emphasis: Graphic Design Program—comprehensive visual communications degree; specialized courses; common core in drawing, painting, anatomy, color theory, printmaking, and sculpture. Communication Arts—diverse curriculum emphasizes broadcast production while also providing training in film and video production; course listings include Video Graphics I; Fundamentals of Media Graphics; Motion Graphics; Video Animation.

Facilities/Equipment: Computer graphics lab includes Macintosh and IBM systems; Photoshop; Pagemaker; Quark Xpress; Illustrator Freehand; Macromind Director; Premiere and Adobe Dimensions; complete film, video and television production and postproduction.

Guide POV: This university offers a full major in graphic design; concentrations in computer graphics, cartoon and animation, illustration, or publication/editorial design; in addition, the Communication Arts Department presents eight media concentrations; topics include electronic graphics systems for television, frame-by-frame video animation, object animation, character animation, and special effects.

SCHOOL OF VISUAL ARTS
209 E. 23rd St., New York, NY 10010
(212) 592-2100
Private professional arts institution. Coed, urban location. Undergraduate enrollment: 2,750. Graduate enrollment: 320.

Calendar: Semesters.

Degrees Offered: B.F.A., Film/Video/Animation. B.F.A., M.F.A., Computer Art.

Curricular Emphasis: Film/Video/Animation Department—directing; screenwriting; cinematography; editing; animation; video art; studio and field production with ENG; course listings include Introduction to Film Animation; Animation Drawing I and II; Action Analysis and Timing; Camera and Editing; Special Effects; Puppet Animation; Animation Workshop I and II; Video Art; Video Image Processing; Animation Thesis. Computer Art Department—course listings include Computer Animation; Computer Graphics I, II, and III; 3-D Animation; Computer Drawing; 3-D Modeling and Animation; Computer Design; MacGraphics; Film and Video with the Computer; Digital Photography; Desktop Animation; Scripts and Animation; Computers in Art; 3-D Illustration and Design; Image Making; workshops.

Facilities/Equipment: Two Oxberry animation cameras; two pencil animation video systems; optical bench for film; Moviola and Steenbeck editing machines with sound track analyzation equipment; computer graphics lab with IBM and Macintosh computers; Amiga; Easel; Dr. Halo; Deluxe Paint; variety of other systems and software; complete film, video and television production and postproduction.

Guide POV: Providing quality instruction for animators and computer artists, this institution—which started as a school of cartooning and illustration and is now the country's largest independent art school—offers a media program with sequential course listings in animation, as well as thorough training in film and video production; 24-hour access to equipment; separate program in computer art and graphics covers computer animation for film and video as well as a variety of other projects in computer art and design; both undergraduate and graduate programs in computer art are offered; program maintains 1:1 student to computer ratio; separate program in Illustration and Cartooning; emphasis throughout on individual projects; animation students are expected to complete a short Thesis Film in any animation technique creating characters, design, and sound tracks.

SKIDMORE COLLEGE
Saratoga Springs, NY 12866-1632
(518) 584-5000
Private comprehensive institution. Coed, small town location. Undergraduate enrollment: 2,200.

Calendar: Semesters.

Degrees Offered: B.S., Art.

Curricular Emphasis: Art Department—there are four advanced studio courses in computer imaging; each student uses 35mm camera; airbrush; studies in 3-D computer animation and video production; graphic design; computer imaging projects for television, books, magazines, and posters.

Facilities/Equipment: Computer graphics lab in the art building; variety of software; UNIX operating system; Macintosh and Silicon Graphics workstations using Wavefront animation software; video animation.

Guide POV: Skidmore College's Art Department offers advanced computer graphics instruction within the context of a studio art degree; emphasis on individual and group projects in computer animation and graphic design using advanced computer imaging techniques; diverse projects include those in video animation, photo-montage, scientific visualization, advertising design, and book publishing.

STATE UNIVERSITY OF NEW YORK AT BINGHAMTON
Vestal Pkwy. E., Binghamton, NY 13902-6000.
(607) 777-2000
State comprehensive institution. Coed, urban location. Undergraduate enrollment: 8,315.

Calendar: Semesters.

Degrees Offered: B.A., Cinema.

Curricular Emphasis: Beginning to advanced production with emphasis on film and video as art forms; digital electronic artmaking; topical studies in cinema; course listings include Film Artmaking I and I; Analog Electronic Artmaking; Digital Electronic Artmaking; Advanced Electronic Artmaking.

Facilities/Equipment: Animation stands (Oxberry and Bolex); JandK computer-controlled optical printers; video artmaking studio with Amiga computers; film to video transfer suite; complete film and video production and postproduction; switcher/special effects generators.

Guide POV: This quality program offers professional production training with a strong emphasis on film and video art; projects in character and computer animation; exploration of new media; attention to experimental forms.

STATE UNIVERSITY OF NEW YORK AT BUFFALO
Hayes-A 3435 Main St., Buffalo, NY 14260-6020
(716) 645-6902/6878
State comprehensive institution. Coed, urban location. Undergraduate enrollment: 18,831. Graduate enrollment: 8,812.

Calendar: Semesters.

Degrees Offered: Department of Media Study—B.A., Media Study; M.A., Humanities. Department of Art—B.A., B.F.A., Communication Design; B.F.A., Computer Art.

Curricular Emphasis: Department of Media Study—students are offered training in production of independent film, video and digital arts projects;

emphasis on animated, narrative, ethnographic and documentary forms; film theory, history, and analysis; critical focus on image making codes; graduate program is interdisciplinary. Department of Art—students are offered course listings that include Computer Art and Design; Visual Symbology and Syntax; Time Based Imaging; Motion Imaging; Modeling and Simulation; Image Synthesis, and Interactive Computer Art.

Facilities/Equipment: Students in the Department of Media Study are equipped with an animation stand; complete 16mm film and video production and postproduction; two Amiga computer labs, one with five Amiga 500 and two Amiga 2000 computers; peripherals include DCTV, DigiView, sound sampler and a Toaster; the second lab has three Amiga 4000 computers, one with a Personal Animation Recorder, a second with AMILink A-B roll editor and a Toaster and the third Amiga 4000 has a SunRise Studio 16 audio board; Computer Art and Communication Design majors make use of computer graphics labs that include 60-plus Mac computer systems, ranging from LC3 to Power PC and Quadra 800, and color Ink Jet dye-sublimation and laser printers with video input and output.

Guide POV: Students at this university who wish to pursue studies in computer graphics are offered a choice between two quality programs: first, undergraduates in the Department of Media Study approach independent and experimental film, video and digital arts production with a special interest in the integration of new media technologies; students work in film, video, and digital arts before choosing one or more concentration areas; secondly, the Department of Art offers students majoring in either Computer Art or Communication Design a program that focuses on the computer as a unique tool and medium for communication and expression, both in publication and in artists' productions.

STATE UNIVERSITY OF NEW YORK AT OSWEGO

Oswego, NY 13126
(315) 341-2500
State comprehensive institution. Coed, suburban location. Undergraduate enrollment: 8,000.

Calendar: Semesters.

Degrees Offered: B.A., Communication Studies.

Curricular Emphasis: Communication Studies—broadcast production with advanced training in principles of television graphics design emphasizing creative innovation and manipulation of graphic materials; attention to design, illustration, mounting, lettering, coloring, and transparency production; additional course in computer graphics through Computer Science Department emphasizes algorithms and data structures.

Facilities/Equipment: Computer graphics lab with Amiga computers; television and video production and postproduction.

Guide POV: Within the comprehensive Broadcasting and Mass Communications major, students receive a core curriculum dealing with American broadcasting history and management; diverse electives in broadcast production, cable television, computer graphics, and other areas.

STATE UNIVERSITY OF NEW YORK AT PURCHASE

735 Anderson Hill Rd., Purchase, NY 10577

(914) 251-6000

State comprehensive institution. Coed, suburban location. Undergraduate enrollment: 4,000.

Calendar: Semesters.

Degrees Offered: B.F.A., Film; Professional Training Program for Directors.

Curricular Emphasis: At the conclusion of the sophomore year, students choose a concentration in either experimental, narrative, or documentary filmmaking; in-depth instruction in film animation; training in video production; professional program leads to degree in motion picture directing; students participate in national film and video festivals.

Facilities/Equipment: Animation stand; complete film and video production and postproduction; 10-track mixing studio.

Guide POV: Aspiring filmmakers at SUNY Purchase's School of the Arts produce, write, direct, and edit their own work, completing at least one original film per academic year; advanced projects in film animation.

STATE UNIVERSITY OF NEW YORK AT STONY BROOK

Stony Brook, NY 11794-1901

(516) 689-6000

State comprehensive institution. Coed, suburban location. Undergraduate enrollment: 11,310. Graduate enrollment: 6,320.

Calendar: Semesters.

Degrees Offered: B.S., M.S., Ph.D., Computer Science.

Curricular Emphasis: Computer Science—course listings include Fundamentals of Computer Graphics; Computer Graphics; 3-D Graphics; Special Topics in Computer Graphics; Image Analysis; Computer Vision; Seminar in Computer Graphics; Seminar in Image Analysis; User Interface Development; Digital Simulation and Modeling; Projects.

Facilities/Equipment: Computer graphics lab with Sun; SGI; HP; PHIGS; variety of other systems and software.

Guide POV: Students at this competitive state university may pursue undergraduate and graduate training in the field of computer graphics with special attention to new research in the areas of digital simulation and modeling, image analysis, and computer vision; software engineering; advanced projects.

SUFFOLK COUNTY COMMUNITY COLLEGE

533 College Rd., Selden, NY 11784

(516) 451-4110

State and county two-year institution. Coed, suburban location. enrollment: 19,000.

Calendar: Semesters.

Degrees Offered: A.A.S., Broadcast Telecommunications.

Curricular Emphasis: Broadcast and corporate audio-video production and management.

Facilities/Equipment: Film—35mm screening facilities; animation stand; complete Super-8 production and postproduction; complete television and video production and postproduction.

Guide POV: Students planning careers as media production technicians or managers receive two-year training through this practical program; emphasis on variety of production techniques, including computer graphics, for both broadcast and nonbroadcast media; additional training in cel animation; video art; basic film production.

SYRACUSE UNIVERSITY
Syracuse, NY 13244
(315) 443-1033
Private comprehensive institution. Coed, urban location. Undergraduate enrollment: 11,000. Graduate enrollment: 4,000.

Calendar: Semesters.

Degrees Offered: B.F.A., M.F.A., Art Media Studies.

Curricular Emphasis: Diverse curriculum includes courses in filmmaking, computer graphics, composition animation, photography, advanced video postproduction techniques, screenwriting, sound techniques, and experimental production along with requirements in film and video theory, history and criticism; separate undergraduate filmmaking tracks in either film art or film drama; students choosing film art track take variety of studio art electives; computer graphics listings include Introduction to Computer Graphics for the Visual Arts (two semesters); Intermediate Computer Graphics for the Visual Arts (two semesters); Advanced Computer Graphics for the Visual Arts (two semesters); Graduate Computer Graphics for the Visual Arts (two semesters); separate concentration in Art Video.

Facilities/Equipment: 16mm Oxberry animation studio; optical printer studio; complete film and video production and postproduction including Amiga toaster and special effects equipment for video; computer graphics lab includes Macintosh II FX with Nu-Vista board; VAX 8810 network; Sun workstations; Tek cluster; Silicon Graphics Iris; numerous PCs; connection machine.

Guide POV: The School of Art and Design of Syracuse University is one of the oldest and most highly-rated in the country, offering students a curriculum in which freshmen explore twenty different programs of study before choosing a concentration; undergraduate and graduate programs in filmmaking (including animation), art video, and computer graphics; emphasis on experimental and narrative filmmaking.

TOMPKINS CORTLAND COMMUNITY COLLEGE
170 North St., Box 139, Dryden, NY 13053
(607) 844-8211
County two-year institution. Coed, rural location. enrollment: 2,000.

Calendar: Semesters.

Degrees Offered: A.S., A.A.S., Television and Radio; A.A.S., Graphic Design/Computer Graphics.

Curricular Emphasis: Television and Radio—broadcasting students may specialize in visual production by taking electives through the Art Department that include Graphic Design I and II; Design I and II; Computer Graphics I and II; Photography. Graphic Design and Computer Graphics—sequential training in computer graphics as well as in drawing, design, and graphic design; additional studies in portable video techniques, illustration, photography, typography, and art history.

Facilities/Equipment: Television production and postproduction includes video special effects equipment; computer graphics lab with variety of systems and software.

Guide POV: This community college of SUNY offers broadcast students a visual production specialization which prepares computer graphics technicians for careers at television stations or video production houses; the broadly-designed Graphic Design/Computer Graphics Program prepares students for careers in design studios and creative agencies.

North Carolina

■■■■■■■■■■■■■ ■ ■ ■ ■ ■ ■ ■ ■ ■ ■ ■ ■ ■ ■

BARTON COLLEGE
600 W. Lee St., Wilson, NC 27893
(919) 399-6300
Private comprehensive institution. Coed, urban location. Undergraduate
enrollment: 1,300.

Calendar: Semesters.

Degrees Offered: B.A., B.S., Communications (focus in Film/Video).

Curricular Emphasis: Electronic media theory and culture; critical studies in
media writing; video and broadcast television production; media management.

Facilities/Equipment: Complete video and television production and postproduction.

Guide POV: This private nonprofit college offers undergraduates a video
major centering on studio and on-site production; computer graphics effects
training for video and television production; advanced computer graphics
studies for commercial design applications.

DUKE UNIVERSITY
Durham, NC 27706
(919) 684-8111
Private comprehensive institution. Coed, urban location. Undergraduate
enrollment: 6,500. Graduate enrollment: 4,500.

Calendar: Semesters.

Degrees Offered: Certificate in Film and Video.

Curricular Emphasis: Film and Video Program—independent film and video
production; theory, history, and cultural criticism; student filmmaking collective; visiting film and video artists.

Facilities/Equipment: Animation stand; complete film, video, and television
production and postproduction; computer graphics lab.

Guide POV: Students at Duke University produce independent work in both
film and video; projects in film animation; video art.

NORTH CAROLINA STATE UNIVERSITY
Raleigh, NC 27695-8104
(919) 515-2011
State comprehensive institution. Coed, suburban location. Undergraduate
enrollment: 21,000. Graduate enrollment: 4,000.

Calendar: Semesters.

Degrees Offered: B.A.. Communication (concentration in Mass Communication); Film Minor offered by Departments of English, Communication, and
Multidisciplinary Studies.

Curricular Emphasis: Film Minor—critical studies; experimental and animated production. Communication Department—criticism; television and video production; broadcast journalism.

Facilities/Equipment: Animation stand; Super-8 cameras and editing; complete video and television production and postproduction.

Guide POV: Comprehensive and professional television and video training is offered through the Department of Communication including digital postproduction techniques; a separate Film Studies Minor offers studies in criticism and theory along with basic film production training, including experimental animation; attention to individual projects.

PEMBROKE STATE UNIVERSITY
Pembroke, NC 28372.
(919) 521-6378
State comprehensive institution. Coed, small town location. Undergraduate enrollment: 3,100. Graduate enrollment: 200.

Calendar: Semesters.

Degrees Offered: B.A., Mass Communications.

Curricular Emphasis: Telecommunications—broadcast production course listings include Computer Animation and Graphics; Advanced TV Production; Internship I and II; additional courses in news journalism and media management; student-staffed television facility serving over 500,000 homes telecasts 24-hours daily over microwave interconnect system linked to cable companies in five communities; production of live and taped programming.

Facilities/Equipment: Complete television and video production and postproduction includes A/B roll and nonlinear editing; control track and time code; computer animation and graphics lab.

Guide POV: Pembroke State University, part of the University of North Carolina system, offers complete technical training in broadcasting along with theoretical studies in mass communication; students use advanced computer graphics and nonlinear editing techniques; limited enrollment in production classes; supportive atmosphere; extremely active student-operated television station; tuition for in-state students is lowest of any four-year institution in the nation.

SCHOOL OF COMMUNICATION ARTS IN RALEIGH
American Center for Computer Imaging and Animation
3220 Spring Forest Rd., Raleigh, NC 27604
(919) 981-0971
Private two-year institution. Coed, urban location. enrollment: 300.

Calendar: Six-month and nine-month terms.

Degrees Offered: Certificates offered in Computer Graphics Design, Computer Art and Animation, and Multimedia and Advanced 3-D Computer Animation.

Curricular Emphasis: Computer Graphics Design Program—courses enable students to design and produce graphics for printed communications and desktop presentations. Computer Art and Animation Program—course listings are geared to students who will utilize PC-based software for commercial studio applications in both print and video production and for interactive digital presentations. Advanced 3-D Computer Animation program—courses oriented toward requirements for feature film, video and industrial production. Multimedia Program—training combines several disciplines in Digital Medial Production in which students bring entertainment, games, children's stories, encyclopedias, music, world maps and so on to the desktop computer.

Facilities/Equipment: 65 workstations for computer graphics and animation with Macintosh, PC and Silicon Graphics; production software includes SoftImage; Betacam postproduction; advanced media labs set up to incorporate desktop video, digital audio, mixed media production and interactive authoring.

Guide POV: Pointed instruction is offered in several disciplines; the Advanced 3-D Computer Animation program is oriented toward computer applications in feature film, video, and industrial production; the Computer Art and Animation program prepares students for commercial studio positions in both print and video production and for interactive digital presentations; the Computer Graphics Design program works with students on designing and producing graphics with an emphasis on printed media and desktop communications; and the Multimedia program incorporates a variety of disciplines; students receive accelerated instruction with every class held in a computer studio; graduates work in the entertainment, business and industrial industries as computer animators, video graphics artists and designers, multimedia artists, directors and producers, and advertising illustrators; sister-school in Minneapolis, MN.

SOUTHWESTERN COMMUNITY COLLEGE
Webster Rd., Sylva, NC 28779
(704) 586-4091
State two-year institution. Coed, rural location. enrollment: 1,400.

Calendar: Quarters.

Degrees Offered: A.A.S., Radio and Television Broadcast Technology.

Curricular Emphasis: Course listings include Computer Graphics; Computer Literacy; Television Systems; Television Production I and II; sponsored projects in corporate video programs, public service videos, and advertising.

Facilities/Equipment: Complete television production and postproduction; video toaster system; Super-8 filmmaking.

Guide POV: Students at this small community college learn all aspects of broadcast operations, including computer graphics generation for television, media management, technical troubleshooting, media writing, production and performance; individual attention to projects.

UNIVERSITY OF NORTH CAROLINA AT CHAPEL HILL
Chapel Hill, NC 27599-6235
(919) 962-2211
State comprehensive institution. Coed, urban location. Undergraduate enrollment: 16,000. Graduate enrollment: 8,000.

Calendar: Semesters.

Degrees Offered: B.A., M.A., M.S., Ph.D.

Curricular Emphasis: Department of Communication Studies—this liberal arts major emphasizes writing, practice, and film/media theory; student television production unit; film and television production companies. Computer Science—graduate course listings include Virtual Worlds; Computer Vision; Picture Processing and Pattern Recognition; Raster Graphics.

Facilities/Equipment: Animation stand; complete film, video and television production and postproduction; computer graphics lab includes Pixar; PS300; VG; Adage; variety of other systems and software.

Guide POV: Founded in 1795, this selective university offers film and television production training within a strong media studies curriculum; strong emphasis on theory and writing; individual production projects including cel animation; graduate program is theory-oriented with additional electives in production; this is one of the oldest mass media programs in the South; in addition, the Computer Science Department offers advanced graduate studies in computer graphics; emphasis on newest technologies; advanced research; students may participate in joint programs with Duke University and North Carolina University.

UNIVERSITY OF NORTH CAROLINA AT GREENSBORO
Greensboro, NC 27412
(919) 334-5000
State comprehensive institution. Coed, urban location. Undergraduate enrollment: 8,000. Graduate enrollment: 2,500.

Calendar: Semesters.

Degrees Offered: B.A., Media Studies; M.F.A., Film and Video Production.

Curricular Emphasis: Broadcasting/Cinema—Undergraduate film, video and broadcast production and theory including limited training in film animation; graduate film and video production and theory; Carolina Film and Video Festival (national competition).

Facilities/Equipment: Complete film, video, and television production and postproduction.

Guide POV: Limited enrollment at this university promotes support to serious undergraduate and graduate projects in film, video, and television; interested students may pursue projects in film animation; strong emphasis on developing creative potential; university sponsors exchanges in Europe, Australia, and Central America; practicum work built into requirements for graduate program.

WAKE FOREST UNIVERSITY
1832 Reynolda Rd., Winston-Salem, NC 27109
(919) 759-5000
Private comprehensive institution. Coed, suburban location. Undergraduate enrollment: 3,500.

Calendar: Semesters.

Degrees Offered: B.A., Speech Communication.

Curricular Emphasis: Critical studies; media writing; audio-film-video production.

Facilities/Equipment: Animation stand; complete film, video, and television production and postproduction.

Guide POV: Established in 1834, this private university offers students a small program in media criticism and production, including advanced projects in film animation.

WINSTON-SALEM STATE UNIVERSITY
601 Martin Luther King Dr., Winston-Salem, NC 27110
(919) 750-2000
State comprehensive institution. Coed, urban location. Undergraduate enrollment: 2,700.

Calendar: Semesters.

Degrees Offered: B.A., Mass Communications.

Curricular Emphasis: Mass Communications Department—Radio-Television sequence prepares students for careers in production, performance, management and sales; includes computer graphics techniques for broadcasting; film animation studies possible for interested students.

Facilities/Equipment: Animation stand; custom-designed 3/4" television studio includes wireless lavaliere microphone system, state-of-the-art control room and postproduction equipment; computer graphics.

Guide POV: Students learn computer graphics techniques in the context of a broadcast production curriculum; expanding computer facilities; individual projects in cel animation.

North Dakota

■■■■■■■■■■■■■■■■■■■■■ ■ ■ ■ ■ ■ ■ ■

NORTH DAKOTA STATE UNIVERSITY
Fargo, ND 58105
(701) 237-8011
State comprehensive institution. Coed, urban location. Undergraduate enrollment: 10,000. Graduate enrollment: 10,000.

Calendar: Semesters.

Degrees Offered: B.A., M.A., Mass Communication.

Curricular Emphasis: Electronic media theory and culture; broadcast journalism; broadcast production; media management.

Facilities/Equipment: Television production and postproduction; University Computer Lab.

Guide POV: The program in broadcast journalism provides basic training in producing special effects for television; in addition, the computer science department offers course work in computer graphics, system simulation, and robotics.

UNIVERSITY OF NORTH DAKOTA
Grand Forks, ND 58201
(701) 777-2011
State comprehensive institution. Coed, urban location. Undergraduate enrollment: 10,000. Graduate enrollment: 1,100.

Calendar: Semesters.

Degrees Offered: B.A., M.A., Communication.

Curricular Emphasis: School of Communication—electronic media theory and culture; media writing; broadcast production; student-produced "Studio One" rated best college-produced news program by National College Broadcast Association.

Facilities/Equipment: Complete 3/4" television production and postproduction includes Intergroup 9600 switcher; Pinnacle Prism DVE; Laird CG.

Guide POV: Computer graphics effects for television are explored within the context of an active broadcasting program featuring a variety of student productions; advanced study and application of graphic design techniques, styles, and processes as used in mass media; attention to individual projects.

Ohio

■■■■■■■■■■■■■■ ■ ■ ■ ■ ■ ■ ■ ■ ■

ACA COLLEGE OF DESIGN

2528 Kemper Lane, East Walnut Hills, Cincinnati, OH 45206
(513) 751-1206
Private two-year arts institution. Coed, urban location. enrollment: 100.

Calendar: Quarters.

Degrees Offered: A.A., Computer Graphics Design; two-year diploma program.

Curricular Emphasis: A 22-month program is geared to the art student interested in learning design techniques with special attention to the latest computer technologies; studies in both print and motion arts media; emphasis on advertising.

Facilities/Equipment: Computer graphics lab includes Macintosh computers with color monitors; color scanner; video scanning system; laser printer; additional exterior hard drives and memory; PMS color correct and color separation capabilities; Director, Freehand, Aldus, Persuasion, and Swivel 3-D animation software packages.

Guide POV: This two-year institution provides solid preparation for those seeking careers in graphic design at advertising agencies, television stations, and video production houses, as well as in publishing; advanced computer graphics studies possible; emphasis on art and design applications.

ANTIOCH COLLEGE

795 Livermore, Yellow Springs, OH 45387
(513) 767-7331
Private comprehensive institution. Coed, small town location. Undergraduate enrollment: 550.

Calendar: Quarters.

Degrees Offered: B.A., Communication and Media Arts (with emphasis in Film, Video, Documentary Arts, Journalism, or Photography).

Curricular Emphasis: Separate concentrations in film, video, and documentary arts production, as well as in journalism and photography; emphasis on experimental and independent forms; course work balances theory and practical training; studies in cultural criticism; curriculum grounded in socially responsible media practice; cooperative education program available in which students alternate quarters of work/internship and study.

Facilities/Equipment: Animation stand; complete film, video, and television production and postproduction.

Guide POV: Antioch College offers an individualized program of study emphasizing independent film and video production; projects in film animation; 24-hour access to postproduction facilities.

BOWLING GREEN STATE UNIVERSITY
Bowling Green, OH 43403
(419) 372-2531
State comprehensive institution. Coed, suburban location. Undergraduate enrollment: 16,000. Graduate enrollment: 2,600.

Calendar: Semesters.

Degrees Offered: B.A.

Curricular Emphasis: Art Department—course listings include Introduction to Computer Art; 3-D Animation; Problems in Computer Art; Advanced Problems in Computer Art; Simulation or Special Techniques.

Facilities/Equipment: Computer graphics lab with Atari Mega 2 and 3; animation software; laser printer; genloc board; Amiga 1000s; Paint and Sculpt software; Lumena; complete film, video and television production and post-production.

Guide POV: Undergraduates majoring in art at this state university undertake advanced computer animation projects; other media production courses offered through the Film Studies Program and the Department of Radio-Television-Film.

CENTRAL STATE UNIVERSITY
Wilberforce, OH 45384
(513) 376-6011
Public comprehensive institution. Coed, small town location. Undergraduate enrollment: 3,000.

Calendar: Quarters.

Degrees Offered: B.A., Fine Arts.

Curricular Emphasis: Fine Arts Department—course listings include Computer Graphics Workshop; special projects.

Facilities/Equipment: Computer graphics lab with Amiga 500; 2000; camera; camcorder; genlock board; Sculpt-Animate 3-D/4-D software.

Guide POV: Fine Arts majors at this state university may train as computer graphics artists for careers in print and motion arts media; emphasis on developing personal portfolio.

COLLEGE OF MOUNT SAINT JOSEPH
5701 Delhi Rd., Cincinnati, OH 45233-1670
(513) 244-4200
Private comprehensive institution. Coed, urban location. Undergraduate enrollment: 2,500. Graduate enrollment: 300.

Calendar: Semesters.

Degrees Offered: B.A., Communication Arts (students may select emphasis in Visual Media); A.A., B.A., B.F.A., Graphic Design.

Curricular Emphasis: Humanities Department—film, video, and television production, including animation, documentary, and news production. Art Department—training offered in graphic design, digital photography and animation.

Facilities/Equipment: Animation stand; complete film, video, and television production and postproduction; computer graphics lab.

Guide POV: The Visual Media emphasis includes production training in film, corporate video, and broadcast television; students may produce animated projects in film; computer graphics training for careers in design as well as at video production houses and television stations.

DENISON UNIVERSITY
Granville, OH 43023
(614) 587-0810
Private comprehensive institution. Coed, small town location. Undergraduate enrollment: 1,950.

Calendar: Semesters.

Degrees Offered: B.A., Cinema.

Curricular Emphasis: Department of Theatre and Cinema—cinema studies are taught in a liberal arts setting; even balance of production and film studies course load; all production in 16mm or S-VHS video; film animation training; Artist-In-Residence Program.

Facilities/Equipment: Oxberry animation stand; J-K optical printer; complete film and video production and postproduction.

Guide POV: The quality-oriented Cinema Program is designed for the motivated film/video student wishing to explore the possibilities of cinematic art; narrative, animated, documentary and avant-garde works; additional course listings in cinema history/theory, screenwriting, and film analysis; study abroad program allows for semester of studying cinema in another country; there is a New York Arts Semester in which students may be paired with artists working in NYC.

FRANKLIN UNIVERSITY
201 S. Grant Ave., Columbus, OH 43215-5399
(614) 341-6237
Private comprehensive institution. Coed, urban location. Undergraduate enrollment: 26,000. Graduate enrollment: 7,000.

Calendar: Semesters.

Degrees Offered: B.S, Computer Science.

Curricular Emphasis: Computer Science—course work in computer graphics trains students in the manipulation and display of 2-D and 3-D objects; other topics include hidden surface algorithms, shading algorithms, and animation techniques; emphasis on interactive computer graphics.

Facilities/Equipment: Computer graphics lab with variety of hardware and software; complete video and television studio and field equipment.

Guide POV: The computer science student may concentrate on computer graphics studies with an emphasis on interactive computer graphics; in addition, a practical program in communications focuses on the acquisition of electronic media production skills; study abroad possible at Richmond College in London.

OBERLIN COLLEGE

173 W. College St., Oberlin, OH 44074-1191

(216) 775-8121

Private comprehensive institution. Coed, rural location. Undergraduate enrollment: 3,000.

Calendar: Semesters.

Degrees Offered: B.A., B.S.

Curricular Emphasis: Art Department—course listings include Computer Imaging; Projects. Computer Science Department—course listings include Computer Imaging; Introduction to Graphics; Computer Graphics; Projects.

Facilities/Equipment: Complete video production and postproduction; computer graphics lab with Macs; DEC; SGI.

Guide POV: This private college offers the art major instruction in creating, manipulating, and recording computer images; emphasis on translating images created on computer into traditional media of drawing and painting; the computer science major with a strong background in mathematics is offered two semesters of computer graphics instruction; topics include perspective displays and clipping; splines and fractals; hidden surfaces; color and shading; algorithms; two- and three-dimensional transformations; other topics include artificial intelligence; computer application development; structured programming; software development; there is a Semester-in-London Program for qualified students.

OHIO STATE UNIVERSITY

Columbus, OH 43212

(614) 292-6446

Public comprehensive institution. Coed, urban location. Undergraduate enrollment: 50,000. Graduate enrollment: 10,000.

Calendar: Quarters.

Degrees Offered: Media Arts—B.F.A., M.F.A. Theatre Department—B.A., B.F.A., M.A.; M.F.A., Directing Program in Cinema.

Curricular Emphasis: Art (Media Arts Program)—undergraduate and graduate course listings include Microcomputer Graphics I and II; Computer Animation Production I, II, and III; Character Animation by Computer; 3-D Computer Modeling; Introduction to Multimedia; graduate concentration in computer graphics and animation; advanced topics at the Center include virtual reality; image manipulation; geometric modeling. Theatre Department—undergraduate and graduate course work includes film animation training; film/video production; graduate directing program. Computer Science Department—course listings include 3-D Image Generation I and II; Geometric Modeling; Projects.

Facilities/Equipment: Animation stand; Super-8, 16mm and 35mm cameras; complete film, video and television production and postproduction; computer graphics lab includes Amiga 2000; Sun NFS; Convex C-1; Hewlett-Packard color graphics workstations; Hypercube; Butterfly; Encore; Cray; Transputer; variety of other systems and software.

Guide POV: The Advanced Computing Center for the Arts and Design at Ohio State University conducts research and instruction in computer graphics and animation for students from a variety of disciplines including art and computer science; undergraduate course work and special graduate art concentration in computer graphics and animation; computer science students explore geometric modeling and 3-D image generation; undergraduate and graduate training is offered in film/video through the Department of Photography and Cinema, and includes film animation projects; well-equipped production facilities open to students at all levels.

UNIVERSITY OF CINCINNATI

Cincinnati, OH 45221-0091

(513) 556-6000

State comprehensive institution. Coed, urban location. Undergraduate enrollment: 31,000. Graduate enrollment: 5,200.

Calendar: Quarters.

Degrees Offered: B.F.A., M.F.A., Art; B.F.A., Electronic Media; B.S., Graphic Design.

Curricular Emphasis: School of Art—undergraduate and graduate studies in electronic art stressing computer-based applications, which either output to videotape or are interactive; live action production; experimental animation. Electronic Media Department—study of radio, sound recording, television, video production and other forms of electronic media communication; broadcast journalism and corporate video emphasis; computer graphics. Graphic Design—this is a five-year professional practice program leading to careers in communication design, visual design, or graphic design; applications in film, video messages, corporate symbols, advertisements, photographic images, etc.

Facilities/Equipment: Animation stand; animation drawing tables; film chain; RGB camera for animation grab; complete film, video, and television production and postproduction including 3/4" SMPTE editing suite with Videographics and special video effects; computer graphics lab with Macintosh; Sun; Wavefront software; NuVista; color, slide, black and white and 3-D scanners; variety of other systems and software.

Guide POV: An innovative and well-equipped film and video program is offered through the Art Department, emphasizing interactive media, electronic arts, and experimental animation; emphases on both artistic and technical merit; exploration of alternative applications to current technology; separate undergraduate Electronic Media Program offers career training in broadcasting with a news/documentary sequence; includes computer graphics training for television; in addition, there is a well-rated five-year Graphic Design Program.

UNIVERSITY OF TOLEDO

2801 W. Bancroft St., Toledo, OH 43606-3390

(419) 537-2072

Public comprehensive institution. Coed, suburban location. Undergraduate enrollment: 17,000. Graduate enrollment: 5,000.

Calendar: Quarters.

Degrees Offered: B.A., B.F.A., Art. B.A., Film; B.F.A., Film/Video. B.S., M.S., Ph.D., Engineering.

Curricular Emphasis: Department of Art—the Cyber Arts program within the Department of Art addresses two-dimensional, three-dimensional and interactive media, encouraging experimental approaches to the mixing of technology and traditional media. Theatre, Film, and Dance Department—instruction in film and video production, history and theory with special attention to experimental film and video, including one course in film animation. Computer Science and Engineering—course listings include Computer Graphics I, II and III; Special Topics.

Facilities/Equipment: The Department of Art's Digital Studio maintains 15 Networked Macintosh computers consisting of CIs, AV Quadras and AV Power PC; color scanner; laser and color printers; film recorder; CD read/write; all computers have Internet access and all Cyber Arts students have e-mail accounts; adjacent to the Digital Studio are a 3-D fabrication room and a complete workshop; in addition, the film department houses an Oxberry Media Pro 16mm animation stand (Bolex camera); film and video production and postproduction including JK optical printer; S-VHS video including Video Toaster and Amiga graphics.

Guide POV: Through the Department of Art's innovative, recently-designed Digital Studio program, students integrate traditional media and new technology, exploring digital animation, photography, interactive media, and other areas; in addition, the film production program provides training for those working in video as well and promotes the independent exploration of varied forms, including film animation; the School of Engineering offers diverse course listings with special attention to problems in computer graphics; topics include interactive graphics, three-dimensional geometry, texture mapping, ray tracing, shading, and animation techniques.

WRIGHT STATE UNIVERSITY
Dayton, OH 45435
(513) 873-3333
State comprehensive institution. Coed, suburban location. Undergraduate enrollment: 13,000. Graduate enrollment: 4,000.

Calendar: Quarters.

Degrees Offered: B.A., Film Studies; B.F.A., Film Production.

Curricular Emphasis: Department of Theatre Arts—film and video production and theory treated equally; narrative, documentary, and experimental forms treated equally; training in film animation; video art; university-subsidized filmmaking grants for students; university filmmakers association; commercial theatre screenings of student films; workshops and master classes with industry professionals.

Facilities/Equipment: Animation stand; complete film, video, and television production and postproduction.

Guide POV: Undergraduates choosing a motion picture concentration within the lively Department of Theatre Arts are offered extensive practical training in film and video in addition to studies in media theory; projects in film animation; separate B.F.A. program with required 16mm senior practicum.

XAVIER UNIVERSITY

3800 Victory Pkwy., Cincinnati, OH 45207
(513) 745-3000
Private comprehensive institution. Coed, urban location. Undergraduate enrollment: 4,100. Graduate enrollment: 2,300.

Calendar: Semesters.

Degrees Offered: A.A., B.A., Communication Arts (emphasis in Electronic Media).

Curricular Emphasis: The Electronic Media Concentration offers courses in video production, video postproduction, video graphics, television directing, broadcast news and sports production, broadcast performance, and media management.

Facilities/Equipment: Complete video and television production and postproduction; computer graphics lab with high resolution paint system.

Guide POV: Founded in 1831, this private university offers an emphasis in electronic media that includes advanced postproduction training with attention to electronic graphics and video paint system operation, and teaches the integration of computer-generated animation with live/tape video and character generation.

YOUNGSTOWN STATE UNIVERSITY

410 Wick Ave., Youngstown, OH 44555-3150
(216) 742-3000
State comprehensive institution. Coed, urban location. Undergraduate enrollment: 14,179. Graduate enrollment: 1,275.

Calendar: Quarters.

Degrees Offered: B.F.A., Art (emphasis in Graphic Design). B.A., Telecommunications Studies (emphasis in Electronic Media).

Curricular Emphasis: Art Department—emphasis in Graphic Design includes course listings in Computer Graphics at several levels, a complete Graphic Design sequence and special projects. Telecommunications Department—emphasis in Electronic Media includes training in video graphics and special effects as well as directing, scriptwriting, and operations management.

Facilities/Equipment: Television production and postproduction; computer graphics lab with variety of paint/animation systems and software.

Guide POV: This commuter university provides a solid program in graphic design that includes special projects in computer animation as well as print media; special attention to development of personal style in computer imagery, encompassing both color systems and desktop publishing; in addition, a practical telecommunications program offers video postproduction graphics and special effects training; finally, the upper-division computer science major is offered studies in the algorithms of computer graphics.

Oklahoma

■■■■■■■■■■■■■■■■■■■■ ■ ■ ■ ■ ■ ■

NORTHEASTERN OKLAHOMA A&M COLLEGE
200 I St. NE, Miami, OK 74354-0001
(918) 542-8441
State two-year institution. Coed, small city location. enrollment: 2,000.

Calendar: Semesters.

Degrees Offered: A.S., A.A., Radio-TV-Film; Two-Year Certificate.

Curricular Emphasis: Radio-TV-Film Department—technical knowledge of equipment with an emphasis on training for immediate employment in the media industries; college students participate in national video festivals and competitions, such as the Hometown Video Festival and the Chicago International Festival.

Facilities/Equipment: Television and video production and postproduction including state-of-the-art chip cameras; digital graphics laboratory.

Guide POV: Comprehensive media instruction is offered at this community college; strong emphasis on practical studies for career employment, including digital graphics training for technical support positions in television.

OKLAHOMA STATE UNIVERSITY
Stillwater, OK 74078-0195
(405) 744-5000
State comprehensive institution. Coed, small city location. Undergraduate enrollment: 21,000. Graduate enrollment: 4,000.

Calendar: Semesters.

Degrees Offered: B.A., B.S., Journalism and Broadcasting. M.S., Mass Communications.

Curricular Emphasis: Radio-Television-Film—production training with diverse curriculum emphasizing broadcasting; individual projects in cel animation; training includes computer graphics for television broadcasting.

Facilities/Equipment: Animation stand; special effects library; complete film, video and television production and postproduction; computer graphics lab with variety of systems and software.

Guide POV: Undergraduate and graduate degree programs are offered to those seeking professional training in television production; character animation workshops are available to interested individuals; in addition, advanced graphics training with an emphasis on interactive computer graphics, modeling, simulation, robotics and computer-aided design offered through the Mechanical and Aerospace Engineering Department; Semester at Sea program.

ROSE STATE COLLEGE
6420 SE 15th St., Midwest City, OK 73110
(405) 733-7311
State two-year institution. Coed, small town location. enrollment: 10,000.

Calendar: Semesters.

Degrees Offered: A.A.S., Broadcasting (option in Production or Technology).

Curricular Emphasis: Production option includes intensive radio and television broadcast writing, production, and ENG/video editing training; computer graphics techniques; music video production; multipurpose on-campus television studio is designed for producing instructional video tapes.

Facilities/Equipment: Complete television and video production and postproduction including computer graphics.

Guide POV: For students seeking to enter the field of television production, this professional two-year program provides practical training that includes postproduction special effects; advanced students integrate computer graphics into their productions; diverse curriculum with projects in music video and instructional video production.

UNIVERSITY OF OKLAHOMA
520 Parrington Oval, Norman, OK 73019
(405) 325-0311
State comprehensive institution. Coed, urban location. Undergraduate enrollment: 20,000. Graduate enrollment: 2,000.

Calendar: Semesters.

Degrees Offered: B.A., M.F.A., Film/Video; B.A., Radio/TV/Film; M.A., Journalism/Mass Communication.

Curricular Emphasis: School of Art, Video/Film Department—production and theory taught as part of a fine arts curriculum; projects include experimental, animated, narrative, documentary, and film/video art. School of Journalism/Mass Communication Department—film and video production; emphasis on broadcast journalism.

Facilities/Equipment: Animation stand; complete film, video, and television production and postproduction; computer graphics lab.

Guide POV: Both the School of Art and the School of Journalism offer professional studies in film and video production with advanced projects in both film animation and computer graphics art and animation.

UNIVERSITY OF TULSA
600 S College Ave., Tulsa, OK 74104
(918) 631-2000
Private comprehensive institution. Coed, urban location. Undergraduate enrollment: 4,000. Graduate enrollment: 1,000.

Calendar: Semesters.

Degrees Offered: B.A., B.S., Communication.

Curricular Emphasis: Mass communication emphasis includes television and video production training with an emphasis on news/documentary; video art; computer graphics.

Facilities/Equipment: Complete television and video production and postproduction; computer graphics lab.

Guide POV: This private university offers competitive studies in video and television production; includes computer graphics training; undergraduates have good success rate entering major graduate cinema and television programs.

Oregon

■■■■■■■■■■■■■■■■■ ■ ■ ■ ■ ■ ■ ■

GEORGE FOX COLLEGE
Newberg, OR 97132
(503) 538-8383
Private comprehensive institution. Coed, suburban location. Undergraduate enrollment: 900.

Calendar: Semesters.

Degrees Offered: B.A., Communication/Video Production.

Curricular Emphasis: Communication Arts Department—technical and production-oriented video training; core requirements in both production and theory.

Facilities/Equipment: The Video Communication Center, including studio, audio bay, control room, and video editing suites, is used for the technical aspects of the major and is also used by the college for contracted work; complete video and television production and postproduction includes Amiga computer with CG software; video toaster; Mac II with graphics software.

Guide POV: Founded in 1891 by Oregon Quakers, this well-equipped private college offers students a major in Communication Arts that integrates the areas of speech communication, drama, journalism, and media; students may also choose the Communication/Video Production major which combines a strong production and theory core with extensive electives; 50 percent of graduates enter broadcasting field while 50 percent enter corporate/industrial market.

LANE COMMUNITY COLLEGE
4000 E. 30th Ave., Eugene, OR 97405
(503) 747-4501
State two-year institution. Coed, urban location. enrollment: 9,000.

Calendar: Ten-week terms.

Degrees Offered: A.A.S., Broadcasting/Visual Design and Production; A.A.S., Radio Production; certificates.

Curricular Emphasis: Media Arts and Technology Department—varied course listings in film, radio, video, and television production and postproduction; computer graphics; scriptwriting; corporate media; still photography.

Facilities/Equipment: Complete film, video and television production and postproduction including switchers; character generators; computer graphics.

Guide POV: Lane Community College offers students a diverse program with training in film, television, radio, and photography, along with several courses in film and electronic media theory and criticism; postproduction digital effects.

MOUNT HOOD COMMUNITY COLLEGE
26000 SE Stark St., Gresham, OR 97030
(503) 667-6422
District two-year institution. Coed, suburban location. enrollment: 1,200.

Calendar: Semesters.

Degrees Offered: A.A.S., Visual Art/Graphic Design.

Curricular Emphasis: Visual Arts/Graphic Design—course listings include Computer Graphics; Graphic Design; workshops; Computer Art gallery shows.

Facilities/Equipment: Computer graphics lab with Macintosh computers and power Macs; scanners; digitizing cameras; tablets; laser printers; color printers.

Guide POV: The one-year computer graphics program offers hands-on training in paint systems, illustration, digital imaging, and animation; the two-year graphic design program offers practical career training to those working in both print and motion graphics media.

NORTHWEST FILM CENTER

Portland Art Museum, 1219 SW Park Ave., Portland, OR 97205
(503) 221-1156
Regional media arts center. Coed, urban location. Undergraduate enrollment: 1,000.

Calendar: Two 15-week terms per academic year as well as a separate 10-week summer session.

Degrees Offered: B.F.A., Filmmaking and Animation (co-offered with the Pacific Northwest College of Art); Certificate Program in Film.

Curricular Emphasis: Hands-on production classes with professional film/videomakers; sequential training in film animation techniques; three major film festivals sponsored per year; Video/Filmmaker-In-Residence Program; video art installations.

Facilities/Equipment: Animation stand; complete 16mm film and video production and postproduction; digital sound design; digital video editing; access to computer graphics lab through Pacific Northwest College of Art.

Guide POV: Classes at this lively media arts center are primarily designed for the working professional who is either already in film/video or wishing to make a career transition; through affiliations with the Pacific Northwest College of Art and Marylhurst College, the Film Center offers accredited semester-long courses in Filmmaking and Animation toward the B.F.A. degree; the nondegree Certificate Program is a 14-course sequence that culminates in the production of an original short film; students take up to four years to complete certificate requirements.

OREGON STATE UNIVERSITY

Corvallis, OR 97331
(503) 737-0123
State comprehensive institution. Coed, small town location. Undergraduate enrollment: 12,400. Graduate enrollment: 2,500.

Calendar: Quarters.

Degrees Offered: B.S., M.S., Ph.D., Computer Science.

Curricular Emphasis: Department of Computer Science—variety of course listings; includes advanced projects in computer graphics.

Facilities/Equipment: Computer graphics lab with variety of systems and software.

Guide POV: Students may engage in research projects involving new applications in computer graphics.

PACIFIC NORTHWEST COLLEGE OF ART
1219 SW Park Ave., Portland, OR 97205
(503) 226-4391
Private professional arts college. Coed, urban location. Undergraduate enrollment: 250.

Calendar: Semesters.

Degrees Offered: B.F.A., Graphic Design/Illustration; B.F.A., Filmmaking and Animation (co-offered with the Northwest Film Center).

Curricular Emphasis: Departments of Graphic Design/Illustration—training in motion graphics as well as design, illustration, and advanced computer graphics technology; there is a thesis semester; students may incorporate curriculum of new Electronic Imaging Program dedicated to advanced experimental concepts in computer arts and imaging.

Facilities/Equipment: Computer graphics lab especially designed for fine and graphic arts majors with paint programs, animation, and specialized graphic design applications including MacPlus; SE; IIs; scanners; Dunn camera; genlock board; Colorfreeze 24; ImageStudio; Aldus; Adobe Freehand; Pixelpaint.

Guide POV: The Department of Graphic Design trains students in commercial communication for careers in print and electronic graphics; curriculum includes instruction in advanced computer graphics and animation systems and software; design projects; electronic imaging; separate degree program in Filmmaking and Animation offered in conjunction with Northwest Film Center, located adjacent to the College.

PORTLAND STATE UNIVERSITY
Portland, OR 97207
(503) 725-3000
State comprehensive institution. Coed, urban location. Undergraduate enrollment: 8,000. Graduate enrollment: 4,000.

Calendar: Quarters.

Degrees Offered: B.S., M.S., Computer Science.

Curricular Emphasis: Department of Computer Science—diverse course listings; advanced projects in computer graphics.

Facilities/Equipment: Computer graphics lab with variety of systems and software including Tektronix X terminals, both color and grey scale; NeXT, Sun, MS-DOS and Macintosh workstations; support for X terminals provided by Intel workstations; laser printers.

Guide POV: Students attending this commuter university may study advanced applications of computer graphics research through the small, solid Computer Science Department; flexible program designed to meet needs of individual students; program enjoys working relationship with local industries such as Tektronix, Sequent, and Intel.

UNIVERSITY OF OREGON
Eugene, OR 97403-1206
(503) 346-3111
Public comprehensive institution. Coed, urban location. Undergraduate enrollment: 15,000. Graduate enrollment: 4,000.

Calendar: Quarters.

Degrees Offered: B.A., B.S., M.S., B.F.A., M.F.A.

Curricular Emphasis: Fine and Applied Art—film/video/computer production with an experimental arts and animation approach; developing an understanding of time as a design consideration; investigation of continuity, movement and communication in time-based media; students work in both film and digital animation. Computer and Information Science Department—course listings include Computer Graphics; Advanced Computer Graphics; Advanced Rendering Techniques.

Facilities/Equipment: Animation compounds and stands; complete film, video, and television production and postproduction; computer graphics lab with variety of systems and software including Sun SPARC stations; Tek 4325; Iris 3030; SGI; Macintosh.

Guide POV: Through the innovative Fine and Applied Art Department, experimental, animated, and documentary film production training is offered with an emphasis on individual projects; alumni work as film and computer animators, multimedia designers, and graphic media artists and executives; in addition, the School of Journalism provides students with telecommunications training, including postproduction effects; finally, the Computer and Information Science Department offers undergraduate and graduate computer graphics training.

Pennsylvania

■■■■■■■■■■■■■■■■■■■ ■ ■ ■ ■ ■   ■

ALBRIGHT COLLEGE
13th and Exeter St., Reading, PA 19612-5234
(215) 921-2381
Private comprehensive institution. Coed, suburban location. Undergraduate
enrollment: 1,000.

Calendar: Semesters.

Degrees Offered: B.A., B.S., Art.

Curricular Emphasis: Art Department—film and video experimental and animated production; critical theory explored in context of modern visual/fine arts media; monthly visits by American and foreign experimental film and video artists; cooperative relationship with Berks Filmmakers. Computer Science Department—course listings include Introduction to Computer Graphics; Image Processing.

Facilities/Equipment: Animation stand; film library of avant-garde/experimental films and videotapes; complete film and video production and postproduction; computer graphics lab includes 486s; Macs; Suns; IBM PCs and clones.

Guide POV: Albright College offers a highly-charged fine arts program that focuses on the production of innovative noncommercial/experimental film and video; strong visiting artist series supports cutting-edge atmosphere; animated projects; in addition, Computer Science Department offers students with a strong mathematics background computer graphics instruction and image-processing methodologies.

BUCKS COUNTY COMMUNITY COLLEGE
Swamp Rd., Newtown, PA 18940
(215) 968-8000
County two-year institution. Coed, rural location. enrollment: 9,000.

Calendar: Semesters.

Degrees Offered: A.A., Cinema; Telecommunications; Digital Animation Track Graphic Design; Digital Illustration Track.

Curricular Emphasis: Communications Program—film production including animated, narrative, documentary, and experimental filmmaking; television and video production. Computer Graphics Track—Digital Animation; Digital Illustration; Digital 3-D Modeling; Graphic Design Illustration or Advertising; Television Studio Production; Advanced Television Postproduction.

Facilities/Equipment: Animation stand; computer graphics laboratory with variety of systems and software; complete film, video and television production and postproduction; digital audio and multitrack recording.

Guide POV: This lively community college offers students solid training in film, television and video production, cel animation, digital three-dimensional modeling, digital animation and computer illustration; quiet, semi-rural location close to Philadelphia and New York City; internships available.

CARNEGIE MELLON UNIVERSITY
Pittsburgh, PA 15213
(412) 268-2000
Private comprehensive institution. Coed, urban location. Undergraduate enrollment: 4,500. Graduate enrollment: 3,000.

Calendar: Semesters.

Degrees Offered: B.F.A., M.F.A., Art; B.S., M.S., Ph.D., Computer Science.

Curricular Emphasis: Art Department/Electronic Media Studios/Electronic and Time-Based Work—Electronic Media Studio I and II; Three-Dimensional Media Studio I and II; Two-Dimensional Media Studio I, II, III and IV; Computer Drawing and Painting I, and II; Computer Graphic Programming I and II; 2-D Computer Animation; 3-D Computer Modeling and Animation; Interactive Multimedia; Video Production and Postproduction I and II; Performance and Installation; Digital Photography; Networking and Telecommunications; Special Topics; M.F.A. Art and Computer; Projects. Computer Science—great variety of advanced graphics projects; special interest in computer graphics; computer vision; artificial intelligence; robotic manipulation; other areas.

Facilities/Equipment: State-of-the-art computer graphics lab with IBM PCs; XTs; ATs (PGA or VMI); RTs; plotters; printers; Matrix film recorders; Macs; 3-D Graphics; TrueVision; video output; variety of other systems and software.

Guide POV: This selective private university, formed by the merger of the Carnegie Institute of Technology and the research-oriented Mellon Institute, offers an innovative, extremely solid and complete curriculum in computer-based art and animation at both the undergraduate and graduate levels; Art Department places strong emphasis on new artmaking technologies; the Computer Science Department is one of the top-ranked in the nation and is active in graphics research at all levels.

COMMUNITY COLLEGE OF BEAVER COUNTY
One Campus Dr., Monaca, PA 15061-2588
(412) 775-8561
County two-year institution. Coed, suburban location. enrollment: 2,869.

Calendar: Semesters.

Degrees Offered: A.A.S., High Technology Communications.

Curricular Emphasis: High Technology Communications—course listings include Video-Displayed Graphics; Media Images; Digital Video Imaging; there is training in both broadcast and nonbroadcast video production including news, fiction, and local commercial advertising.

Facilities/Equipment: Computer lab for video graphics; video photography; desktop audio workstation; MIDI; desktop publishing; complete video production and postproduction.

Guide POV: Designed for students seeking immediate employment upon graduation, this practical two-year video program covers both broadcast and nonbroadcast production; graduates employed as computer graphics animators and video production technicians.

DREXEL UNIVERSITY
32nd and Chestnut Sts., Philadelphia, PA 19104-9984
(215) 895-2000
Private comprehensive institution. Coed, urban location. Undergraduate enrollment: 6,200. Graduate enrollment: 3,000.

Calendar: Quarters.

Degrees Offered: B.S., Film and Video Production.

Curricular Emphasis: Department of Performing and Cinema Arts, Film and Video Production—critical studies; film and video production; film animation; writing for the visual media; required creative or analytical project in senior year.

Facilities/Equipment: Animation stand; complete film and video production and postproduction; Design and Imaging Studio; Center for Automation Technology.

Guide POV: Undergraduates attending Drexel University are offered practical training in both film and video production; students may undertake film animation projects; in addition, advanced computer graphics course work is available through both the Art and Computer Science Departments; microcomputer requirement for all students; cooperative education program with full-time professional internships.

EAST STROUDSBURG UNIVERSITY
East Stroudsburg, PA 18301
(717) 424-3600
State comprehensive institution. Coed, small town location. Undergraduate enrollment: 5,000. Graduate enrollment: 500.

Calendar: Semesters.

Degrees Offered: B.S., Media; B.S., Communication and Technology.

Curricular Emphasis: Department of Media, Communication and Technology—television production; basic film production including animation; microcomputer applications.

Facilities/Equipment: Animation stand; complete film, video and television production and postproduction with three off-line editing systems including A/B roll editing; Amiga Toaster; special effects.

Guide POV: Undergraduates at this state university located in the Pocono Mountains are offered a communications program that features small classes with individualized instruction; film animation projects; video effects for television.

EDINBORO UNIVERSITY OF PENNSYLVANIA
Edinboro, PA 16444
(814) 732-2406
Public comprehensive institution. Coed, small town location. Undergraduate enrollment: 6,339. Graduate enrollment: 665.

Calendar: Semesters.

Degrees Offered: B.F.A., Applied/Media Arts (Cinema).

Curricular Emphasis: Art Department (Cinema Area)—character animation; computer animation; live-action filmmaking including documentary, narrative fiction, and experimental approaches; film studies; frequent visits by guest animators and filmmakers; Alternative Film Festival.

Facilities/Equipment: Animation stands; rotoscope unit; computer animation lab with variety of systems and software including Amiga computers; black and white film processor; film transfer unit; complete film and video production and postproduction; digital sound recording studio.

Guide POV: This small university offers a quality, individually-tailored cinema program to fine arts students; training in film production includes work in both character and computer animation; alumni work as paintbox/animation artists, character layout artists, and independent animators and filmmakers; additional training through majors in photography, painting, drawing, sculpture, and communication graphics.

GETTYSBURG COLLEGE
Gettysburg, PA 17325
(717) 337-6000
Private comprehensive institution. Coed, small town location. Undergraduate enrollment: 2,500.

Calendar: Semesters.

Degrees Offered: B.S.

Curricular Emphasis: Mathematics and Computer Science Department—course listings include undergraduate studies in interactive computer graphics systems.

Facilities/Equipment: Computer graphics lab with variety of systems and software including MS/DOS computers.

Guide POV: Interactive computer graphics systems are explored through the selective Mathematics and Computer Science Department.

INDIANA UNIVERSITY OF PENNSYLVANIA
Indiana, PA 15705
(412) 357-2100
Public comprehensive institution. Coed, small town location. Undergraduate enrollment: 12,000. Graduate enrollment: 2,000.

Calendar: Semesters.

Degrees Offered: B.F.A., M.F.A., Art.

Curricular Emphasis: Art Department—course listings include Computer Graphics and Electronic Imagery; undergraduate and graduate projects. Computer Science Department—course listings include Computer Graphics; Undergraduate/Graduate Projects.

Facilities/Equipment: Computer graphics lab includes Macs; scanners; digitizers; output to video; other university resources include NeXT; DEC 5000s.

Guide POV: Art students may learn advanced computer graphics and animation techniques at both the undergraduate and graduate level; attention to developing individual portfolio; computer graphics training also provided through Computer Science Department at both the undergraduate and graduate levels.

KING'S COLLEGE
River St., Wilkes-Barre, PA 18711
(717) 826-5900
Private comprehensive institution. Coed, urban location. Undergraduate enrollment: 1,750.

Calendar: Semesters.

Degrees Offered: B.A., Mass Communications.

Curricular Emphasis: Mass Communications—broadcast news production; basic film production; computer graphics techniques; graphic design.

Facilities/Equipment: Complete television and video production and postproduction including 3/4" SP video editing suite with computer graphics capabilities; basic film production and postproduction; computer graphics lab includes Mindset; Zenith; Targa 16; AutoCAD; PageMaker; video output; PCs; other systems and software.

Guide POV: This private college provides mass communications training to students pursuing careers in television production as well as print mediums, including advertising and public relations; attention to computer graphics effects for video; graphic design techniques; in addition, there is a computer graphics curriculum for computer science majors.

KUTZTOWN UNIVERSITY
Kutztown, PA 19530-0730
(215) 683-4000
Public comprehensive institution. Coed, small town location. Undergraduate enrollment: 7,500. Graduate enrollment: 635.

Calendar: Semesters.

Degrees Offered: B.S., M.S.

Curricular Emphasis: Computer Science—undergraduate and graduate course listings include Introduction to Computer Graphics; Seminar in Computer Graphics; Computer Graphics I and II; Projects. Telecommunications Department—all aspects of electronic communication including television broadcast and nonbroadcast production, media management, and microwave and satellite distribution of programming.

Facilities/Equipment: Computer graphics lab includes Unisys-A9; Tektronix 4112/4115; complete video and television production and postproduction including on-line and off-line video editing systems.

Guide POV: The Computer Science Department offers both undergraduate and graduate studies in computer graphics; in addition, students choosing the telecommunications major are offered hands-on digital postproduction training through a variety of student productions; accelerated degree program.

LA SALLE UNIVERSITY

20th and Olney Ave., Philadelphia, PA 19141
(215) 951-1000
Private comprehensive institution. Coed, urban location. Undergraduate enrollment: 3,400. Graduate enrollment: 1,065.

Calendar: Semesters.

Degrees Offered: B.A., Communication.

Curricular Emphasis: Communication—film and electronic media history and criticism; film narrative and animated production; television production work emphasizes fiction, news/documentary, and instructional/industrial.

Facilities/Equipment: Animation stand; basic film, video and television production and postproduction including Imix Video Cube; Non-Linear Video Editor; Video Toaster 4000; Pro Tools Non-Linear Audio Editing.

Guide POV: La Salle University offers both cinema and television studies; there is training in film and television animation for the interested undergraduate; computer science majors may elect graphics training.

PENNSYLVANIA STATE UNIVERSITY

University Park, PA 16802
(814) 865-4700
State comprehensive institution. Coed, small town location. Undergraduate enrollment: 31,000. Graduate enrollment: 600.

Calendar: Semesters.

Degrees Offered: B.A., M.F.A., M.A.

Curricular Emphasis: Film and Video/School of Communications—diverse course listings; animation projects.

Facilities/Equipment: Animation stand; complete film, video and television production and postproduction; computer graphics lab.

Guide POV: Founded in 1855, this state university offers a rigorous four-year program featuring production training in both film and video; students work in narrative, documentary and experimental forms, including film animation.

PITTSBURGH FILMMAKERS

477 Melwood Ave., Pittsburgh, PA 15213
(412) 681-5449
Private comprehensive institution. Coed, urban location. Undergraduate enrollment: 1,200.

Calendar: Semesters.

Degrees Offered: B.F.A., Film and Video Production (offered in conjunction with Point Park College).

Curricular Emphasis: Narrative, documentary, experimental, and animated film/video productions; digital imaging; still photography; history and theory; Pittsburgh Filmmakers operates a first-run 35mm movie theatre; special showcases; major grant funding available for students in film, video, and television.

Facilities/Equipment: Bench and flatbed editing suites; interlock sound mixing studio; Oxberry animation stand; complete film, video and television production and postproduction; digital imaging and digital editing.

Guide POV: Pittsburgh Filmmakers is an independent media arts center; Point Park College offers a B.F.A. in Film and Video Production through this institution; Carnegie Mellon University, Duquesne University and Carlow College offer the art center's complete course listings for elective credit; the University of Pittsburgh offers all production courses as a complement to their own major in Film Studies; courses also available on a noncredit basis to independent students; encouragement of individual creative expression; sequential training in film animation.

POINT PARK COLLEGE

Wood St. and Blvd. of the Allies, Pittsburgh, PA 15222
(412) 391-4100
Private comprehensive institution. Coed, urban location. Undergraduate enrollment: 2,900. Graduate enrollment: 100.

Calendar: Semesters.

Degrees Offered: B.F.A., Film and Video Production (in conjunction with Pittsburgh Filmmakers).

Curricular Emphasis: Department of Fine, Applied, and Performing Arts—film and video production training, including film animation, given at Pittsburgh Filmmakers facilities.

Facilities/Equipment: Film and video equipment, including animation stand, through Pittsburgh Filmmakers; 3/4" television studio; video editing suites.

Guide POV: Point Park College offers a B.F.A. program in Film/Video through Pittsburgh Filmmakers located off-campus; includes film animation training; co-op program in Visual Arts and Design is offered with the Art Institute of Pittsburgh; some television postproduction effects training through Journalism and Communications Department.

TEMPLE UNIVERSITY

Broad and Montgomery Sts., Philadelphia, PA 19122
(215) 204-7000
State comprehensive institution. Coed, urban location. Undergraduate enrollment: 24,000. Graduate enrollment: 10,000.

Calendar: Semesters.

Degrees Offered: B.A., M.F.A., Radio/Television/Film; B.F.A., Art; M.F.A., Graphic Arts and Design.

Curricular Emphasis: Radio/Television/Film—diverse program includes projects in film animation; new media; computer graphics; computer editing; M.F.A. program emphasizes independent production; graduate animation workshops explore varied approaches from cards and cels to computer imagery. Graphic Arts and Design—course listings include Experimental Film; Animated Film.

Facilities/Equipment: Cine studio; animation stand; complete film, video and television production and postproduction; Betacam and 1" available in local production houses for advanced graduate projects; computer graphics lab includes variety of systems and software; video disc capabilities.

Guide POV: Undergraduate and graduate students in the production-oriented Film, Television, and Media Studies Department may undertake projects in both film and computer animation; a rigorous M.F.A. program emphasizes socially-aware independent film and video production; separate Graphic Arts and Design program offers training in animation and other experimental film techniques with an emphasis on the creative use of optical printing; additional computer graphics/imaging processing studies available through the Computer and Information Sciences Department.

UNIVERSITY OF PENNSYLVANIA
34th and Walnut, Philadelphia, PA 19104-6376
(215) 898-5000
Private comprehensive institution. Coed, urban location. Undergraduate enrollment: 10,000. Graduate enrollment: 12,000.

Calendar: Semesters.

Degrees Offered: B.S., M.S., Ph.D., Computer Science and Engineering.

Curricular Emphasis: Computer Science and Engineering—substantial advanced research in computer graphics with topics that include human occupants in 3-D environments; animation control techniques; language-based interfaces; 3-D computer graphics techniques; interactive system design; task-oriented computer animation; natural language and animation.

Facilities/Equipment: Computer Graphics Research Laboratory with state-of-the-art systems and software including Iris 4-Ds; HP 3xx workstations; Sun SPARCstation 1 color workstations; IBM AT personal computers; microVAX dedicated for image capture, processing and display; teaching robot.

Guide POV: Most selective, this private university conducts advanced research in the area of visual communication with computers; special interest in advanced interactive techniques; modeling and simulation; language and animation; robotics.

UNIVERSITY OF PITTSBURGH
Fifth Avenue and Bigelow, Pittsburgh, PA 15260
(412) 624-4141
State-related comprehensive institution. Coed, urban location. Undergraduate enrollment: 19,000. Graduate enrollment: 10,000.

Calendar: Semesters.

Degrees Offered: B.A., Film Studies; B.F.A., Studio Arts.

Curricular Emphasis: Film Studies—theoretical approach; film animation projects through Pittsburgh Filmmakers; special relationship with Carnegie Museum of Art. Studio Arts—course listings include Computer Graphics; Projects.

Facilities/Equipment: Animation stand; complete film, video, and television production and postproduction; computer graphics lab with Sun 3/CXP;

IBM ATs; video digitizers; cameras; software for paint, image analysis, and modeling.

Guide POV: The interdisciplinary Film Studies Program at this selective university provides a theoretical foundation for graduate production work; by special arrangement with Pittsburgh Filmmakers, film animation courses are made available for credit; in addition, the Studio Arts Department offers students the opportunity to learn computer animation techniques; interactive computer graphics may be studied through the Computer Science Department at the undergraduate and graduate levels; there is a Semester at Sea Program.

UNIVERSITY OF PITTSBURGH AT BRADFORD
300 Campus Dr., Bradford, PA 16701
(814) 362-7500
State-related comprehensive institution. Coed, small town location. Undergraduate enrollment: 1,200.

Calendar: Semesters.

Degrees Offered: B.A., Communication.

Curricular Emphasis: Communication Arts—television production and programming; digital effects; computer graphics; media-related trips to NYC and Buffalo; sponsored video productions for independent clients.

Facilities/Equipment: Complete television and video production and postproduction including 1/2" and 3/4" (both standard and SP) with A/B roll; four editing bays; two three-tube studio cameras; digital effects; Grass Valley switching; Video Toaster 2.0.

Guide POV: Featuring practical training in broadcast journalism as well as corporate video production, this program trains students to produce computer graphics effects for television and video.

UNIVERSITY OF PITTSBURGH AT JOHNSTOWN
Johnstown, PA 15904
(814) 269-7000
State-related comprehensive institution. Coed, small town location. Undergraduate enrollment: 3,000.

Calendar: Trimesters.

Degrees Offered: B.S., Computer Science.

Curricular Emphasis: Computer Science—undergraduate students may undertake advanced graphics projects with special attention to interactive computer graphics.

Facilities/Equipment: Computer graphics lab includes AT&T PC 6300/7300; AT&T DMD 5620; VAX; GKS; Plot 10; Macintosh; IBM PCs.

Guide POV: Computer science majors with a strong background in mathematics and physics receive training in interactive computer graphics and undertake advanced undergraduate projects.

UNIVERSITY OF SCRANTON

Scranton, PA 18510

(717) 941-7400

Private comprehensive institution. Coed, urban location. Undergraduate enrollment: 4,500. Graduate enrollment: 700.

Calendar: Semesters.

Degrees Offered: B.A., Communication.

Curricular Emphasis: Communication—critical studies in film; media writing; audio-film-video production; film animation; computer graphics; television journalism; cable television; communication law; advertising.

Facilities/Equipment: Animation stand; complete film, video, and television production and postproduction; computer graphics lab.

Guide POV: Operated by the Jesuit order, this private university offers diverse course listings in the field of communication with core requirements in the liberal arts; students may then choose emphasis in broadcasting/film, which blends theory and training; film animation projects; separate radio/television production emphasis; digital video effects.

UNIVERSITY OF THE ARTS
PHILADELPHIA COLLEGE OF ART AND DESIGN

320 S. Broad at Pine St., Philadelphia, PA 19102

(215) 875-4800

Private college of art and design within a university of visual and performing arts. Coed, urban location. Undergraduate enrollment: 1,400.

Calendar: Semesters.

Degrees Offered: B.F.A., Film-Video/Animation.

Curricular Emphasis: Photography/Film-Video/Animation—experimental work exploring the creative possibilities of media; sequential training in both film animation and computer imaging; senior animation workshops; there is an animation concentration; department encourages interaction with the Illustration Department and among the Schools of Dance, Music, and Theatre; Black Maria Film Festival; collaborative projects in experimental media.

Facilities/Equipment: Two Oxberry animation stands; JK optical printer; computer animation and processing facilities; film and video library; complete 16mm film production; complete 1/2" video; Amiga and Macintosh computer labs.

Guide POV: A nonprofit institution, this is the nation's only university devoted exclusively to professional training in the visual and performing arts; program encourages the exploration of film, video, animation, and multimedia techniques; both traditional and experimental animation techniques are explored, with training in film animation and computer-generated motion graphics; there is cross-registration with The Pennsylvania Academy of Fine Arts.

Rhode Island

■■■■■■■■■■■■■■■■■■■■■■■■ ■ ■ ■

BROWN UNIVERSITY

Providence, RI 02912

(401) 863-1000

Private comprehensive institution. Coed, urban location. Undergraduate enrollment: 5,000. Graduate enrollment: 1,500.

Calendar: Semesters.

Degrees Offered: B.A., Modern Culture (students may select emphasis in Video). B.S., M.S., Ph.D., Computer Science.

Curricular Emphasis: Computer Science—course listings include Introduction to Computer Graphics; Interactive Computer Graphics; Undergraduate/Graduate Projects. Modern Culture—theory and analysis of media; film and video production.

Facilities/Equipment: Center for Modern Culture and Media includes video studio; complete film and television production and postproduction; computer graphics lab includes Suns; variety of other systems and software.

Guide POV: This small selective film/video program offers 24-hour access to production facilities; experimental video projects; in addition, computer science majors pursue advanced research with special attention to interactive computer graphics; students enjoy quality computer facilities; cross-registration with Rhode Island School of Design.

RHODE ISLAND SCHOOL OF DESIGN

Two College St., Providence, RI 02903-2791

(401) 454-6100

Private professional arts institution. Coed, urban location. Undergraduate enrollment: 2,000. Graduate enrollment: 100.

Calendar: Semester plus winter session.

Degrees Offered: B.F.A., B.G.D.

Curricular Emphasis: Film, Animation and Video Program—production-based curriculum for artists in cel and computer animation, film, and video. Graphic Design Program—professional degree program in visual communication, covering original design as it applies to film graphics, publications design, packaging and other areas.

Facilities/Equipment: Two Filmmaker and one Master Series animation stand; IBM RS-6000 computer workstation running Wavefront 3-D animation software; variety of other graphics systems and software including Mac Plus; SE; II; Amigas; video digitizers; printers; plotters; complete film and video production and postproduction; 8-track mixing studio with MIDI/video/tape chase.

Guide POV: A highly regarded fine arts college, Rhode Island School of Design offers those undergraduate students gaining entrance into the Film, Animation and Video Program opportunities to work in film and digital animation while refining conceptual and aesthetic skills; the program emphasizes individual authorship, craftsmanship and innovation in time arts; traditional drawing and design skills counterbalanced with advanced technology; each student must produce a finished work in order to graduate; the separate Bachelor of Graphic Design degree, instituted in 1989, was the first of its kind in graphic design education; various three-to-six week travel courses available.

ROGER WILLIAMS UNIVERSITY
Ferry Rd., Bristol, RI 02809-2921
(401) 253-1040
Private comprehensive institution. Coed, suburban location. Undergraduate enrollment: 2,200.

Calendar: Semesters.

Degrees Offered: Individualized Minor in Film Studies.

Curricular Emphasis: School of Humanities—film history, theory/aesthetics, and basic live-action and animation production; the course entitled Filmmaking: Animation introduces the student to a variety of techniques including drawn animation; clay/object animation; cutout animation and animating under the camera.

Facilities/Equipment: Animation stand; film/video library; complete Super-8 production and postproduction.

Guide POV: Roger Williams College offers students an opportunity to construct an individually-tailored program of studies leading to an independent film minor; blend of theory and criticism classes taught along with basic Super-8 production training; varied projects in film animation.

UNIVERSITY OF RHODE ISLAND
Kingston, RI 02881
(401) 792-1000
State comprehensive institution. Coed, small town location. Undergraduate enrollment: 9,000.

Calendar: Semesters.

Degrees Offered: B.A., B.F.A., Art.

Curricular Emphasis: Studio Art—training in principles, techniques and aesthetics of computer art.

Facilities/Equipment: Computer graphics lab with Macintosh; software.

Guide POV: Computer graphics training is approached within a fine art context; emphasis on the development of individual style along with acquisition of technical skills.

South Carolina

■■■■■■■■■■■■■■ ■ ■ ■ ■ ■ ■ ■ ■ ■ ■ ■

BOB JONES UNIVERSITY
Greenville, SC 29614
(803) 242-5100
Private liberal arts institution. Coed, urban location. Undergraduate enrollment: 5,000. Graduate enrollment: 300.

Calendar: Semesters.

Degrees Offered: B.S., M.A., Cinema and Video Production.

Curricular Emphasis: Department of Cinema and Video Production—film, television, and video production; includes individual projects in film animation; university production unit (Unusual Films).

Facilities/Equipment: Animation stand; complete film, video, and television production and postproduction.

Guide POV: Bob Jones University offers undergraduate training in media production within a core curriculum of evangelical Protestant studies; film animation projects.

CLEMSON UNIVERSITY
103 Keith St., Clemson, SC 29634-1503
(803) 656-3311
Public comprehensive institution. Coed, rural location. Undergraduate enrollment: 9,400. Graduate enrollment: 3,000.

Calendar: Semesters.

Degrees Offered: B.S., M.S., Ph.D., Engineering Graphics.

Curricular Emphasis: Course listings include Engineering Graphics with Computer Applications; Interactive Computer Graphics; Computer-Aided Geometric Modeling; Projects.

Facilities/Equipment: Computer center houses VAX8650; Tek terminals; TekniCAD; Sun4/110s; PATRAN; HOOPS; D13000; ANSYS.

Guide POV: Clemson University offers a professional program in engineering graphics for students seeking positions that employ principles of advanced graphic design; students must have strong background in mathematics; variety of undergraduate and graduate projects.

UNIVERSITY OF SOUTH CAROLINA
Columbia, SC 29208
(803) 777-7000
State comprehensive institution. Coed, urban location. Undergraduate enrollment: 20,000. Graduate enrollment: 3,000.

Calendar: Semesters.

Degrees Offered: B.M.A., M.M.A.

Curricular Emphasis: Department of Media Arts—screenwriting; film, audio, and video production; film animation; photography; Carolina Cinematographers Association.

Facilities/Equipment: Animation stand; complete film, video, and television production and postproduction; computer graphics lab.

Guide POV: The stated goal of this lively department is to educate the media production generalist with training in film, audio, video, television, photography, and screenwriting; innovative system of interactive television instruction transmitted statewide; projects in film animation; computer-generated special effects for video.

South Dakota

■■■■■■■■■■■■■ ■ ■ ■ ■ ■ ■ ■ ■ ■ ■   ■

NORTHERN STATE UNIVERSITY
Aberdeen, SD 57401
(605) 622-3011
State comprehensive institution. Coed, urban location. Undergraduate enrollment: 2,500.

Calendar: Semesters.

Degrees Offered: B.A., B.S., B.S.Ed., Art.

Curricular Emphasis: Art Department—course listings include Computer Layout and Illustration; Computer Paint and Design Systems; Computer Animation and Video Design; Advanced Computer Design; Advanced Studio Computer Animation; Projects; variety of electives.

Facilities/Equipment: Computer graphics lab with Apple IIGS; Amiga; video output; toaster; software.

Guide POV: The professional concentration in computer-aided art offered at this state university is composed of an interesting curriculum that allows students to participate in advanced design and animation projects; video art; separate emphasis in commercial design offers related curriculum within the context of general career training for the commercial artist.

SOUTH DAKOTA STATE UNIVERSITY
Brookings, SD 57007-0649
(605) 688-4151
State comprehensive institution. Coed, small town location. Undergraduate enrollment: 6,500. Graduate enrollment: 1,500.

Calendar: Semesters.

Degrees Offered: B.A., B.S.

Curricular Emphasis: Visual Arts—courses include Graphic Design I, II and III; Video Graphics.

Facilities/Equipment: Computer graphics lab with Mac Pluses; MacDraw; Aldus; Amiga; Digiview; Deluxe Paint; Videoscape 3-D; complete video and television production and postproduction.

Guide POV: This is South Dakota's largest state university; Visual Arts majors pursue professional computer graphics training for both print and motion arts media; additional training in computer graphics effects through Journalism and Mass Communication Department.

UNIVERSITY OF SOUTH DAKOTA
414 E. Clark St., Vermillion, SD 57069
(605) 677-5011
State comprehensive institution. Coed, small town location. Undergraduate enrollment: 6,000.

Calendar: Semesters.

Degrees Offered: B.S., M.A., Computer Science.

Curricular Emphasis: Computer Science—undergraduate courses include Computer Graphics; Artificial Intelligence; Software Engineering; Simulation.

Facilities/Equipment: Computer graphics lab with variety of systems and software including two Sun servers; 22 Sun workstations; UNIX operating system; MicroVaxII; PCs.

Guide POV: Undergraduate computer science students study the development of graphics software involving a wide array of hardware, software, and application techniques; graduate emphasis on computer software development.

Tennessee

■■■■■■■■■■■■■■■ ■ ■ ■ ■ ■ ■ ■ ■ ■

CARSON-NEWMAN COLLEGE
Jefferson City, TN 37760
(615) 475-9061
Private comprehensive institution. Coed, small town location. Undergraduate enrollment: 2,000. Graduate enrollment: 100.

Calendar: Semesters.

Degrees Offered: B.A., Art.

Curricular Emphasis: Art Department—computer graphics studies offered through the Advertising Art emphasis; portfolio must be submitted at end of sophomore year before acceptance into area of emphasis.

Facilities/Equipment: Computer graphics lab; complete video and television production and postproduction.

Guide POV: Art majors attending this small private college may undertake advanced projects in computer graphics with special attention to advertising art; a comprehensive television broadcasting curriculum is offered through the Communication Arts Department.

MIDDLE TENNESSEE STATE UNIVERSITY
Murfreesboro, TN 37132
(615) 898-2300
State comprehensive institution. Coed, small town location. Undergraduate enrollment: 17,000. Graduate enrollment: 1,500.

Calendar: Semesters.

Degrees Offered: B.F.A., B.A., B.S.

Curricular Emphasis: Art Department—course listings include Computer Art I and II; Workshop; Projects. Mass Communications Department of Radio/Television/Photography—there is a specialty area in Digital Animation with courses that include Introductory, Intermediate and Advanced Digital Animation; Electronic Graphics for Television; Electronic Multimedia Production, and Digital Photography.

Facilities/Equipment: Mass Communication complex houses Silicon Graphics workstations; Wavefront Advanced Visualizer; Dynamation; Kinemation; Composer and Explore software; Abekas A66 Digital Disc Recorder; Macintosh computers with Adobe Photoshop software; various other hardware peripherals for input and output; access to Digital Audio workstations and Midi lab; art department may also utilize graphics hardware and software tools such as Amigas; DigiPaint; Mac IIs; PixelPaint; Studio 8; Adobe; Aldus; IBM PS/2s; plotters; tablets; scanner; inkjet; VAXstation 3100s; complete video and television production and postproduction.

Guide POV: Art students study computer graphics with special attention to original design and illustration; majors in Mass Communication may choose a specialty area in Digital Animation with an emphasis on careers in television graphics and multimedia production; in addition, computer science majors may explore multidimensional graphic techniques at both the undergraduate and graduate levels.

THE UNIVERSITY OF MEMPHIS
Memphis, TN 38152
(901) 678-2000
State comprehensive institution. Coed, suburban location. Undergraduate enrollment: 16,000. Graduate enrollment: 3,600.

Calendar: Semesters.

Degrees Offered: B.A., B.F.A., M.F.A.

Curricular Emphasis: Art/Applied Design—course listings include Computer Graphics; Graphic Design for Digital Communication; Studies in Computer Animation; Computer Graphics Workshop; Projects.

Facilities/Equipment: Computer graphics lab with IBM XT and ATs; video digitizer; frame controller; Lumena; Genigraphics; Digital Arts 3-D; TIPS; complete film, video and television production and postproduction.

Guide POV: Art students receive career training in computer graphics and animation with special attention to problems in design; additional graphics studies through the Theatre and Communication Arts Department.

UNIVERSITY OF TENNESSEE AT CHATTANOOGA
615 McCallie Ave., Chattanooga, TN 37403-2598
(615) 755-4111
State comprehensive institution. Coed, urban location. Undergraduate enrollment: 6,300. Graduate enrollment: 1,400.

Calendar: Semesters.

Degrees Offered: B.F.A., Art.

Curricular Emphasis: Art Department—Graphic Design concentration; course listings include Computer Graphic Design; Concentration Topic in Graphic Design; Graphic Design I, II, III, and IV; Photography for Graphic Design; Drawing I, II, and III.

Facilities/Equipment: Computer graphics lab with variety of systems and software including Macintosh; Tek; GKS; tablet; audio-video production and editing facilities.

Guide POV: The University of Tennessee at Chattanooga offers art majors a full concentration in graphic design; in addition, communication majors interested in advertising are encouraged to minor in Graphic Design; finally, computer science majors study computer graphics applications and algorithms.

UNIVERSITY OF TENNESSEE AT KNOXVILLE
1715 Volunteer Blvd., Knoxville, TN 37996-2410
(615) 974-3408
State comprehensive institution. Coed, urban location. Undergraduate enrollment: 22,000. Graduate enrollment: 7,000.

Calendar: Semesters.

Degrees Offered: B.F.A., M.F.A.

Curricular Emphasis: Art Department—course listings include all levels of Graphic Design, Computer-Enhanced Design, Media Arts, Digital Photography, Video and Film Design.

Facilities/Equipment: Computer graphics lab with Power Macintosh 8100/80 and Power Macintosh 8100/80AV workstations; thermal wax color printer and black and white laser printer output; flatbed scanners; video and digital photography input; ethernet connectivity; the Video and Film lab maintains production and postproduction facilities; there is also a full service photography lab.

Guide POV: Founded in 1794 and the original campus of the state's university system, this institution offers art students a degree program in Studio Art or Graphic Design; the Graphic Design concentration provides career training for the fields of graphic design, illustration, desktop publishing, interactive multimedia, graphical interface design, and low-end video and animation; this program is augmented with an annual visiting designer residency; students can take advantage of a regularly scheduled overseas summer workshop in Britain; the Media Arts concentration focuses on film, video, photography, and performance art; interrelated programs offered by the university in advertising, computer science, information science, broadcasting and cinema studies; notably, the Computer Science Department offers advanced undergraduate and advanced work in the field of interactive computer graphics.

Texas

■■■■■■■■■■■■■■■■■■■■ ■ ■ ■ ■ ■ ■ ■ ■

BAYLOR UNIVERSITY
Waco, TX 76798
(817) 755-1011
Private comprehensive institution. Coed, urban location. Undergraduate enrollment: 11,500. Graduate enrollment: 1,400.

Calendar: Semesters.

Degrees Offered: B.S., M.S., Computer Science.

Curricular Emphasis: Computer Science—diverse course listings; survey of computer graphics hardware and software; advanced projects.

Facilities/Equipment: Computer graphics lab with variety of systems and software.

Guide POV: Students may pursue advanced projects involving a variety of computer graphics applications; emphasis on systems and software design.

OUR LADY OF THE LAKE UNIVERSITY
411 SW 24th St., San Antonio, TX 78207-4689
(210) 434-6711
Private comprehensive institution. Coed, suburban location. Undergraduate enrollment: 3,000. Graduate enrollment: 700.

Calendar: Semesters.

Degrees Offered: B.A., Art; B.A., B.A.S., Communication Arts.

Curricular Emphasis: Art Department—course listings include Computer Design; Graphics; Desktop Publishing. Media Department—course listings include Introduction to Cinema; Graphics; Desktop Publishing.

Facilities/Equipment: Video production and postproduction; computer graphics lab; Media Center.

Guide POV: Both Media and Art majors apply computer graphics techniques for print and video media; in addition, art students create computer art projects; additional film studies through English Department; university offers Weekend College Program.

PRAIRIE VIEW A&M UNIVERSITY
Prairie View, TX 77446
(409) 857-3311
Public comprehensive institution. Coed, small town location. Undergraduate enrollment: 4,500. Graduate enrollment: 700.

Calendar: Semesters.

Degrees Offered: B.S., Computer Science.

Curricular Emphasis: Computer Science—graphics topics include interactive systems; surface reconstruction; recent developments; simulation and modeling.

Facilities/Equipment: Computer graphics lab.

Guide POV: Students in this department are offered a broad curriculum that places emphasis on concepts and problem-solving skills so that graduates may assume variety of programming, analysis, management, and research positions.

RICE UNIVERSITY
6100 Main, Houston, TX 77251
(713) 527-8101
Private comprehensive institution. Coed, urban location. Undergraduate enrollment: 3,000. Graduate enrollment: 1,000.

Calendar: Semesters.

Degrees Offered: B.A., B.F.A., Art and Art History (emphasis in Film).

Curricular Emphasis: Art and Art History—film animation; electronic media theory and culture; film theory/aesthetics; film and video production within a visual/media arts context.

Facilities/Equipment: Animation stand; film/video library; complete film, video and television production and postproduction; Media Center.

Guide POV: Rice University offers comprehensive film and video studies within a visual/media arts context; students in this small department may produce animated as well as narrative and documentary works; in addition, advanced graphics projects are pursued at all levels through Computer Science Department; admission to university is most selective.

SOUTHERN METHODIST UNIVERSITY
CENTER FOR COMMUNICATION ARTS
Dallas, TX 75275-0276
(214) 768-2000
Private comprehensive institution. Coed, suburban location. Undergraduate enrollment: 6,000. Graduate enrollment: 4,000.

Calendar: Semesters.

Degrees Offered: B.A., Cinema; B.A., TV/Radio.

Curricular Emphasis: Center for Communication Arts—electronic media theory and culture; critical studies in film; media writing; audio-film-video production; media management.

Facilities/Equipment: Center for Communication Arts houses computer graphics lab as well as complete film, video and television production and postproduction;16-track audio sweetening rooms; window dubbing.

Guide POV: This private university offers strong degree programs in both film and video production that combine technical, creative, historical and economic studies; training includes advanced computer-based special effects for video; Southwest Film Archive; summer SMU-In-London Program.

SOUTHWEST TEXAS STATE UNIVERSITY
San Marcos, TX 78666
(512) 245-2111
State comprehensive institution. Coed, urban location. Undergraduate enrollment: 16,500. Graduate enrollment: 2,500.

Calendar: Semesters.

Degrees Offered: B.A., B.S., M.S., Computer Science.

Curricular Emphasis: Computer Science Department—course listings include Computer Graphics; Advanced Computer Graphics; Projects; Computer Vision; Language Processing; Networks; Operating Systems.

Facilities/Equipment: Computer graphics lab includes a wide range of equipment from Pentium PCs to DEC Alpha Workstations; laser printers; scanners; variety of software.

Guide POV: Computer science students attending this state university, founded in 1899, may pursue graphics research and special projects at both the undergraduate and graduate levels.

TARRANT COUNTY JUNIOR COLLEGE
828 Harwood Rd., Hurst, TX 76054.
(817) 788-6903
County two-year institution. Coed, urban location. enrollment: 26,000.

Calendar: Semesters.

Degrees Offered: A.A.S., Media Communications.

Curricular Emphasis: Media Communications—critical studies; media writing; computer graphics and animation; film and television/video production.

Facilities/Equipment: Animation stand; film library; complete Super-8 film production and postproduction; complete video and television studio and location; computerized video editing; computer graphics and animation.

Guide POV: Tarrant County Junior College is a large, comprehensive community college with locations at three urban campuses; the Media Communications Program is designed to train students in television production with an emphasis on the corporate/industrial market; diverse curriculum includes basic film and digital animation and video art projects.

TEXAS A&M UNIVERSITY
College Station, TX 77843
(409) 845-3211
State comprehensive institution. Coed, small town location. Undergraduate enrollment: 31,000. Graduate enrollment: 9,000.

Calendar: Semesters.

Degrees Offered: B.A., B.S., M.A., M.S., Ph.D.

Curricular Emphasis: Visualization Lab—undergraduate and graduate courses include 3-D Modeling and Animation; 3-D Computer Animation I and II; Computing Environments; Environmental Simulation; Digital Synthesis Techniques; Experimental Visualization Techniques.

Facilities/Equipment: Computer graphics lab includes Suns; Iris 4-D; Abekas; NeXT; variety of other systems and software.

Guide POV: Through a well-equipped Visualization Lab, students in both arts and sciences may elect advanced training in computer animation with either design, motion arts, or engineering applications; experimental research projects in the field of visualization as well as related areas.

TEXAS CHRISTIAN UNIVERSITY
Bellaire Dr. N., Fort Worth, TX 76129
(817) 921-7000
Private comprehensive institution. Coed, urban location. Undergraduate enrollment: 6,000. Graduate enrollment: 1,000.

Calendar: Semesters.

Degrees Offered: B.S., Radio/TV/Film; B.S., Broadcast Journalism; M.S., Media Studies.

Curricular Emphasis: Radio/TV/Film—critical studies; audio-video production; film animation; broadcast management.

Facilities/Equipment: Animation stand; 6000-film library; multimedia studio; multitrack studio; complete film, video, and television production and postproduction.

Guide POV:. Affiliated with the Disciples of Christ, Texas Christian University offers film animation studies within the context of a broad media arts program; stress on broadcast production and critical/cultural studies; there is a Disney media internship program available for qualified majors.

TEXAS TECH UNIVERSITY
West Broadway and University, Lubbock, TX 79409-5015
(806) 742-2011
State comprehensive institution. Coed, urban location. Undergraduate enrollment: 19,000. Graduate enrollment: 5,500.

Calendar: Semesters.

Degrees Offered: B.A., Telecommunications; M.A., Mass Communications.

Curricular Emphasis: Corporate telecommunications; broadcast journalism; program material produced for local public television station.

Facilities/Equipment: Multi-image lab; complete video and television production and postproduction including Grass Valley switching; stereo audio including DAT; Laird CG; additional graphics systems and software through Computer Science lab.

Guide POV: Students attending this large public university are offered a communications major with both undergraduate and graduate specializations in television/video production and management; students produce professional digital effects; in addition, computer science majors focus on principles and methods for designing, implementing and applying graphics packages.

UNIVERSITY OF HOUSTON AT CLEAR LAKE
2700 Bay Area Blvd., Houston, TX 77059
(713) 283-7600
State upper-division comprehensive institution. Coed, suburban location. Undergraduate enrollment: 7,500.

Calendar: Semesters.

Degrees Offered: B.A., Applied Design and Visual Arts; B.A., Media Studies.

Curricular Emphasis: Applied Design and Visual Arts—course listings include Computer Graphics; Graphic Design I and II; Illustration; Film and Videotape Making I and II; Photography I and II. Media Studies Program—critical studies; media writing; film-video production; computer graphics.

Facilities/Equipment: Computer graphics lab with variety of graphic systems and software; complete television and video production and postproduction; Super-8 film production and postproduction.

Guide POV: There is a Graphic Communication emphasis for studio artists which includes training in computer graphics; art majors may also elect courses in film and photography; in addition, students accepted into the Media Studies Program will have occasion to produce works in both film and video; this program emphasizes corporate communications and trains students in producing computer-generated effects for video production, television broadcasting, and corporate advertising.

UNIVERSITY OF NORTH TEXAS
Denton, TX 76203-3108
(817) 565-2000
State comprehensive institution. Coed, urban location. Undergraduate enrollment: 27,500. Graduate enrollment: 3,500.

Calendar: Semesters.

Degrees Offered: B.A., M.A., M.S., Radio, Television and Film. B.A., M.A., Art.

Curricular Emphasis: Radio, Television, and Film Department—short film production projects in narrative, documentary, experimental genres, including animation; broadcast television production; corporate film/video; computer-generated special effects. Art Department—course listings include Computer Applications in Arts; Projects.

Facilities/Equipment: Animation stand; complete film, video, and television production and postproduction; satellite downlink; computer graphics lab with Apple; Mac II; WASATCH; Artronic; variety of other systems and software.

Guide POV: Undergraduate media arts majors at this public university may concentrate on the production of animated shorts; graduate program emphasizes research as well as documentary and corporate video production; art students also pursue computer art and animation projects.

UNIVERSITY OF TEXAS AT AUSTIN
Austin, TX 78712
(512) 471-3434
State comprehensive institution. Coed, urban location. Undergraduate enrollment: 38,000. Graduate enrollment: 12,000.

Calendar: Semesters.

Degrees Offered: B.S., M.A., Radio-Television-Film; M.F.A., Film/Video Production; Ph.D., Communication; B.S., M.S., Ph.D., Computer Science.

Curricular Emphasis: Radio-Television-Film Department—production studies include 16mm and video; screenwriting; media studies with strong international and critical dimensions. Computer Science Department—course listings include Computer Graphics; Systems Modeling; Graph Theory; other topics.

Facilities/Equipment: 35mm screening facilities; sound mixing room; film library; complete film, video and television production and postproduction includes four color studios; 24 video and film editing stations; computer graphics lab with variety of systems and software.

Guide POV: One of the nation's largest single-campus universities, this state institution offers solid programs both in production and media studies; diverse graduate production program requires combined film and video training; special graduate research interest in experimental film and electronic media design; in addition, the computer science curriculum provides in-depth examination of techniques for realistic image synthesis, covering such topics as advanced geometric modeling methods, animation and dynamic simulation, scientific visualization, and high-performance graphics architectures.

UNIVERSITY OF TEXAS AT EL PASO

El Paso, TX 79968
(915) 747-5000
State comprehensive institution. Coed, urban location. Undergraduate enrollment: 14,000. Graduate enrollment: 2,500.

Calendar: Semesters.

Degrees Offered: B.A., B.F.A., M.A., Art.

Curricular Emphasis: Art Department—there is a graphic design major which trains students for careers in both motion arts and print media; variety of projects.

Facilities/Equipment: Computer graphics lab with variety of systems and software; complete video and television production and postproduction.

Guide POV: Students attending this state university are offered a professional degree program in graphic arts that covers a variety of applications; upperclassmen elect internships at television stations, design firms, art studios, or advertising agencies.

Utah

■ ■

BRIGHAM YOUNG UNIVERSITY
Provo, UT 84602
(801) 378-4636
Private comprehensive institution. Coed, urban location. Undergraduate enrollment: 26,000. Graduate enrollment: 2,500.

Calendar: Semesters.

Degrees Offered: B.A., B.F.A., Film; Ph.D., Theatre and Film; B.A., Broadcast Communication; M.A., Communications; B.S., M.S., Ph.D., Computer Science.

Curricular Emphasis: Department of Theatre and Film—separate degree programs for students pursuing film studies or film production/writing; Ph.D. program for film scholars. Department of Communications—comprehensive training in all aspects of broadcast communication; graduate program is management and theory-oriented, with additional broadcast production training in the documentary form. Computer Science Department—variety of graphics courses for both undergraduates and graduates.

Facilities/Equipment: Animation stand; complete film, video, and television production and postproduction including CMX editing suites; computer graphics lab with variety of systems and software.

Guide POV: Comprehensive film and television training is provided at this selective private university; film department offers cel animation instruction; broadcast communication majors receive extensive television production training and use advanced computer graphics techniques; in addition, the Computer Science Department offers a graphics curriculum geared to research, design and engineering.

SOUTHERN UTAH UNIVERSITY
351 W. Center St., Cedar City, UT 84720
(801) 586-7700
State comprehensive institution. Coed, small town location. Undergraduate enrollment: 5,000. Graduate enrollment: 200.

Calendar: Quarters.

Degrees Offered: B.A., B.S.

Curricular Emphasis: Communication Department—broadcast news production; communication graphics; media writing; directing; technical broadcasting; communication law; program material produced for local commercial station and for entire schedule of local cable channel.

Facilities/Equipment: Complete video and television production and postproduction; graphics workstations for video; computer graphics lab with VAX 11/780; Chromatics 7900; Mac IIs; 80286 computers.

Guide POV: A small program featuring a great deal of hands-on training in broadcast television production is offered; students produce computer-based animation for television broadcasts; there is also a graphics curriculum for computer science students.

UNIVERSITY OF UTAH
Salt Lake City, UT 84112.
(801) 581-7200
State comprehensive institution. Coed, urban location. Undergraduate enrollment: 19,000. Graduate enrollment: 5,000.

Calendar: Quarters.

Degrees Offered: B.A., M.F.A., Theatre and Film. B.S., M.S., Ph.D., Computer Science.

Curricular Emphasis: Theatre and Film Department—broad-based degree with 50 credits in film required, 25 optional; production training; graduate program emphasizes film and video production and screenwriting. Computer Science Department—course listings include Introduction to Computer Graphics I-IV; Computer Graphics Applications Programming; Computer Vision; Advanced Computer Vision; Computer-Aided Geometric Design; Projects; special topics.

Facilities/Equipment: Animation stand; complete film and video production and postproduction; CAGD Lab with SGI ONYX RE2 superworkstations; SGI 4D20 Indigo2 Extreme Graphics workstations; Sun, HP, IBM and DEC workstations; film recorder; Abekas digital video recorder; multisource frame accurate video editing station; sound room; color Postscript Printers; AVCAD Poster Printer; VLSI Lab; Scientific Visualization Lab; Vision and Robotics Lab; Digibotics 3-D Digitizer; Advanced Manufacturing Laboratory (NC Mills, Lathes, EDM, etc.)

Guide POV: The film program emphasizes narrative screenwriting and the production of socially relevant documentaries; undergraduate and graduate training in film animation; volunteerships at Sundance Film Festival; international student film festival; Utah Film and Video Festival co-sponsors several activities with university and holds its festival every spring; in addition, a strong computer science program concentrates on graphics in terms of new research, with studies in 3-D visualization techniques, hidden line and surface removal, interactive graphics, and photographing computer-generated grayscale images, among others.

UTAH STATE UNIVERSITY
Logan, UT 84321
(801) 750-1000
State comprehensive institution. Coed, urban location. Undergraduate enrollment: 18,000. Graduate enrollment: 2,500.

Calendar: Quarters.

Degrees Offered: B.S., M.S., Computer Science. B.A., B.S., Communication (with emphasis in Broadcasting or Media Management).

Curricular Emphasis: Computer Science Department—course listings include Introduction to Computer Graphics; Computer Graphics; Advanced Computer

Graphics; Projects. Communication Department—topics include television production; writing for media; mass media management.

Facilities/Equipment: Television/Video—complete 1" and 3/4" studio; complete 3/4" location; video toaster; computer graphics lab includes HP 700s;
various SGI machines.

Guide POV: Computer science majors may undertake both undergraduate
and graduate projects in computer graphics; topics include studies in 2-D and
3-D animation; 3-D surface representation; hidden surface removal; color,
shading and ray tracing; research interests include photorealistic images; very
large database animation, and scientific visualization; in addition, communication majors, following a sequential program, learn all aspects of mass media
production, including the production of special effects.

WEBER STATE UNIVERSITY
Ogden, UT 84408-2001
(801) 626-6455
State comprehensive institution. Coed, urban location. Undergraduate enrollment: 12,000.

Calendar: Quarters.

Degrees Offered: B.S., B.A., B.F.A., Visual Arts.

Curricular Emphasis: Visual Arts—course listings include Computer-Aided
Art and Design; Advanced Computer-Aided Art and Design; Computer Animation and Interactive Media.

Facilities/Equipment: Computer graphics lab with Macintosh SEs; IIS;
Quadras; animation, paint and multimedia software.

Guide POV: This public commuter university offers undergraduates computer
graphics training for both print and interactive media within the Department
of Visual Arts.

Vermont

■■■■■■■■■■■■■■■■■■■ ■ ■ ■ ■ ■ ■ ■ ■

BENNINGTON COLLEGE

Bennington, VT 05201

(802) 442-5401

Private comprehensive institution. Coed, rural location. Undergraduate enrollment: 550. Graduate enrollment: 50.

Calendar: Semesters.

Degrees Offered: B.A., M.F.A.

Curricular Emphasis: All students at this small innovative college are encouraged to press their own CD-ROMs or audio CDs as part of their curriculum; work reflects individual student's area of interest; tutorials on new media techniques offered by faculty.

Facilities/Equipment: New Media Center houses 12 Power Macintosh 7100/66 stations with 24 megs of RAM; wide variety of card upgrades and software; S-VHS video editing deck; color scanner; magneto-optical drive; supplemental Pocket Hammer drive with memory of two gigabytes; Center for Audio Technologies houses electronic music studio, computer instructional studio, and digital audio studio.

Guide POV: Bennington College is committed to integrating creative computer applications to every program of studies; each student in the college assembles a digital portfolio; undergraduates in the Mathematics and Computers Program explore principles of color graphics and animation; special topics generated by student interest; particular interest in multimedia applications integrating dance, music, writing and art; comprehensive CD-ROM interactive college viewbook created by students is available.

LYNDON STATE COLLEGE

Lyndonville, VT 05851

(802) 626-9371

State comprehensive institution. Coed, small town location. Undergraduate enrollment: 1,000. Graduate enrollment: 100.

Calendar: Semesters.

Degrees Offered: A.S., B.S., B.A., Communication Arts and Sciences.

Curricular Emphasis: Communication Arts and Sciences—the concentration in Graphic Design includes instruction in visual design and on-line video graphics; live and taped program material produced for local cable television; corporate video projects produced for local clients.

Facilities/Equipment: Computer graphics studio with variety of systems and software; complete video and television production and postproduction.

Guide POV: Lyndon State College offers a well-equipped media program integrating oral and visual communication with writing and dramatic arts; blend of aesthetics and practical training in video technologies; advanced training for special effects artists using computer-generated motion graphics.

SAINT MICHAEL'S COLLEGE
Winooski Park, Colchester, VT 05439
(802) 655-2000
Private comprehensive institution. Coed, suburban location. Undergraduate enrollment: 1,750. Graduate enrollment: 850.

Calendar: Semesters.

Degrees Offered: B.S., Computer Science.

Curricular Emphasis: Department of Computer Science—curriculum covers introductory courses, electives, and the following core courses: Data Structures and the Analysis of Algorithms; Introduction to Machine Organization and Assembly Language Programming; Organization of Programming Languages; Principles of Operating Systems; Computer Architecture; Math Foundations for Computer Science I and II; Probability and Statistics.

Facilities/Equipment: Computer graphics majors have exclusive use of a MicroVAX with a UNIX operating system; in addition, the campus provides two Digital VAX 4000 mainframe computers through six networked labs throughout the campus.

Guide POV: Located just outside of Burlington, this selective college offers computer science majors training in computer graphics with special attention to designing graphics software; topics include line generation, polygon generation, two- and three-dimensional transformations, segmentation, windowing and clipping.

UNIVERSITY OF VERMONT
Burlington, VT 05405
(802) 656-3131
State comprehensive institution. Coed, large town location. Undergraduate enrollment: 9,000. Graduate enrollment: 1,000.

Calendar: Semesters.

Degrees Offered: B.A., Art.

Curricular Emphasis: Art Department—course listings include Cel Animation; Computer Art; Filmmaking; Video Production; Computer Graphics for Designers.

Facilities/Equipment: Computer graphics studio with variety of systems and software; animation stand.

Guide POV: Art majors at the University of Vermont enjoy the opportunity to explore both cel and computer animation and receive training in both film and video production; small classes.

Virginia

COLLEGE OF WILLIAM AND MARY
Williamsburg, VA 23187
(804) 221-4000
State comprehensive institution. Coed, small town location. Undergraduate enrollment: 6,000. Graduate enrollment: 2,300.

Calendar: Semesters.

Degrees Offered: B.S., M.S., Ph.D., Computer Science.

Curricular Emphasis: Undergraduate course listings include Computer Graphics; Stochastic Models for Computer Science; Simulation; Analysis of Algorithms; Software Engineering; Survey of Artificial Intelligence; other areas.

Facilities/Equipment: Computer graphics lab with variety of systems and software.

Guide POV: Chartered in 1693, this is the second-oldest college in the United States; undergraduate computer science majors are introduced to topics in graphics such as coordinate systems, the relationship between continuous objects and discrete displays, fill and flood algorithms, two-dimensional geometric transformations, clipping, zooming, panning and windowing; topics from three-dimensional graphics include representations for objects; geometric and projection transformations; geometric modeling; hidden line/surface removal algorithms; graduate students pursue long-term advanced projects.

GEORGE MASON UNIVERSITY
Fairfax, VA 22030-4444
(703) 993-1000
State comprehensive institution. Coed, suburban location. Undergraduate enrollment: 10,000. Graduate enrollment: 8,000.

Calendar: Semesters.

Degrees Offered: B.A., Art; M.A., M.F.A., Visual Information Technologies.

Curricular Emphasis: Art Department—undergraduate course listings include Computer Art and Animation; Computer Graphics I and II; Exhibition Projects; Graphic Design I and II; Visual Thinking; emphasis on high-resolution imaging using computer both as tool and medium; areas addressed include complex menu structures, rotations and scaling, color mapping and palette design, font generation, and video digitizing techniques. Visual Information Technologies—this graduate art program offers course listings that include Conceptual Arts: Computer Imaging; 2-D Computer Imaging; 3-D Computer Imaging; Computer Animation; Special Topics; computer imaging applications explored in areas of painting, printmaking, sculpture, mixed media, illustration, video, and animation; advanced computer animation projects.

Facilities/Equipment: Computer graphics lab with variety of systems and software; animation; paint; video digitizer; complete video production and post-production.

Guide POV: Undergraduate art students may elect computer art/animation courses which include lab assignments addressing both technical and aesthetic challenges; graduate art program, Visual Information Technologies, focuses on electronic and digital media technology with attention to computer imaging/animation as well as graphic design; graduate students may concentrate on assembling advanced computer animation portfolio; additional graphics training offered through Computer Science Department, emphasizing software design, and Speech Communication Department, emphasizing computer-based effects for video.

HOLLINS COLLEGE

Roanoke, VA 24020
(703) 362-6000
Private comprehensive women's institution, suburban location. Undergraduate enrollment: 800.

Calendar: Semesters.

Degrees Offered: B.A., Theatre Arts (Film Concentration).

Curricular Emphasis: Theatre Arts—film history, criticism, and theory; strong emphasis on writing program; film/video production including film animation projects.

Facilities/Equipment: Animation stand; film library. complete film and video production and postproduction.

Guide POV: Critical film studies, creative writing, and film production techniques are emphasized at this private women's college; students undertake independent and experimental projects in film animation.

RADFORD UNIVERSITY

Radford, VA 24142
(703) 831-5000
State comprehensive institution. Coed, small city location. Undergraduate enrollment: 9,500. Graduate enrollment: 800.

Calendar: Semesters.

Degrees Offered: B.A., B.S., Communication.

Curricular Emphasis: Telecommunications Program—mass communication theory; broadcast writing; radio and television broadcast production; news journalism; corporate/industrial video production; media management.

Facilities/Equipment: Complete Super-8 film production and postproduction; complete television and video production and postproduction; Center for Media Arts Technology houses variety of computer graphics systems and software.

Guide POV: Radford University offers professional training in all aspects of broadcast television and corporate/industrial video production; additional computer graphics courses through both the Art and Computer Science departments.

UNIVERSITY OF VIRGINIA
Charlottesville, VA 22906
(804) 924-0311
State comprehensive institution. Coed, suburban location. Undergraduate enrollment: 12,500. Graduate enrollment: 6,500.

Calendar: Semesters.

Degrees Offered: B.S., M.S., Ph.D., Systems Engineering; B.S., M.S., Ph.D., Computer Science.

Curricular Emphasis: Both the engineering and computer science curriculums offer computer graphics training.

Facilities/Equipment: Academic Computing Center with variety of systems and software, including over 200 PCs and Macintosh systems; Sun; NeXT; Silicon Graphics; Hewlett-Packard; Digital; high-performance graphics workstations.

Guide POV: The School of Engineering and Applied Science offers students a strong, diverse curriculum for those interested in advanced computer graphics research; other areas of interest include human-computer interaction; parallel computers and systems; VLSI design; staffed facilities are open continuously; department has strong research orientation.

VIRGINIA COMMONWEALTH UNIVERSITY
Richmond, VA 23284
(804) 367-0100
State comprehensive institution. Coed, urban location. Undergraduate enrollment: 12,000. Graduate enrollment: 6,500.

Calendar: Semesters.

Degrees Offered: B.F.A., M.F.A., Communication Arts and Design.

Curricular Emphasis: Communication Arts and Design Department—course listings include Media Arts Survey; Computer Graphics I and II; Computers in Graphic Design; Computers in Illustration; Visual Communication Workshop.

Facilities/Equipment: Computer graphics lab with variety of systems and software, including Apple IIe; Amiga 500/2000; tablet; digitizer; MacPlus; Laserwriter; Imagewriter.

Guide POV: This is a solid Visual Communications program which trains computer graphic artists for careers in illustration and design, particularly for positions in advertising agencies and design studios.

VIRGINIA INTERMONT COLLEGE
1013 Moore St., Bristol, VA 24201-4298
(703) 669-6101
Private comprehensive institution. Coed, small town location. Undergraduate enrollment: 500.

Calendar: Semesters.

Degrees Offered: B.A., B.S., Photography (concentration in computer imaging).

Curricular Emphasis: Photography Department—critical studies in film; basic video production; computer imaging.

Facilities/Equipment: Computer imaging lab; 1/2" video; switcher/special effects generator.

Guide POV: Students attending this small private college are offered course listings in video production that include techniques of computer imaging and video art; art majors also explore advanced techniques in computer art.

VIRGINIA POLYTECHNIC INSTITUTE AND STATE UNIVERSITY

Blacksburg, VA 24061-0311
(703) 231-6000
State comprehensive institution. Coed, rural location. Undergraduate enrollment: 20,000.

Calendar: Semesters.

Degrees Offered: B.S., M.S., Ph.D., Computer Science; M.I.S. (Master of Information Systems).

Curricular Emphasis: Course listings include Computer Graphics; Simulation and Modeling; Theory of Algorithms; Modeling and Evaluation of Computer Systems; Systems Simulation; Digital Picture Processing; Human Computer Interaction; Artificial Intelligence; other topics; undergraduate and graduate projects.

Facilities/Equipment: Computer graphics lab with Macintosh; Amiga; other systems and software.

Guide POV: This public university offers the computer science major sequential instruction in computer graphics applications; emphasis on hardware and software systems and design; attention to long-term projects.

VIRGINIA STATE UNIVERSITY

Petersburg, VA 23806
(804) 524-5902
State comprehensive institution. Coed, suburban location. Undergraduate enrollment: 3,500.

Calendar: Semesters.

Degrees Offered: B.F.A., Visual Communication, Art and Design or Teaching of Art in the Schools.

Curricular Emphasis: Art and Design Department—course listings include Introduction to Computer Graphics; Computer Graphics; Projects; Printmaking; Drawing; Painting; Sculpture.

Facilities/Equipment: Computer graphics lab with IBM and Macintosh systems; variety of graphics software.

Guide POV: This small program trains computer artists for careers in illustration and design; students experiment with variety of styles; attention to individual projects.

VIRGINIA WESTERN COMMUNITY COLLEGE
3095 Colonial Ave. SW, Roanoke, VA 24015
(703) 857-7272
State two-year institution. Coed, urban location. enrollment: 6,500.

Calendar: Semesters.

Degrees Offered: A.A.S., Radio/Television Production Technology.

Curricular Emphasis: Television design and videography; introductory and advanced radio/television production; varied seminar studies on film genres, popular culture, photography, and other areas; media writing; media management; program material produced for various nonprofit outlets.

Facilities/Equipment: Complete 4-camera full-color 3/4" studio and location; 12-input switcher; Laird CG with paint graphics and camera capture; U-matic control track and time-code editing.

Guide POV: This small community college offers a solid training program in broadcast media; studio is a teaching facility; strong hands-on approach; student videographers learn to produce computer-generated special effects for video production, television broadcasting, and corporate advertising.

Washington

■■■■■■■■■■■■■■■■■■■■■ ■ ■ ■ ■ ■ ■

BELLEVUE COMMUNITY COLLEGE
3000 Landerholm Circle S.E., Bellevue, WA 98007
(206) 641-0111
State two-year institution. Coed, suburban location. enrollment: 14,000.

Calendar: Quarters.

Degrees Offered: A.A., Media Communication and Technology; Certificate Programs in Video Media and Computer Media.

Curricular Emphasis: New digital technologies; interactive multimedia design and application; electronic media theory and culture; television/video production.

Facilities/Equipment: Interactive Multimedia Lab includes 15 interactive multimedia workstations with Macintosh and PC; complete television and video production and postproduction.

Guide POV: Located in a suburban area east of Seattle, this community colleges features an innovative curriculum that includes training in interactive multimedia design and application; advanced video/computer students create special projects.

EASTERN WASHINGTON UNIVERSITY
Cheney, WA 99004-2496
(509) 359-6200
State comprehensive institution. Coed, small town location. Undergraduate enrollment: 8,000. Graduate enrollment: 300.

Calendar: Quarters.

Degrees Offered: B.S., M.S., Computer Science; B.A., Radio/Television (emphasis in production/performance).

Curricular Emphasis: Computer Science Department—graduate curriculum includes advanced training in computer animation. Radio-Television Department—audio-video production; computer graphics.

Facilities/Equipment: Computer graphics lab includes SGI 4-D animation; variety of other systems and software; complete video and television production and postproduction.

Guide POV: Undergraduates attending this public university are offered a comprehensive major in Radio-Television with attention to all aspects of production, including computer-generated graphic effects; in addition, computer science graduate students explore advanced computer animation projects with attention to both technical and aesthetic considerations.

SEATTLE CENTRAL COMMUNITY COLLEGE
1701 Broadway, Seattle, WA 98122
(206) 587-3800
State two-year institution. Coed, urban location. enrollment: 3,500.

Calendar: Quarters.

Degrees Offered: A.A.S., Applied Video Communications Program.

Curricular Emphasis: Computer graphics, video and television production; media law and management.

Facilities/Equipment: Complete 1" and 3/4" studio; complete 3/4" and 1/2" location; Amiga Toaster; Amiga 500.

Guide POV: Offering communication students a particularly varied curriculum, this community college provides a solid technical core for television special effects artists; additional course listings in critical thinking and analysis; group learning activities such as role playing and conceptualization are utilized in small, seminar-style classes; professional video facilities.

THE EVERGREEN STATE COLLEGE
Olympia, WA 98505
(206) 866-6000
State comprehensive institution. Coed, rural location. Undergraduate enrollment: 3,000.

Calendar: Quarters.

Degrees Offered: B.A.

Curricular Emphasis: Expressive Arts: Film/Video Program—history, theory, and production of nonfiction media stressing experimental, animated and documentary forms.

Facilities/Equipment: Oxberry animation stand; JK optical printer; complete film and video production and postproduction; computer graphics.

Guide POV: This progressive state college offers students an intensive, interdisciplinary media arts program stressing nonfiction imagemaking; program encourages development of personal forms of expression; exploration of film animation techniques; entry to program is selective; Evergreen was the first college in America to create its entire curriculum around interdisciplinary learning; all majors are student-designed.

WASHINGTON STATE UNIVERSITY
Pullman, WA 99164-2520
(509) 335-3564
State comprehensive institution. Coed, small town location. Undergraduate enrollment: 16,000. Graduate enrollment: 2,000.

Calendar: Semesters.

Degrees Offered: B.S., M.S., Ph.D., Computer Science. B.A., M.A., Communication.

Curricular Emphasis: Electrical Engineering and Computer Science—course listings include Computer Graphics; Applied Graphics; Digital Image Processing; Graph Theory; Advanced Graphics; Animation Programming; Advanced Animation; Modeling and Simulation of Ecological Systems. Edward R. Murrow School of Communication—broadcast news; broadcast production; media law and ethics.

Facilities/Equipment: Computer graphics lab with Silicon Graphics 4-D/70T workstations; Amiga PCs; HP-Apollo workstations; IBM, DEC, Tektronix, NeXT, and AT&T workstations; variety of other systems and software; complete video and television production and postproduction.

Guide POV: Students choosing the broadcast sequence at this state university will find a demanding program emphasizing news writing and production; attention to computer graphics training for motion arts media; in addition, the well-equipped Computer Science Program emphasizes latest trends in graphics research, including advanced training in computer animation.

WESTERN WASHINGTON UNIVERSITY
Bellingham, WA 98225-9009
(206) 650-3000
State comprehensive institution. Coed, urban location. Undergraduate enrollment: 10,000.

Calendar: Semesters.

Degrees Offered: B.A., Communication (concentration in Broadcast Media Studies).

Curricular Emphasis: Communication—electronic media theory and culture; television/video production; program material produced for cable television includes news and documentary, fiction, and video art.

Facilities/Equipment: Animation stand; computer graphics lab; film, video and television production and postproduction.

Guide POV: Located 90 miles north of Seattle, this university offers professional film and video production training, including the production of computer-based animation for video and television as well as projects in independent film animation.

West Virginia

BETHANY COLLEGE
Bethany, WV 26032
(304) 829-7000
Private comprehensive institution. Coed, small town location. Undergraduate enrollment: 900.

Calendar: Semesters.

Degrees Offered: B.A., Communications.

Curricular Emphasis: Media theory and practice; media writing; audio-video production including computer graphics; international and organizational communication; course listings include Computer Graphics and Applied Design; Television Graphics; Graphic Design Practice.

Facilities/Equipment: Complete Super-8 film production and postproduction; complete video and television production and postproduction; computer graphics lab.

Guide POV: Students at Bethany College receive comprehensive computer graphics instruction with special attention to the design of visual symbols for television; studies combine principles of graphic art with requirements of broadcast production; January term is voluntary and experimental.

MARSHALL UNIVERSITY
Huntington, WV 25755
(304) 696-3170
State comprehensive institution. Coed, urban location. Undergraduate enrollment: 10,000. Graduate enrollment: 2,300.

Calendar: Semesters.

Degrees Offered: B.A., Journalism; M.A.J.

Curricular Emphasis: School of Journalism and Mass Communications—broadcasting sequence covers all aspects of broadcast production including graphics.

Facilities/Equipment: Macintosh and IBM computer labs; complete video and television production and postproduction.

Guide POV: Founded in 1837, Marshall University offers broadcasting students a curriculum with a balanced mixture of practical and theoretical studies; variety of computer graphics projects emphasize television special effects.

WEST LIBERTY STATE COLLEGE
West Liberty, WV 26074
(304) 336-5000
State comprehensive institution. Coed, rural location. Undergraduate enrollment: 2,800.

Calendar: Semesters.

Degrees Offered: B.S., Art (Graphic Design); B.S., Communications (Radio and Television).

Curricular Emphasis: Art Department (Graphic Design concentration)—curriculum includes Graphic Design I-III; 3-D Graphic Design; Computer Graphics I and II. Communications Department—video and television production; basic film production; video art.

Facilities/Equipment: Computer graphics lab with Apple Microcomputer; tablets; printers; video digitizer; Adobe Illustrator; animation software; complete Super-8 production and postproduction; complete television and video production and postproduction.

Guide POV: Art majors explore principles of high resolution graphics with attention to aesthetic potentials as well as technical considerations; a minor in Graphic Design is also available; in addition, communication majors may undertake advanced projects in video art.

WEST VIRGINIA STATE COLLEGE
Institute, WV 25112
(304) 768-9842
State comprehensive institution. Coed, suburban location. Undergraduate enrollment: 4,500.

Calendar: Semesters.

Degrees Offered: A.A.S., B.S., Communications (concentrations in Filmmaking, Broadcasting); B.A., Art.

Curricular Emphasis: Communications Department—film animation; video art; media writing and production; required internships; full-length feature films produced and distributed by students and faculty. Art Department—comprehensive training in principles of advanced graphic design with possible specialization in computer graphics; experimental processes.

Facilities/Equipment: 35mm film screening facilities; animation stand; complete film, video and television production and postproduction; computer animation lab.

Guide POV: West Virginia State College is the only institute of higher learning in the state offering comprehensive training in filmmaking, film animation, and screenwriting; faculty and students produce and internationally distribute full-length feature films; separate concentration in broadcast production; throughout, students encouraged to explore personal creativity while mastering technical skills; diverse course listings; special interest in new technologies; students may focus on graphics projects using new computer animation facilities; in addition, art majors may explore advanced graphic design; computer art.

WEST VIRGINIA UNIVERSITY
Morgantown, WV 26506-6001
(304) 293-0111
State comprehensive institution. Coed, small town location. Undergraduate enrollment: 16,000. Graduate enrollment: 6,000.

Calendar: Semesters.

Degrees Offered: B.S., Statistics.

Curricular Emphasis: Statistics and Computer Science Department—course listings include Computer Graphics; Interactive Computer Graphics; Projects.

Facilities/Equipment: Computer graphics lab includes Mac SEs and IIs; variety of software; television and video production and postproduction.

Guide POV: Interactive graphics may be explored at this state university; additional emphases on software development; artificial intelligence; there is a comprehensive evening class schedule for working adults.

Wisconsin

∎∎∎∎∎∎∎∎∎∎∎∎∎∎∎∎∎∎∎ ∎ ∎ ∎ ∎ ∎ ∎ ∎

BELOIT COLLEGE
700 College St., Beloit, WI 53511
(608) 363-2000
Private comprehensive institution. Coed, urban location. Undergraduate enrollment: 1,162.

Calendar: Semesters.

Degrees Offered: B.A., Theatre Arts Department.

Curricular Emphasis: Electronic media theory and culture; media writing; video production.

Facilities/Equipment: Video and television production and postproduction; computer graphics lab.

Guide POV: Intensive television production studies at Beloit College are offered through the Theatre Arts Department; emphasis on scriptwriting and analysis as well as new technologies.

MARQUETTE UNIVERSITY
Milwaukee, WI 53233
(414) 288-7700
Private comprehensive institution. Coed, urban location. Undergraduate enrollment: 9,200. Graduate enrollment: 2,000.

Calendar: Semesters.

Degrees Offered: B.A., Broadcast and Electronic Communication; M.A., Communication.

Curricular Emphasis: Broadcast news; production; corporate communication; entertainment television; media writing; new technologies; interactive technologies.

Facilities/Equipment: Complete video and television production and postproduction including two fully-equipped color studios; extensive computer graphics platforms with facilities for animation; digital video effects.

Guide POV: Both television and corporate video production may be studied with advanced projects in computer-based animation; diverse assignments; studies in media law and ethics; special interest in emergent and interactive technologies; additional training through Fine Arts Department centers on applications for graphic designers and illustrators.

MILWAUKEE AREA TECHNICAL COLLEGE
700 W. State St., Milwaukee, WI 53203
(414) 278-6600
State two-year institution. Coed, urban location. enrollment: 4,600.

Calendar: Semesters.

Degrees Offered: A.A., Television and Video Production.

Curricular Emphasis: All aspects of television and video production; students produce a variety of programming.

Facilities/Equipment: Three television studios; electronic graphics including ArtStar and WaveFront; analog switching; digital video effects; High Definition and Beta Test for broadcast; Ampex Alex character generators; Sony 9000 edit controllers.

Guide POV: Students attending this two-year college receive extensive television/video production experience; professional facilities; practical emphasis; students may train as television special effects artists and videographers.

SAINT NORBERT COLLEGE
De Pere, WI 54115
(414) 337-3181
Private comprehensive institution. Coed, suburban location. Undergraduate enrollment: 2,000.

Calendar: Semesters.

Degrees Offered: B.A., Art.

Curricular Emphasis: Art Department—course listings include Graphics I-III; Advertising Graphics; Advanced Drawing and Illustration; Computer Graphics; Projects.

Facilities/Equipment: PC computer graphics lab with specialty software; Mac lab with desktop publishing and design software; basic video and television production and postproduction.

Guide POV: Art students are offered a special graphic communication major with electives in advertising and marketing.

UNIVERSITY OF WISCONSIN AT EAU CLAIRE
Eau Claire, WI 54701
(715) 836-2637
State comprehensive institution. Coed, urban location. Undergraduate enrollment: 9,000.

Calendar: Semesters.

Degrees Offered: B.A., Communication Arts.

Curricular Emphasis: Department of Communication and Theatre Arts—television writing and production.

Facilities/Equipment: Computer graphics lab; complete video and television production and postproduction.

Guide POV: This member of the University of Wisconsin System offers students a variety of production opportunities in the context of a solid liberal arts curriculum; students explore a variety of computer-based animation techniques for motion arts media.

UNIVERSITY OF WISCONSIN AT GREEN BAY
Green Bay, WI 54302
(414) 465-2000

State comprehensive institution. Coed, rural location. Undergraduate enrollment: 6,000. Graduate enrollment: 400.

Calendar: Semesters.

Degrees Offered: B.A., M.A., Communication.

Curricular Emphasis: Communication Processes—course listings include
Designing Multiple Media Applications of Photography; special projects.

Facilities/Equipment: Complete video and television production and postproduction; electronic photography computer studio; graphic communications
lab.

Guide POV: Communication students at this large rural campus of the University of Wisconsin may study photography with an emphasis upon programmed multi-image designs that integrate photography, graphics, and
sound; computer art.

UNIVERSITY OF WISCONSIN AT MADISON
1527 University Ave., Madison, WI 53706
(608) 262-1234
State comprehensive institution. Coed, urban location. Undergraduate enrollment: 30,000. Graduate enrollment: 11,000.

Calendar: Semesters.

Degrees Offered: B.A., M.A., Ph.D., Communication Arts; B.S., B.F.A., M.F.A.,
Art.

Curricular Emphasis: Communication Arts Department—film history, theory
and criticism; some courses in film and video production including cel ani-
mation. Art Department—course listings include Computer-Mediated Art;
Computer Imaging Techniques; Advanced Graphic Design Technology;
Artist's Video; Advanced Research in Graphics; Graduate Graphics Workshop
I and II.

Facilities/Equipment: Animation stand; complete film and video production
and postproduction; computer graphics lab with variety of systems and software including Amiga; PS2; digitizers; A/V equipment; Video Toaster; Macs;
extensive archives collection at Wisconsin Center for Film and Theater
Research.

Guide POV: This public university places a great emphasis on the formal
study of film and television history, theory, and criticism; there is training for
serious scholars as well as for undergraduates seeking a strong theoretical
background for graduate production work; support to independent film animation projects; in addition, fine arts majors explore the aesthetic and technical possibilities of video and computer art, including interactive works, animation, and kinetic imagery.

UNIVERSITY OF WISCONSIN AT MILWAUKEE
Milwaukee, WI 53211
(414) 229-1122
State comprehensive institution. Coed, urban location. Undergraduate enrollment: 25,000. Graduate enrollment: 4,500.

Calendar: Semesters.

Degrees Offered: B.F.A., M.F.A.

Curricular Emphasis: Department of Film and Video—interdisciplinary fine arts production program in film and video stressing imaginative exploration of personal and cultural questions through experimental forms; international conferences through the Center for Twentieth Century Studies on varied topics relating to media and culture.

Facilities/Equipment: Animation stands; magnetic film to optical sound recording; film and video production and postproduction including video studio; film archives; computer animation lab with a variety of systems and software.

Guide POV: Students are offered a small, interdisciplinary program emphasizing avant-garde and experimental production as part of a fine arts curriculum; exposure to a variety of cinematic styles; faculty includes figures in the American and European avant garde; students undertake both film and computer animation projects; video art; multimedia; exploration of new technologies.

UNIVERSITY OF WISCONSIN AT OSHKOSH

800 Algoma Blvd., Oshkosh, WI 54901
(414) 424-1234
State comprehensive institution. Coed, urban location. Undergraduate enrollment: 9,600. Graduate enrollment: 1,600.

Calendar: Semesters.

Degrees Offered: B.A., B.S. Communication (students may select emphasis in Radio-TV-Film); B.S., B.A., B.E., B.F.A., Art.

Curricular Emphasis: Communication Department—dramatic film and animation; corporate video and advertising; industrial video; video art; independent film and video; documentary film and video; creative aesthetics; International Film Series; Oshkosh Film Society; advanced students undertake paid assignments producing corporate videos for outside clients. Art Department—course listings include 2-D Computer Art; 3-D Computer Art; Computer Animation; Interactive Computer Art.

Facilities/Equipment: Oxberry animation stand; complete film, television and video production and postproduction including 1" video special effects; computer graphics lab includes Mac IIs; SEs; Pluses; Pixar II; Sun 3/150; film recorder; variety of software.

Guide POV: Communication majors are offered advanced production training in both film and video; diverse curriculum; Oshkosh Film Society receives allocation for 16mm student projects; advanced works in film animation; art majors explore new concepts in three-dimensional computer art, computer animation for film, video and computer screen, as well as trends in interactive computer art and principles of graphic design.

UNIVERSITY OF WISCONSIN AT PARKSIDE
900 Wood Rd., Kenosha, WI 53144
(414) 595-2345
State comprehensive institution. Coed, suburban location. Undergraduate enrollment: 4,000.

Calendar: Semesters.

Degrees Offered: B.S., Computer Science.

Curricular Emphasis: Computer Science and Engineering Department—course listings include Computer Graphics; Artificial Intelligence I and II; Robotics and Automation; Image Processing; Software Applications Engineering; Projects.

Facilities/Equipment: Computer graphics lab with high performance IBM PC and Apple Macintosh microcomputers; variety of software.

Guide POV: Computer science majors may choose a computer engineering concentration that offers an option in intelligent systems; variety of software engineering and digital logical design projects with special attention to computer graphics applications.

UNIVERSITY OF WISCONSIN AT STEVENS POINT
Stevens Point, WI 54481-3897
(715) 346-0123
State comprehensive institution. Coed, small city location. Undergraduate enrollment: 8,400.

Calendar: Semesters.

Degrees Offered: B.A., Art with emphasis in graphic design/computer graphics.

Curricular Emphasis: Art Department—course listings include Computer Images in Design; Computer Graphics Design; Graphic Design; Environmental Design; Product Design; Computer-Aided Design; Technical Drawing; Design Typography.

Facilities/Equipment: Computer science lab with Gateway Pentium 60; Summa Sketch III Tablets; AutoCad software; HPA-D Pen Plotter.

Guide POV: Art majors may select courses in computer graphics that focus on digital design applications.

UNIVERSITY OF WISCONSIN AT WHITEWATER
Whitewater, WI 53190
(414) 472-1234
State comprehensive institution. Coed, small town location. Undergraduate enrollment: 9,300. Graduate enrollment: 1,300.

Calendar: Semesters.

Degrees Offered: B.A., B.S., Speech Communication (students may select emphasis in Radio-TV); M.S., Communication.

Curricular Emphasis: Electronic media theory and culture; media writing; audio-video production; computer graphics.

Facilities/Equipment: Complete video and television production and postproduction including advanced graphics; digital audio studio.

Guide POV: Located near Milwaukee and Chicago, this university offers a dynamic, growing Radio and Television Program with a strong production emphasis; coursework, practica, and internships stress applying audio and video communication in variety of broadcast, corporate, industrial, and new technology settings; advanced training for television special effects artists.

Wyoming

■■■■■■■■■■■■■■■■■■■ ■ ■ ■ ■ ■ ■ ■

UNIVERSITY OF WYOMING
P.O. Box 3435, Laramie, WY 82071
(307) 766-1121
State comprehensive institution. Coed, urban location. Undergraduate enrollment: 9,300. Graduate enrollment: 1,700.

Calendar: Semesters.

Degrees Offered: B.S., M.S., Ph.D., Engineering; B.A., B.S., M.S., Ph.D., Computer Science; Ph.D., Mathematics and Computer Science.

Curricular Emphasis: Computer Science Department—course listings include Computer Graphics; Digital Image Processing; System Simulation; Computer Vision; Analysis of Algorithms; Computer Design; Software Engineering; other topics. Engineering Department—course listings include Computer Graphics Applications for Engineers; Digital Image Processing; Projects.

Facilities/Equipment: Computer graphics lab with Prime; Tektronix; Macs; VAXs; variety of software.

Guide POV: This public multicampus school offers solid graphics instruction for a variety of applications through both the computer science and engineering departments; highly diverse engineering curriculum provides variety of degree programs with a strong emphasis on underlying principles, practice and theory; additional graphics curriculum through Geography Department explores principles of computer-assisted mapping and design used in cartography.

Profiles

Henry Selick
Animation Filmmaker

I'm convinced that now is the most exciting time in history to be an animation filmmaker. Animation is enjoying enormous success with mainstream cartoon features like Disney's *Aladdin, The Little Mermaid,* and *Beauty and The Beast.* At the same time, one of the funniest shows on network television remains "The Simpsons," and cable television's "Ren and Stimpy" is among the most imaginative. Other evidence of the liveliness of today's animation can be seen everywhere—in television commercials, short films, and even station IDs. Newly-fashioned computer-animated dinosaurs roared in Spielberg's *Jurassic Park,* while old-fashioned hand-animated puppets came to life in *The Nightmare Before Christmas,* the feature I recently directed for producer Tim Burton.

I was born in 1952 and was into music, bugs, birds, lions, horses, and drawing. Character animation on television and in the Disney films fascinated me, as did Ray Harryhausen's stop-motion creatures in *The Seventh Voyage Of Sinbad,* and *Mighty Joe Young.* I especially loved *The Night on Bald Mountain,* and *The Legend of Sleepy Hollow* sequences from *Fantasia.* An old pop-up *Pinnochio* book of my father's seemed magical. But what especially caught my attention, was a series of lovely stop-motion silhouette films on a local kiddie show called "Claude Kershner's Terrytoon Circus." Years later I learned that these were segments from *The Adventures of Prince Achmed,* a feature by the German animator, Lotte Reiniger. The images were haunting and being pure silhouettes, required a lot of imagination to make them work. It was a good early lesson for me: *Audience participation is essential for art to live.*

After studying science, writing, and anthropology at Rutgers University in 1974, then painting, photography, illustration, printmaking, and sculpture at Syracuse University and St. Martin's Art School in London (all the while playing and composing for rock bands and being confused about what to do with my life), the proverbial light bulb flashed on. I was watching a New York public television station as an animated short emerged. Some strange hand-drawn turning boxes appeared that would stop, open, then reveal some startling live-action image. So, when signing up for my final semester at Syracuse, I was pleased to see that they offered an animation course. The teacher, Bruce McCurdy, was a wonderfully energetic and aware man who taught our class basic techniques and exposed us to the fabulous work of Norman McLaren, Caroline Leaf and Ishu Patel of the Canadian Film Board, along with some innovative films made by students from the California Institute of the Arts. I subsequently made my first shorts, *Wall Street Shuffle* (cut-out animation) and *Tube Tales* (cel animation). I was now focused and excited, and decided to further pursue animation studies at Cal Arts.

Once there, I studied character animation with Disney pros, and received a Student Academy Award nomination for *Tube Tales.* But most importantly, I trained with Jules Engel, head of the experimental animation program. Jules, a brilliant filmmaker, designer, and painter, was the person who helped develop my "vision." He showed me some of his own abstract works, as well as the films of such greats as Jan Lenica and Raoul Servais, and some United Productions of America shorts that I had never seen, such as the impeccable *Rooty Toot Toot,* and *The Tell-tale Heart.* I was also exposed to Jan Svankmajer's *Jabberwocky,* Jiri Trnka's *The Hand,* and Disney classics like *Mickey's Band Concert.* Jules gave me a new visual vocabulary where I could now imagine Wassily Kandinsky or Marc Chagall paintings coming to life, and see animation as a legitimate art form.

During my two years at Cal Arts I needed a part-time job, so I applied at the Walt Disney Studio and was hired. There I worked with Eric Larsen, a sweet, patient and great teacher, one of Disney's original "nine old men." After graduation, I continued to work at the Disney Studio, in-betweening and animating on various projects, until finally becoming a full animator on *The Fox and the Hound.* At the same time, with the help of a grant from the American Film Institute, I labored on my own experimental short film called *Seepage,* which combined an abstract storyline with life-sized stop-motion cut-outs, cel animation and animated watercolors. I found myself straddling the fence between traditional character animation and experimental filmmaking. It was at this time that I hooked up with Tim Burton, a young and talented malcontent who drew funny dark cartoons and was, like myself, a Cal Arts grad struggling to find a way to express himself.

When *Seepage* was finally completed, it did garner a number of festival awards but was considered a bit too strange by the Tournee of Animation committee, not to mention the folks at Disney. Ready for a change, my wife, Heather and I pulled up stakes and moved to San Francisco to work on a beautiful but obscure cut-out feature called *Twice Upon a Time.* I worked on it like crazy until 1983. Unfortunately ,the film was only released in two theaters, and died shorly thereafter.

1983 to 1987 proved to be a struggle though a very educational time. My life changed in 1987 when I started doing short pieces for MTV. At last I was getting paid to write, produce, direct, animate, and design my own work through my own company. And I eventually put together a core group with whom I'd like to work with for the rest of my life. People like designer Ron Davis, armature maker Tom St. Amand, and animators Eric Leighton, Trey Thomas, Tim Hittle, and Anthony Scott. After three years of badgering, MTV agreed to back a short film of mine called *Slow Bob in The Lower Dimensions,* a combo live-action, stop-motion and cut-out animated piece that was to be a five minute pilot for a continuing series that would explore different animation techniques in each new adventure.

Tim Burton had already achieved major success, having created some of the most exciting and unusual hit films in Hollywood history. I had lost touch with him for a while, but Rick Heinrichs, his collaborator on almost every project, had kept in contact with me and brought us together. Tim very much liked my demo reel and was particularly impressed with *Slow Bob...* I assembled an entire studio in San Francisco to do *The Nightmare Before Christmas,* forming a group of most of my collaborators on other projects, eventually creating a crew of 110 people. Especially important was putting together a small international team of brilliant stop-motion animators. We worked for almost three years on the project. Tim Burton was in the pipeline on everything, keeping us on track with his story and sense of design.

With *The Nightmare Before Christmas* completed, I can finally say that my professional life is going well while my personal life with Heather has been further enriched by the 1991 adoption of our very animated son, Harry.

It took a lot of education and experience to find out what I really wanted to do. But it's better to be a late bloomer (I didn't start directing my first feature until I was thirty-eight), than never bloom at all. It's been a tough balancing act, and I hope to continue on the razor's edge between "art" and "commerce" for a long time to come.

John Lasseter

Computer Animator, Director

■■■■■■■■■■■■■■■■■ ■ ■ ■ ■ ■ ■ ■ ■

"There is no particular mystery to animation...it is really very simple. And like anything that is simple, it is about the hardest thing in the world to do." Bill Tytla, 1937.

I have always enjoyed an abiding interest in animation, especially computer animation. I received my B.F.A. in Film from the California Institute of the Arts in 1979. While there, I produced two animated films, each winners of the Student Academy Award for Animation: *Lady and the Lamp,* and *Nitemare.* Now, as vice president of Creative Development at Pixar, I am currently directing my first animated feature to be released by Buena Vista Distribution.

Computer animation is an artistic medium that has grown out of science. However, most of the images and animation created in this new medium were produced by the scientists who wrote the software tools—like having all the paintings in the world created by the chemists who made the paint.

The most important thing to understand is that computer animation is not an art form unto itself. Animation is the art form. The computer is just another medium within this art form, as are pencils, clay, sand, and puppets. In fact, I think of the computer as a big, expensive pencil that uses electricity. Sometimes it takes several people to operate the pencil. But until it is picked up by the hand of an artist, it is as useless as a pencil laying about on a desk. Computer animation isn't done by computers any more than clay animation is done by clay.

Animation is not only an art form, it is a method of communication and a means of entertainment—an art form wherein ideas must be visually communicated. To communicate ideas clearly by visual means, one must first learn the fundamentals of graphic design. It is the vocabulary and grammar of graphic communication.

You must design your image so that it communicates your idea clearly. But in doing so, you do not need to make it unappealing or boring. It is important to understand that visually communicating an idea is not enough. It must also be interesting and entertaining. Once this is achieved you can be sure that your idea will have far more impact and the audience will both absorb and retain it.

As soon as an image starts to move, the principles of animation take effect. In the computer animation industry one might think that to animate means to move an object from point A to point B. The dictionary definition of the verb animate is "to give life to." In order to give life to movement, one just cannot move an object without reason. Every movement in an animated scene must have a reason for being. That is the basis for character animation. One must learn animation's fundamental principles, such as timing, staging, anticipation, follow through, squash and stretch, overlapping action, slow in and slow out, etc.

So often in the computer animation field, people with little animation experience will sit in front of a computer and merely move a few objects around, and in doing so, consider themselves animators. Whether drawn by hand or computer, the success of character animation lies in the personality of the characters. Without an underlying thought process, the actions of a character are just a series of unrelated motions. With a thought process to connect them, actions bring a character to life. Technological advances are not what make an animation project great, it is the personalities. Chuck Jones, in discussing the importance of personality in character animation, stated, "All great cartoon characters are based on the human behavior we recognize in ourselves."

With all four of my short films, I strived to integrate human characteristics into the objects I chose as my subjects. In *Luxo Jr.*, a little lamp steals the spotlight with his playful antics; *Red's Dream* reveals what a lonely unicycle dreams about; and in *Knickknack,* a glass-domed snowman is done in by his own machinations to join a lively crowd tempting him on the outside.

I believe that *Tin Toy* was the first computer animated film to win an Academy Award, because Tinny, the wind-up toy, managed to humorously and poignantly convey so many human emotions; the very emotions we might feel were we in his shoes. All of these objects have their own personalities, their own raison d'être, which serve to drive the films, as well as make them memorable.

It is important to remember that the principles of filmmaking or film grammar are vital to the film as a whole. How the story is constructed, the staging and pacing of action and the editing of shots are just some of the principles involved.

If an idea does not further the story, no matter how compelling it may be, it should not be there. Everything within a single frame of film—the characters, the object, the set and even the space around the objects—should be there for a purpose.

Computer animation is unique in that it combines the techniques of varied mediums: graphic design, animation, story writing, live-action filmmaking, and computer science. But as with any artistic medium, the most vital element is creativity.

Nick Park

Animator, Director

■■■■■■■■■■■■■■■■■■ ■ ■ ■ ■ ■ ■ ■ ■ ■

Like many other animators, my fascination with animation started at an early age. I was born and grew up in Lancashire, England where my parents and teachers recognized that I had an ability to draw. Their encouragement gave me a sense of pride and spurred me on to continue drawing. Combined with my love of art, I would enjoy writing stories with a strong comedy theme during school lessons. Basically, I wanted to make people laugh. Like most children, I loved watching animated films, especially cartoons, not only because they were a lot of fun, but I was intrigued to know how they were made. By the age of 12, my fervor for drawing had not abated and my school notebooks were covered with cartoons. This brought me to the attention of one teacher who said, "Park, you will never make a living out of cartoons. It's just not art!"

Then at breakfast one morning, I read about a competition to make a simple zoetrope on the back of a cereal packet. The prize was a Super-8 movie camera and projector. I entered the competition, dreaming of the films I would make if I won. I didn't win, but the idea of making films was now firmly planted in my head. I remember seeing a documentary about Walt Disney and how he started off by drawing a mouse character. So I came up with my own characters, one of which I called Walter the Rat, and I was ready to go into production.

I was 13 when Walter the Rat debuted. Using a cheap notepad, I produced a flip book, with Walter walking along, then drinking some cider and falling over. It was my first attempt at drawn animation. Though it was a crude start, the film took an entire week to make. Unfortunately it got lost at the lab and couldn't be traced. I didn't realize it at the time, but this was just a taste of the trials and frustrations of an animator. Undaunted, I decided to have another go, but this time using felt cut-out characters on a felt-covered background. As I didn't own any lights, I set up on an easel in direct sunlight. The film, *Rat and the Beanstalk,* was shot in a day and lasted all of two minutes.

My catalog of films increased. After school and homework, I would spend evenings and weekends making animated films in my makeshift attic studio. I varied the techniques with paper cut-outs and cel animation (using tracing paper, as I couldn't afford cels), along with puppet and clay animation. When I finished, I entered the BBC's Young Animator's Film Competition, and although I didn't win, they still wanted to show my film with the winners on TV. I received instant fame in my school, and at the age of 15, thought I had reached the pinnacle of my career.

Unsatisfied with the quality of standard-8mm, I wanted to move up to Super-8. In order to raise the money, I took a summer job in a chicken-packing factory. However, as the picture quality improved with that gauge, the flaws became more apparent. This was my first lesson in taking greater care with the animation and helped me to appreciate how humor can be achieved through simplicity. My major influences at the time were Terry Gilliam's abrupt cut-out animation for "Monty Python," and Bob Godfrey's shakily-drawn "Rhubarb" series.

When the tutors in college discovered that I made films, they couldn't believe that I had kept it secret. Both they and my parents encouraged me to apply for a degree in animation, so I enrolled at Sheffield Polytechnic, Faculty of Art and Design, and earned a B.A. in Communication Arts.

After graduation I gained a place at the National Film and Television School in Beaconsfield near London, where I specialized in animation. It was there that I began work on *A Grand Day Out,* my first 35mm film using clay animation. Subsequently, I was offered a job by Aardman Animations Ltd. in Bristol, and finished the film there. I also had the opportunity to animate a number of commercials, including a series for Access credit cards and Dura-cell batteries.

It was during the postproduction of *A Grand Day Out* that I made a film as part of Aardman's "Lip Synch" series for Channel 4 called *Creature Comforts.* Both films earned nominations for British Academy awards, but the former actually won the coveted award. The following year, *Creature Comforts* became the basis of a successful campaign for electrical appliances and heating, scooping many advertising industry awards. Both films went on to pick up numerous citations, and in 1991, both were nominated for the Oscar for best animated short, with *Creature Comforts* winning.

There followed a number of opportunities to pursue many interesting projects both in Britain and America. However, since before the Academy Awards, I had had plans in development for Wallace and Gromit, the heroes of *A Grand Day Out,* so I decided to stay put, and in 1993, completed my longest film to date, a half-hour comedy thriller entitled *The Wrong Trousers.*

Looking back at my education, it is interesting to note that I was largely self-taught and did not actually have any formal animation training. The courses I attended were unstructured, and although I enjoyed the freedom at that time, I might have benefited from a more academic approach. However, I did appreciate being able to learn the basic film crafts of storytelling, direction, writing, and editing.

Now working full-time as a director/animator, I regret not taking the opportunity to study filmmaking more seriously, especially since I consider myself more as a filmmaker who animates, than an animator. Overall, the most valuable aspect of my education has been to make my own films without commercial pressure and to nurture my own style and ideas. My animation has developed over the years, but my fascination with the magic of animation that began years ago has remained undiminished.

Bill Hanna

Animation Director, Producer

■■■■■■■■■■■■■■■■■■■ ■ ■ ■ ■ ■ ■ ■

The year was 1930, and our country was going through the worst depression it had ever experienced. Unfortunately, I was experiencing that same depression. I had dropped out of college—a case of necessity—and was looking for the same thing millions of other Americans were looking for: a job.

Luckily, I knew a man working for a company named Pacific Title and Art, in Hollywood, California. They made titles and subtitles for motion pictures and were financing a cartoon production company called Harmonising Cartoons, owned and operated by Hugh Harman and Rudolph Ising. You can see where the name Harmonising Productions came from, can't you? It was a small cartoon company, and I landed a job there. That was where I first met Friz Freleng and Walter Lantz. They were both animators at that time, and very good I might add. I was hired primarily as a cel washer—a cel is the sheet of clear acetate placed over animation drawings, traced with India ink, then painted various colors on the reverse side. After they were photographed, I would wash the ink and paint off the cels and they were used again and again until the scratches from the pens began to show up on screen. These same cels now are being sold in art galleries throughout the world from prices ranging from hundreds to thousands of dollars, depending upon the particular cel.

Rudolph Ising was a night person, and within weeks of being hired, I was spending most of my evenings working late with him on stories. Also, because I played the saxophone, I worked part-time with Hugh Harman whenever music was involved. By the end of my first year with Harmonising Cartoons, I had become head of the inking and painting department. Soon I was working full-time with both Rudy and Hugh on stories and music respectively, and was able to create the timing and direction of the animation because of my musical experience. By 1936, I was writing and producing. In 1937 I was offered a job at MGM to produce and direct there, and I couldn't pass up the opportunity. It was at that time that I met Joseph Barbera, an artist that MGM had hired out of New York.

It wasn't long after that Joe and I started working as a team, combining our talents. My musical background had helped me to acquire a solid sense of timing, and Joe was a great gag comedy writer. We were both sticklers for detail and together we produced our first Tom and Jerry cartoon, *Puss Gets The Boot,* which was nominated for an Academy Award. In 1943 we did win an Oscar for *Yankee Doodle Mouse,* which turned out to be the first of seven such awards that our Tom and Jerry cartoons would receive over the following nine years. Twenty years later, after more than 160 Tom and Jerry cartoons, MGM closed their animation department. So we wound up opening our own studio, Hanna-Barbera Productions, which has since grown to be the largest in the world.

For the next 25 years, Hanna-Barbera Productions concentrated on producing cartoons for television. In addition, there were a few features for theatres, which involved characters originally created for television, such as Yogi Bear, the Flintstones, and the Jetsons. To name all of the cartoon series and characters Hanna-Barbera has created over the years would take some research, though I am sure the cartoon series would approach one hundred and would involve thousands of cartoon characters.

We are always looking for young animators with talent and vision, either fresh out of art or film school or who have been working in the field for several years. Our new president, Fred Seibert, has produced many ACE award-winning programs for HBO and Nickelodeon. He started by designing the innovative kinetic logos for MTV. Today, there are more outlets for the work we produce than ever before. Animation has come of age.

At this moment, both Joe and I are involved in the process of producing and/or directing animated cartoons, something I've been doing continuously for the past 63 years. When I was a child and I would misbehave, my mother used to say to me, "Enough is enough!" But I don't know when I'll have enough sense to stop.

Faith Hubley
Animation Filmmaker

My love affair with animation began long ago. Fortunately through animation, I have been able to express my passion for the arts, mythology, and astronomy, and above all, to celebrate life.

When I was 18 I arrived in Los Angeles to begin a career in the cinema, armed with high hopes and little money. Since it was 1943 and all the men were being drafted, Columbia Pictures hired me as a messenger. That was how women were able to break into the business, and I wanted to learn everything.

Racing from one department to another, smiling, and asking questions, I began my long education. I was constantly busy painting or playing cello on weekends, while studying acting at night preparing for my directing debut. The years flew by. Finally one of my heroes, composer George Antheil, hired me as music editor for a film called *Spectre of the Rose.* From him I learned of the visceral connection between music and image.

Eventually I was promoted to film editor, and my first assignment was on a documentary with animation called *Human Growth,* which was perhaps the first sex education film. John Hubley of United Producions of America animated the menstrual cycle. To me it looked like a Georgia O'Keefe painting. I realized then that animation was more to my taste than live-action, and after several more years of painting, traveling, and working on various features and documentaries, I was hired as John's assistant on the ill-fated *Finian's Rainbow.* Unfortunately the film collapsed, but we were married, creating one film per year and a family of four children.

Our 22 films dealt with the inner lives of small children *(Moonbird, Windy Day,* and *Cockaboody),* the environment and world peace *(The Hole, The Hat, Urbanissimo, Of Men and Demons, and Eggs),* love *(Tender Game),* life in the universe *(Of Stars and Men),* the future *(Voyage to Next),* and human development *(Everybody Rides the Carousel).*

Music played a vital role and we worked with Benny Carter, Dizzy Gillespie, Quincy Jones, and William Russo. The music of classical composers was used as well, and when it came to dialogue, we drew heavily upon improvisation. We received seven Academy Award nominations and won three times. Our films were often prize winners at the major international film festivals. My dreams seemed to be realized until I was diagnosed with what was thought to be terminal cancer in 1973. Despite that, my first personal film, *Women of the World,* was completed in 1975, and I continued making films alone and in collaboration with John until his unexpected death in 1977.

My films are often inspired by mythology and ancient art. The contemporary painters whose influence I cherish most are Paul Klee and Joan Miro. I love to make films about Mother Earth—her oceans, her children, her beginnings. I ask questions: "Are we alone?" "Who am I?" "What is time?" My feature film *The Cosmic Eye* is a view of life on Earth as seen by three extra-terrestrial jazz musicians, Dizzy Gillespie being the most vocal. The composers with whom I collaborate are Benny Carter, Don Christensen, William Russo, and Elizabeth Swados.

In addition to making films, I teach at Yale University. My students keep me stimulated, my grandchildren keep me young at heart, and the cello and easel remain sources of infinite joy. The storyboard for my current film, *Seers and Clowns,* is almost complete. It will be my eighteenth personal film and the love affair continues. There is so much to learn, to experience, to explore.

My advice to young animators? Fall in love—keep that love alive, nurture it with study, experiment, practice, and never underestimate the need for clarity. If you can visualize a film, you can make that film.

Jules Engel
Artist, Filmmaker, Teacher

■■■■■■■■■■■■■■■■■■ ■ ■ ■ ■ ■ ■ ■

> *"Animation art is concerned with movement through space, and so with time has become the most important element in the art of the 20th century. And it took till this century to discover the art of movement."*
>
> LEN LYE.

Experimental animation is a personal vision, a concrete record of an artist's self-discovery.

My particular emphasis has been to concentrate on the development of a visually inspired, dynamic language, independent of literary and theatrical traditions, demonstrating that pure graphic choreography is capable of nonverbal truth. I have not sought out narratives to bring about graphic expression. Instead, I have chosen to convey ideas and feelings through movements that cannot be transposed into words. Letters forming languages of specific cultures are not the vehicle. The voices are lines, squares, spots, circles, and varieties of color. Though sometimes difficult to comprehend, these are the keys to the pictures.

> *"So we shall have an art which is beyond static painting, beyond cinematographic representation, which we shall not take long to get familiar with; which will have its own admirers particularly skilled in responding to movement, to colors, to mutual penetrations of colors, brisk and leisurely transformations, flows of movement, convergence, and contrast."*
>
> GUILLAUME APOLLINAIRE.

It was not animated films that provided my overture to the art of movement. In my case it came from watching the Ballet Russes de Monte Carlo. It was during their classical performances that I discovered the artistry of movement found in the dance world. Through the choreography of George Balanchine and the magnificent fluidity of dancers like Tamara Toumanova, Danilova, Baronova, David Lichine, and Leonide Massine, my own vision began to emerge. The spectacular unity of body, choreography and music, conveyed with perfect precision, displayed infinite possibilities of gesture.

Another avenue opened for me with the modern dance of Martha Graham. I perceived how a more contemporary art could lead the way for new visions in movement, where an emotional flow is not necessarily explained.

With the concept of movement as a universal expression, I have drawn on sources from diverse disciplines for inspiration: painters like Wassily Kandinsky and Piet Mondrian, sculptors like David Smith, and Alexander Calder with his perpetual moving mobiles, and more recently, from Eduardo Chillida. Those contemporary visual artists serve as stimulating resources and references. I came to realize that fluidity in design, color, and abstraction did not eliminate structure.

I become reflectively creative with ideas about time, rhythm, and structure. I may even infuse conversational rhythm while watching a theatrical production of Anton Chekhov's *Uncle Vanya*. On the other hand, I may become deeply inspired by watching great athletes perform. This takes on a poetic framework of all-consuming motion and grace, visually displaying gentle strength and all the paradoxes of endurance and joy. Picture, for example, Florence Joyner running track, edging around a curve and winning the race. Words are inadequate to describe the visual picture we experience. So, as it exists in my work, movement in itself is the expression that gives us both an aesthetic and an emotional experience.

Movement is the content. Don't merely look at a movement. Feel it. Movement should include *pause and silence*. Movement emerges, only then to disappear. Movement implies advance and reinforces with retreat. Movement is action and our responses to it may be determined by more than the purely kinetic qualities of that motion. It may be affected by our state of mind at any particular moment.

My work is abstract, but it contains an organic element that brings people close to their inner feelings. It does not explain, but within feeling, one can discover answers.

Conductors, composers, and musicians have all spoken to me about my work. They describe the composition, timing, and direction they sense from my films as musical. They are moved by the rhythm and by a "fulfilling process." This is so interesting to me, since I do not rely on music as a starting point. In fact, I add scores to my films after their completion.

Since 1969, I have animated more than 30 abstract films and I prefer to create the graphic choreography from my own sense of timing. Experimental animators like Oscar Fischinger and Norman McLaren have been motivated by music. This work became known as *visual music*. I prefer to call my films *art in motion*. I have, however, made "film to music." An interesting example, that also involved specific colors creating space, occurred when the Disney Studio asked me to storyboard the Chinese and Russian dances for the movie *Fantasia*. After consideration, I decided on a simple approach. I saw the characters as abstract shapes, giving them movement in a small, restricted space. The only problem was to get the studio to accept a black background without texture. In my opinion, the rhythm and motion to music was actually enhanced by the black background. I can appreciate the idea of an all-black background, as it removes the screen corners, and shapes appear to move as though floating in infinite space.

The industry was timid about using color in the same fashion as contemporary painters. As one of the founders of the UPA studio, I helped it become a place where we could be innovative with color and expand the medium creatively. For example, color can create space. And it can be dramatic or expressive of any form or implication.

Experimental film offers a magnificent opportunity to investigate space and time photography, as well as composing in space for spatial disintegration of forms. Composing in space also encompasses the flow of movement, simultaneous rhythm, and forms that interpenetrate. Successive, transformable, and ephemeral forms may disappear, then re-form. You may arrest motion, slow motion, fragment images, change the surface of the screen or the exterior rhythm, even employ cubist composition. The potential is unending.

I am not bound by theory. I am conscious of the shapes and forms I work with, how they grow and develop inside film space and time. I am aware of their action, which presents me with the avenues to move forward, to control, to evolve and finalize. This work is not realized through mathematical formulas. It is gained through visual trial and error. It is a process of perception, a process of discovery.

Ralph Bakshi

Animation Director, Producer

Most students of animation undergo a conservative education in which they emulate the sterile perfection epitomized by classical animation techniques in hopes of finding steady employment after graduation. While financial considerations are important, it seems a shame that more time is not spent helping students develop a personal animation style. While I respect the past, I think it is extremely important that we don't copy it, so that we may explore new directions. Even with dramatic advances in animation techniques, I don't feel that the art of animation has yet moved far from its origins. We still have a lot of areas to examine.

I'm not saying it's easy—far from it. Pulling together the financial resources to make an uncompromisingly personal animated work is a daunting task. If you're lucky enough to get your film made, you still need to get audiences to view it. Despite some exceptions in recent years, the buyers and distributors of animation—both in film and television—are usually unwilling to take chances. They prefer to stick with the accepted, commercial forms of animation aimed particularly at kids. Nevertheless, I strongly believe that animation teachers and their students must decide whether they are willing to settle for the classical ways of doing things, or opt for discovering new methods of visualizing.

My own career in animation has been marked by the fact that I created the screen's first X-rated cartoon feature called *Fritz the Cat,* an adaptation of Robert Crumb's underground comic strip. In my current work, I continue to actively promote the belief that animation is an art form for everyone, adults included. Some of my other film credits include *Heavy Traffic, Coonskin, Hey Good Lookin', Wizards,* and *The Lord of the Rings.* In addition, I have dipped into directing for television with "Tattertown," a prime-time animated series for Nickelodeon, in which I explored making a pure children's story for the first time. The series was a kind of homage to animation, as it used different character types from various periods of animation history. These days, I continue to paint, animate and direct music videos in New York City.

John Whitney
Computer Graphics Director

■■■■■■■■■■■■■■■ ■ ■ ■ ■ ■ ■ ■ ■

After two years of college in the late 1930s, I somehow persuaded myself that I was an artist and practically hitchhiked to Paris. There, I came up with the idea to animate with a movie camera a kind of music that you could see as well as listen to. (I didn't realize that back in my own hometown Walt Disney had a crew of people working on something like that very idea.) In searching for tools to accomplish my goals, I invented and patented mechanisms for motion control and slit-scan processes. My slit-scan machine helped me to anticipate that computers offer the most exact means of visualizing the structural patterns of music. And I have since spent most of my life pursuing the marriage of music and art, using the computer as my instrument.

Pablo Picasso criticized abstractionism in painting, complaining, "Where is the drama?" Yet we do discover great drama in music, the purest abstract art. In this vein, the painter Wassily Kandinsky wrote to composer Arnold Schoenberg in 1911: "The independent life of the individual voices in your compositions is exactly what I am trying to find in my painting." And so too, by an ironic inversion of this quest, the composer Alexander Scriabin envisioned a color counterpoint to music. Who, before today, could imagine how to implement such ideas?

I predict that digital computers are about to reveal enormous potentials for merging music with visual art. It is a momentous, historic fact that color pattern and musical tone can be united in a unique art medium through the technology of computers. After the milestone invention of the *forte piano*, this union eventually will be recognized for what it is: the greatest contribution of technology to the arts. Fast software makes possible the creative manipulation of both color and tone at the computer. Computer graphics is enkindling a new and original art form that intertwines tone with color exactly where Picasso and other critics found no heat at all. I call this relationship between art and music a *complementarity*. Ancient beliefs that color and musical tone possess a magical affinity have acquired a technical basis in truth. For the first time we can design, imagine, and execute patterns of color and tones in an interreactive kind of musical association. Computer powers of calculation take us to the threshold of a world of stunning potentials with which to realize both Kandinsky's and Scriabin's archetypal, curiously identical dream. Often rejected for mechanizing art, a computer is in fact no more or less an action machine than a piano and is the one critical tool with which to advance beyond the frozen gesture of abstract expressionism.

So there may be more to computer graphics than simulation, virtual reality, special effects, loonytoons, or TV commercials. This just may be a new fine art, the first full-scale fine art of modern technology. Computers are the only instrument for creating music interrelated with active color and design. To embrace concepts of complementarity is literally to double the resources for both artistic and musical creativity in general. This could mark the end of obscurity for abstract films and the end of a dry epoch in contemporary classical music. I believe the potential exists for an expanded audience acceptance beyond today's music conventions, beyond MTV, and beyond the ambiance of gallery or concert hall. A popular audiovisual art will evolve. It will be lively, rich in color and texture, and free to integrate video action, photo imagery, and typography, as well as the abstract calligraphy of a special visual design and its musical complement. Would Picasso, Kandinsky, Mondrian, or Bach respect the computer instrument if they were alive today? Would they agree that this is a flame for igniting a new fine art? Could they improve on MTV? Perhaps they could, and so could you.

Bill Melendez
Animation Director, Producer
■■■■■■■■■■■■■■■■ ■ ■ ■ ■ ■ ■ ■ ■ ■ ■

Perhaps I was fortunate in that I started my career in animation and film production purely by accident. Like most children, I naturally took to drawing. Unlike most children, I never outgrew the compulsion. Long after my childhood friends had stopped drawing for fun, I continued drawing seriously—or so I thought. When I went to high school, rather than opting for an art curriculum, I chose mathematics. I arrogantly assumed that I could already draw, therefore, I did not need to take classes in drawing. After high school, in the midst of the Depression, I faced resistance from those unwilling to hire uneducated young artists. But I heard that a studio headed by Walt Disney was looking for young artists to serve as apprentice animators, and although I figured the position was probably beneath me, I hurried over to see about it.

At that time, the Disney Studio was just about to release its first animated feature film, *Snow White and the Seven Dwarfs*. Newly hired, I was shocked to discover I was not nearly up to the caliber of those artists who surrounded me. Fortunately, the studio offered ongoing nightly art classes. There were life drawing classes, action analysis classes, and animal drawing classes. It was quite simply the best thing that had ever happened to me. The teachers were incredibly stimulating, both philosophically and artistically, and encouraged us to study art history. I invested in buying art books—everything from the Renaissance to the Romans, Greeks, Etruscans, and Egyptians. And the more I studied art, the more fascinating the prospect of animating life became. I fell in love with all aspects of the medium, and discovered that by marrying visuals to music and sound, my two-dimensional drawings were magically transformed into a three-dimensional medium: sight and sound. The animator was not only acting out a scene, he was choreographing it. That opened up two additional areas of intensive study for me—music and dance. We were now working on *Pinocchio,* and that experience was also invaluable. I learned as much from the work of those around me as I had from our class instructors.

The Disney Studio trained us to animate as closely as possible to real life. Years later, at UPA, my colleagues and I attempted the opposite approach. We would caricature life like cartoonists, rather than imitate it as does a camera. We tried to reject anthropomorphic subjects and decided to animate human characters in a stylized fashion. Those were exciting times, and artists like John Hubley and Phil Eastman came up with a philosophy that is embodied in this quote:

> "A progressive, intelligent approach to animation and the realization that it is an expressive and not a mechanical medium, is imperative if we want to keep animated cartoons from stagnating. Development and growth of animation is dependent upon varied, significant subject matter presented in an organized form, evolved from elements inherent in the medium. Among the least understood of these elements is the graphic one, in spite of the fact that animation is almost entirely concerned with drawings, drawings which must function in both space and time."

Like all artists, those of us involved in animation as actors (through draw-ing), or as directors (through film), must be involved in the life around us. All aspects of it. Without this involvement, we risk losing control of the very things that make creativity possible. Our best work seems to come from indi-viduals concerned with, and involved in, their society—be it through theater, music, art, politics, charity, whatever.

All of the above, to me, is but art appreciation, and it is applicable every day of one's life to the work at hand: creating life in our chosen field. Today, over 50 years after I first applied at the Disney Studio, I look back in wonder at how I've enjoyed my life. Never have I awakened without immediately looking forward to the day's work.

I always remember that animation is simply the illustration of an action, and posing and designing a film is really the illustration of a story. That is the most fun. All you need do is define the telling of the story: Staging (close-up, medium, or long-shot), the attitude and "spine" of the shot, and the way it fits the overall story's continuity. Best of all, you are the director. You decide, and better yet, you draw.

This gets me to the part that is most difficult to put over: how to convince the young student that it is all possible. The only thing needed is the will to do. All of us involved in the arts must stubbornly assume that we are capable of accomplishing the job at hand, that we can learn to draw, and that we can learn the mechanics of our trade. Above all, we can learn to boldly and aggres-sively express ourselves. When all is said and done, the graphic artist puts him-self on the line each time he pins up his drawings and ideas for all the world to see. The animator does the same when he projects his work, as does the direc-tor, when his film is viewed.

I have directed and animated hundreds of commercials, won seven Emmy awards, and directed five feature films. Of these, *Dick Deadeye, Snoopy Come Home,* and *The Lion, the Witch, and the Wardrobe* are my favorites.

Bretislav Pojar

Animation Filmmaker

■■■■■■■■■■■■■■■■ ■ ■ ■ ■ ■ ■ ■ ■

In the first half of the century, when American film animation was achieving world success with productions from studios such as Disney, Fleisher, and Warner Brothers, European animation barely existed. As a Czech, I lived in a country that produced no animated films at all. I was part of that first generation of Czech animators who started evolving their own techniques and styles after the Second World War. So I suppose I am truly a self-made man.

In 1942, after finishing high school, I tried to find a job because the Germans had closed the universities. So I joined a newly-formed cartoon studio called AFIT, working as a designer. The owner was an Austrian architect with ambitions to become something between a European Disney and Richard Wagner. He liked to do operas in cartoon. Unfortunately, he had a very limited imagination, and everything we drew was rotoscoped from poorly-acting opera singers. The results were awful, yet at the same time we were learning basic animation by secretly studying a few prints of Disney films. With the escalation of the war, the studio closed after one year.

Immediately after the war ended, the people from AFIT established the first Czech cartoon studio, Bratri v Triku. I worked there as an animator while attending art classes at the university. Within one year we had developed our own style of cartooning, different from American animation. Our films were based more on story than on comic characters, and our graphic style was taken from that of Czech book illustration. The main force behind this style was Jiri Trnka, an excellent designer, painter, and set designer, who was invited to be the artistic director. Even though Trnka was not an animator in the strict sense, he gave new direction to our work, straight toward producing animated puppet films.

Historically, puppetry is a very old folk tradition for the Czech people, and Trnka started out by working in a puppet theatre as a schoolboy. Even as a successful artist, puppets remained his greatest love. Through the technique of frame-by-frame shooting in animation, he discovered a way to bring richer life to his wooden heroes. Consequently, after just one very successful year making cartoons in 1946, he decided to leave in order to start a new puppet studio. Trnka invited me to go with him, and my big adventure began.

Apart from some of Trnka's experiences in theatre that were applicable to film, our small group of animators and craftsmen did not know anything about three-dimensional animation. What were we to do with some puppets, two old cameras dating from 1929, and some equipment discarded from live-action productions? Even worse, neither books nor people with this experience could give us help. We discovered and invented everything as we went along, making those first films. We were enthusiastic. We managed. And with each new film we learned more and more. All of this we owe to Trnka's dream to transform wooden puppets into living stars. For me it was both a very useful and a very amusing time. It was at this time that I began making my own animated films. *A Drop Too Much*, my second film, won awards at Cannes and many other festivals, bringing me recognition and a measure of success.

In spite of my excursions into documentary films and live-action films for children, I worked with Trnka throughout his most fruitful years, including his most ambitious project, Shakespeare's *A Midsummer Night's Dream* in 1959. Afterwards, I was offered the chance to develop a second puppet studio in Prague. There, in the following years, I made the majority of my films, though not always with the puppets. But I often recalled my collaboration with Trnka as it gave me the courage to explore and experiment both with subject matter and the technical possibilities.

I made fables, modern fairy tales, lyrical works, and comedies. I made social and political satires that were received very poorly by the authorities, who for a long time forced me to make only children's films. I perfected a technique of using semi-relief puppets, and made the first Czech-speaking puppets, which were very successful in my homeland but not suitable for exporting. It is better in a small country to produce films without words: to make a good foreign language version of an animated film is a privilege reserved only for big productions. I continued to experiment, combining cutouts and puppets with live-action shooting. In fact, the charm of animation remains for me the possibility of creating so many very different worlds. Everything is in your hands, everything depends upon your choice and inventiveness: the subject you have chosen, how you visualize it, how you draw or model the characters and backgrounds, what kind of animation you choose. The choice can be a world close to reality, but also absurd, surrealist, or abstract, or the world of a known painter or sculptor. In many films I attempted to make visual the nonsensical world of the human soul. In *Night Angel*, it is the world perceived by a young blind man. Both the same possibilities and rules apply to sound, which is no less important for a film's impact than is the picture.

Because of the variety of work and freedom of imagination, I enjoyed making personal, nontraditional films, and so continued to explore puppet animation. In my opinion, this was essential at the time. Puppet animation was the stepchild of traditional animation, and it was necessary to spend extra time and care to perfect this art form in order to compensate for years of general neglect. To be honest, to be able to do this was also my good fortune, since not everyone can work in such an independent way, although in the Fifties many solo animators and small production houses did so. But the big production studios certainly preferred to turn out regular series based on well-known characters. These are much more widely seen and therefore more commercially viable.

Computers, media attention, and music videos, together with a growing public interest, are all changing the face of animation. Who knows how things will look tomorrow? To work in animation it is no longer necessary, as it was in my day, to build a road through the forest of the unknown. With technological advances and schools of animation, there is now an entire highway. Evolution does not stop. Today there are infinite new worlds for young animators to explore.

Herbert Klynn
Animation Artist, Producer

■■■■■■■■■■■■■■■■■■■ ■ ■ ■ ■ ■ ■ ■

I am constantly asked how animation can be used, why animation is different from other forms of film techniques, and why animation should be chosen for a particular subject. So I'll attempt to analyze some of the basic reasons why one chooses animation, and what it can do best compared with live-action.

First, animation can use every variety of graphic style and presentation that the animator can devise to illuminate the principles involved. These can range from the wholly imaginative or symbolic images to the simplest diagrammatic representation. Therefore, aesthetic power can be added to purely intellectual symbols. This lifts animation from the level of a purely representational picture or diagram in motion onto a figurative level, where the power of suggestion begins to operate and the imagination, as distinct from the craftsmanship of the animator, is brought into play. This can be particularly useful in the industrial film intended for more general audiences, where demonstration of the nature of what is happening is of greater importance than a detailed and accurate reconstruction of processes.

Included in the graphic style and presentation in the artwork of animation are the advantages of color. Color can be used to emphasize certain lines of action needed to make a point clear, perhaps saving verbal explanation because color differences can convey by eye alone what might well have to be laboriously expressed in words alongside a purely black and white image. Color can also be used symbolically in that kind of subject that involves mood or feelings. Color has seldom been used symbolically in the live-action film except occasionally in avant-garde production. In animation it is consistently being used nonrepresentationally to assist an argument or create a mood.

Animation can be more versitile than live action. It can reduce or accelerate its speed in the presentation of movement in any process that is being explained. It is also more economical, because important elements in a process may be presented in emphatic slow time, while the unimportant can be speeded up or merely flashed by. This process is familiar in live-action, especially in the scientific film using accelerated speeds to show natural processes. In animation, this technique can be extended to demonstrate all forms of movement, including that of machines.

The basic structure of the animation technique is the superimposition of transparent celluloid sheets one over the other, each bearing one moving section only of the final composite moving image. In this way, the sectionalization of a complex moving process can be stripped down by peeling off layer after layer of the total image, so that the whole may truly be seen as the sum of the parts. This process helps clarify an operation stage by stage. For example, one particular element can be isolated and emphasized to the exclusion of the rest, then followed through while other elements are kept in abeyance until their turn comes.

Animation can even superimpose upon the living image the moving diagram that both simplifies and analyzes the working principles within. Much of the plant, machinery, or laboratory equipment used today is highly complex and needs considerable technological understanding to appreciate its principles of operation. The emphatic, memorable use of naturalistic or artificial sound can help to reinforce the image in an incalculable number of ways and so can music to a limited degree,.

Character animation, which is the principal, is the most flexible and free of the many branches of animation, and is traditionally associated with humor, and a flash of humor here and there eases the concentration in any film seeking to present information. It is, therefore, natural for the cartoon medium to relax and slip in a humorous or comic symbol when effective. This leads to consideration of the question of whether the human figure in cartoons should be treated naturalistically or rather if it ought instead to be presented in the form of a caricature. This depends on the nature of the film and the attitude of both sponsor and animator towards their audience. It is a fact about cartoon that the more naturalistic the human figures are the less natural they seem, for cartoon is essentially an artificial medium that thrives on its artificiality. If the need for a naturalistic figure is genuine, this implies that live-action would be more appropriate in this particular case. Human figures in cartoon can range from simplified drawings from those designed and "played" relatively straight, to grotesqueries made up of a few mobile lines. Some element of caricature is usually effective, and need not make its subject unsympathetic to an audience. It can in fact humanize him far more than any typed performance by a live actor in a poor quality live-action film will do.

Finally, there is that particular contribution that the medium of contemporary animation can itself bring to the presentation of any subject, the equivalent of style in writing and composition in visual arts and music. Animation is indeed a unique art form.

Pablo Ferro
Director, Animator, Producer

■ ■

It's hard for me to believe that in 1947 I was a little boy milking cows and farming in a remote part of the Cuban countryside. Twenty years later, I was a New York City filmmaker creating new techniques in the advertising industry.

After our family moved to New York, I attended the School of Industrial Art, and with two friends put together a little animation studio in Brooklyn. Using a book by Preston Blair, we built our own animation boards and stand so we could shoot artwork with a 16mm Bell and Howell camera that photographed single frames.

At the same time I worked as an usher in a Manhattan theatre that showed foreign films, and became friendly with the projectionist. It was here that I saw UPA's *Gerald McBoing Boing,* which impressed me with its originality. I was able to acquire a few frames from the film and my friends and I studied it at great length.

Searching for a style, I began doing EC Comic Horror Books and illustrating stories for Dell Comics. When looking for an animation job I showed my comics, but was only able to get work in the inking department of the animation studios. Finally I got into the animation department of a studio that produced black and white commercials. When the studio changed hands, a lot of Disney artists were brought in, among them Bill Tytla, who had directed and animated the "Night On Bald Mountain" sequence in *Fantasia.* From Tytla, I learned a great deal more about the art of animation.

After working for various studios I eventually developed my own style and together with two partners formed Ferro, Mogubgub and Schwartz. We produced commercials for major firms and won many national and international animation awards. I later founded Pablo Ferro Films. Fortunately, my early use of multiple screens on TV and the quick cut technique (graphics combined with live-action and animation) came to Stanley Kubrik's attention, and he hired me to do the titles, trailer, and opening sequence for *Dr. Strangelove.* That led me to creating numerous titles, logos, trailers, and special effects for such films as *Midnight Cowboy, Harold and Maude, A Clockwork Orange, Stop Making Sense,* and *The Thomas Crown Affair* (where I employed the first use of single projected multiple screens in a feature film). I also found time to make my acting debut as an Indian with severe back problems in Robert Downey's *Greaser's Palace.*

Settling in California, I continued to design titles and sequences for feature films, including *Beetlejuice, Dark Man,* and *The Addams Family.* And I finally was able to finance and direct my first live-action feature *Me, Myself and I,* whose screenplay by Julian Barry I had commissioned some 20 years earlier.

Show business is like a wild roller coaster ride, in which only perseverance keeps you hanging on. Obviously, there is a great gulf between the movie business and cinema as an art form, but you must know how to survive in one so that you can function in the other. And this applies worldwide, not only in America.

Grant Munro

Animation Director, Producer

From a very early age I preferred drawing to the exclusion of every other childhood pursuit. My first brush with animation happened when I was nine. In 1933 Disney's *Three Little Pigs* was about to open in Winnipeg, and as part of a promotional campaign, a local department store sponsored a contest for children. We were asked to submit a sketch of the three live little piglets tethered in the store foyer. I won. At that time I began to make very simple flip books from my dad's prescription pads, a hobby which was to continue through four years of art college, especially during art history and anatomy lectures—probably the reason I failed both subjects.

Following high school it was expected I would follow in my father's footsteps and study medicine. Fortunately, art won out. My big dream was to attend the Art Center School in Los Angeles. The brochure indicated that many of the instructors worked in and/or had a direct line with the Hollywood studios.

But, it was wartime and anyone eligible for the military draft was not permitted to leave Canada to study something that was available on home ground. So I enrolled at the Ontario College of Art, where the distinguished animators George Dunning, Richard Williams, Sidney Goldsmith, and Evelyn Lambart are graduates, and took the commercial course, half expecting to be an illustrator, preferably of childrens' books.

One month prior to graduation, a favorite professor, Franklin Carmichael, arranged an interview for me with a "chap from the National Film Board of Canada." That very shy and modest chap was Norman McLaren, who was recruiting personnel for his small animation unit.

I got the job, and for me it was an indescribably exciting time. None of us had any "single frame" experience. But under McLaren's watchful eye and with a trial-and-error approach, we began to achieve some favorable results. There were no guide books to animation in those days. In retrospect, I believe that *Animated Motion: Parts 1—5* that McLaren and I produced in the early Seventies would have been an invaluable and time-saving reference.

Our methods and techniques were very simple. Any thoughts of cel work and fully animated characters were just not considered. We didn't have the personnel, the equipment, or the money. It was encouraging to have those early efforts praised by the superb animators of the newly established UPA unit. For they, too, used an economy of design and movement and budget.

McLaren, incidentally, used both me and Jean Paul Ladouceur as actors in his 1952 Oscar winning film, *Neighbours,* which was also my first editing experience. Personally, I made, among other shorts, *The Man on The Flying Trapeze* and *My Darling Clementine* at the National Film Board of Canada.

Animation as we all know is not only here to stay, but is expanding internationally at one hell of a rate. The definition of animation is continually being refined—and that is our challenge.

Bruno Bozzetto
Animation Director

■ ■

My grandfather was a great painter. He worked in an enormous and luminous room, covering the walls and ceiling with images. Whenever I would go to the room to see him, I would at first be struck by the pungent odor of turpentine, then by the gigantic paintings, mostly of saints and madonnas that dwarfed me from the highest reaches of that space.

I'm not sure what significance those memories have for me, but I believe that our lives can often be affected by such experiences. At any rate, when I was a boy in Italy, drawing remained a mere hobby. In high school and college I studied everything but drawing. I must confess that, even while admiring Disney both in cinema and in comic strips, my true passion then was not for animated cartoons but live-action films, and I never missed a chance to run off to the local movie theatres. I learned many things from watching movies. I learned that character and story were what really kept the audience glued to their seats. I learned that the success of a film is not based only upon the fame and talent of the actors, but upon numerous other things such as character, plot, photography, rhythm, performance, narrative timing, music, sound effects, etc.

When I was about 15 years old, I started filming documentaries and short narrative films on a Bauer Super-8, using my school friends as subjects and actors. From these experiences I learned the importance of framing, lighting, camera movement, and above all editing, a task that I have always loved.

When I started experimenting with animation at age 18, I had already acquired a good understanding of the cinematic medium. I was convinced that artwork was not the most important thing. Rather, the most important elements were theme, story, and the movements or "performances" of the animated characters.

For me, the true talent of the animator lies not so much in the ability to draw well as it does in knowing how to give life to the movements of the characters by exploiting, with intelligence and humor, even the smallest movements, and by appreciating the value of such things as facial expression and dramatic pause. In short, the animator, although perhaps only subconsciously, must also be an actor, endowed with a great rhythmic and aesthetic sense as well as an extraordinary sense of humor.

Perhaps if I had watched only the animated Disney films, I would never have had the courage to take the leap of faith into this type of work. Disney films fascinated me. At the same time, however, they intimidated me in their level of perfection. Such a degree of excellence seemed inaccessible to me. Encouragement and stimulation came instead through a couple of short pieces from the National Film Board of Canada. These were *History of Sports and Transportation,* by Colin Low, and *Blinkity Blank,* drawn directly on celluloid by the ingenious Norman McLaren. Ultimately, the coup de grâce came from Disney Studios in the form of a rather anomalous short film entitled *Toot, Whistle, Plunk and Boom.* This wonderful piece was directed by the great

Ward Kimball. Together, these films convinced me that one could tell new and intelligent stories based not only on fantasy, but on daily life. And one could do this using the very simplest drawings and animation techniques, which, where creatively employed, could be extremely effective, not to mention fun.

So I made my first short subject. Shortly thereafter, with the financial help of my father, I bought a movie camera and a Moviola (I was an only child, which in my case was perhaps a blessing since I had all possible support from my father, both moral and financial). I then founded the animation studio from which many great talents would later emerge: Guido Manuli, Giovanni Mulazzani, Giuseppe Laganà, and Maurizio Nichetti—many others, too numerous to list, also had their start in that studio.

At first, only advertising work guaranteed the financial survival of the studio. But I acknowledge the value of this work because it taught us many fundamental things about coming up with original ideas and synthesizing them. Above all, it taught us about the organization and technique of production. By forcing us to work within the framework of strict durational time limits and deadlines, we learned precision. The continuous invention of stories, themes, and characters was especially stimulating and contributed greatly to the creative growth of the entire studio.

Aside from commercials, I have always based the characters of my animation pieces on the study of man, his obsessions and behavior, and the development of civilization and the natural world (and therefore on our relationship with nature and animals). I believe that the animated drawing is one of the most fantastic tools man has for dealing with such subjects. It offers us an infinite number of viewpoints and angles from which to observe these great problems. We can study the world from afar or from very near. We can reduce whole centuries down to a few seconds, and we can visualize dreams and thoughts. The effective use of this medium in original ways is a challenge for anybody. The animator is challenged to use creativity and humor while transforming personal feelings into a story for an audience, a story that expresses and shares a personal point of view about the thousands of things that make up life.

If, as an animator, you succeed in giving the audience a good time, you have done a fine job. But if you cause the audience to reflect upon what they have seen, and to look inside themselves, then you have done even better. When I have succeeded in doing this, the enormous pleasure I derived was enough to convince me that all the years I have dedicated to animation were well spent.

In addition to numerous short subjects, I have produced and directed three long animated films at my studio in Milan: *West and Soda, Vip, My Superman Brother,* and *Allegro Non Troppo.* In 1987, I co-produced and directed a full-length, live-action feature film called *Under The Chinese Restaurant.*

Dan McLaughlin

Filmmaker, Professor, Theorist

■■■■■■■■■■■■■■■■■■■ ■ ■ ■ ■ ■ ■ ■ ■

What is the future of animation? Perhaps that is easiest answered by turning the question around. "The future is animation!" The question then is "How do the rest of the people fit in?" The answer to that is for them to learn animation.

For students who apply to the UCLA Animation Workshop, we look for very smart and creative workaholics with great ideas who must do animation or die—a student with a stimulating personality who knows only two limits to animation: imagination and exhaustion.

I believe that a formal education is essential if you are to achieve your full potential in animation—you animate with your brain, not your hand. Students from the UCLA Animation Workshop often end up having their own companies, forging new directions, and creating jobs for others. One of the prime goals of the Workshop is to train you not for the first job you will have, but the last one.

How did I get started in motion pictures? Well, I was born in Hollywood, California and went to work in feature films when I was four months old (my first paycheck went to pay the doctor and hospital costs of my birth). After appearing in over 35 films as an extra, stand-in, and bit player, I decided that live-action movies merely recorded reality in an unethical environment by using assembly line methods, not unlike Detroit. Education to me became more important than life as an extra, so I quit the live-action world at the age of 12. Some of the many memories from that period are of my mother, a hairdresser, designing Betty Grable's hair color, my off-screen fights with the fat kid from the *Our Gang* comedies, and almost being shot by John Wayne for using his makeup.

After serving in the Korean conflict, then working as a shill in Nevada, I entered the Animation Workshop at UCLA. The Workshop had been created in 1947 by Bill Shull, a former Disney animator. I was first attracted to the basic animation course after a fellow student guaranteed that it was a sure "B" course. Later, the philosophy of the workshop: "One person, one film," became my primal and continuing commitment to animation. Having never left UCLA, I am presently a professor in the Department of Film and TV, where my duties include mentoring 33 graduate students in a M.F.A. program. The UCLA Animation Workshop has consistently been one of the top animation programs in the world and our students have won Student Academy Award prizes in four of the past six years.

I really like to think of myself as an independent, experimental filmmaker (structuralist) and poet. I have made 20 animated films, ranging from the traditional to the experimental, which have occasionally won both national and international awards. *Claude* and *God is Dog Spelled Backwards* (which started the style and technique of Kinestsas) are two of my earlier films. My most recent films have been very minimal and very boring. *Red/Green* is a five-minute film consisting only of a dissolve (the world's longest) between the colors red and green, and a one shot film of my left eyeball lasting eight minutes titled *In The Penal Colony.*

I have lectured and had retrospective screenings at many universities and film festivals. One recent honor was to be appointed to the steering committee for the first International Teaching Symposium held in Urbino, Italy. I have had several articles published and have developed an interactive critical analysis system for animation with Phil Denslow. In 1982, I designed an animation studio for the government of Nigeria, directed animation for both Sesame Street and the Amnesty International Human Rights Now World Tour. Additionally, titles for features and legal expert witness work are among my professional activities.

Presently, I am establishing an animation multimedia curriculum, and an interactive system for teaching animation, while finishing an animated film narrated by Burt Lancaster, entitled *The Shapes of Movement, A Short History of Gymnastics.* I am also writing books, planning an international conference on interactive poetry, and doing articles on animation as well as starting more projects, one of which will be a humorous computer animated film.

In teaching, I seek to achieve three stages: information, knowledge, and wisdom. First, the teacher must impart the information that allows one to master the discipline, then guide that information into knowledge—and if we are very lucky, that knowledge will become wisdom.

Stan Lee
Publisher, Writer, Producer
■■■■■■■■■■■■■■■■■■■ ■ ■ ■ ■ ■ ■ ■ ■

Animation: the very word conjures up action, zest, and excitement. I still remember my feeling of elation when as a child I would be in a movie theatre and suddenly the image of Bugs Bunny, Donald Duck, or a number of other cartoon characters would appear, filling the screen with energy, laughter, music, and action. Action was the key word. Exaggerated, improbable, silly, but always hilarious action.

Later, after being exposed to my first full-length animated cartoon, Disney's *Snow White*, I was hopelessly hooked. From that moment on, animation to me was, and still is, one of the greatest art forms on earth.

Even during the years I spent as head writer, editor, and art director at Marvel Comics (then known as Timely Comics), I never lost my love for animation. In fact, for a number of years I supervised the production of dozens of animated-type comic books such as *Terrytoons, Mighty Mouse, Super Rabbit, Buck Duck, Homer the Happy Ghost, Silly Seal,* and *Ziggy Pig.*

Prior to that time, Marvel Comics, from its base in New York, had licensed the rights to various Hollywood producers to make cartoon versions of our characters for television: characters such as Spider Man, The Fantastic Four, The Mighty Thor, The Incredible Hulk, Sub-Mariner, and Iron Man.

While the majority of those cartoon shows were successful, I was never fully satisfied with the quality of either the stories, the characterization, or the animation itself. Therefore, I decided it was time for me to become personally involved. Convincing the Marvel executives that we could do a better job of animating our own characters than any other studio, I moved to Los Angeles where I eagerly set about creating our own animation studio.

And what a studio it is. We were fortunate in being able to attract some of the most talented animators, directors, storyboard artists, and layout artists in the business. Why? Because so many of them had grown up reading our comics. Since many were already enthusiastic Marvel fans, there was little or no orientation time needed and we were able to plunge right into the job of creating cartoons.

Though I had been an animation buff for years, it was then that I gained a true appreciation of the tremendous amount of work, time, and talent that goes into every animated cartoon. In the past, when doing comic books, I was somewhat cavalier about editing the dialogue or artwork. No matter how many things may have needed alteration, there was always time to make last moment changes before we went to press. If any dialogue didn't please me, I'd merely have it "whited out," then relettered. If some artwork wasn't quite up to snuff, I could have the panel or panels redrawn and paste the new versions over the original ones on the sheet of illustration board. But I soon learned that television animation was entirely different. In doing a network cartoon series the pressure on each and every creative person involved with the production is incredibly intense. Time and money are the great leveling factors. You pretty much have to be right the first time. But the joys are immense. Just think how satisfying it is to work in a field where virtually any idea, anything your imagination can conceive, no matter how wild, no matter how spectacular, no matter how indescribably fantastic it might be, can be illustrated and colored, put to music, then brought to life with movement and style. Imagine being associated with an art form that is possibly the most popular of all for young minds, and only now coming into its own as one of the greatest sources of family entertainment.

Animation: the perfect blending of story and art, music and imagery, fantasy and myth. Now, with the advent of computer imaging, interactive technology, and virtual reality, animation is as exciting and as promising as tomorrow, and limited only by the capacity of the human brain itself.

Mark Harris

USC Co-chair, Film and Television Production

■■■■■■■■■■■■■■■■■■ ■ ■ ■ ■ ■ ■ ■ ■

The fundamental goal of our production program at the University of Southern California is to foster creative growth and self-expression through the teaching of filmmaking.

The program is designed to train all students in the essentials of filmmaking, providing them the tools to begin functioning professionally in the industry. At the same time we like to encourage students to explore and experiment, to develop their own voice and vision. The faculty view our school as a laboratory for research and exploration, a community of filmmakers devoted to investigating and expanding the concept and language of the cinema.

The students we are seeking may have little previous training in film, but they should have rich life experiences. Basically, we are seeking students from diverse backgrounds, with an openness to ideas, who are passionate about cinema. They should be intelligent, imaginative, insightful, self-motivated, and disciplined.

The main pedagogical principal underlying the program is that students learn best experientially—by making films they care about. The faculty's role is two-fold. One is to teach basic skills and professional attitudes and to define and communicate the standards for evaluating work. The other is to create a supportive environment that encourages growth, risk-taking, and critical reflection. To accomplish this successfully, there needs to be constant communication and feedback between students, faculty, and staff and continual reevaluation of the faculty's and program's performance.

Recently, we have begun offering an M.A. degree here in animation that features extensive studies in computer graphics, cel animation, writing for animation, and animation history.

Stan Freberg
Writer, Producer, Comedian

In 1992, I was standing in the Television Academy Theatre being honored by ASIFA. June Foray, the president, just handed me the Winsor McCay award. It is inscribed "To Stan Freberg, for his distinguished lifetime contribution to the art of animation." Feeling the way I do about animation as an art, no award I've ever received means more to me.

In 1945, my first professional job in Hollywood was standing next to the great Mel Blanc, supplying what would be the first of many cartoon voices for Warner Brothers Cartoons. I was an 18-year-old actor trying to break into show business. I would take the bus from my home in Pasadena to downtown Hollywood, hitting the radio networks, reading for producers, then riding back to Pasadena again. Finally one day an agent got me an audition for Warner Brothers Cartoons

Standing at a microphone behind a curtain in a projection room, I went through a series of original voices and impersonations (FDR, Jimmy Durante, Peter Lorre, Edward R. Murrow) for a room full of writers and directors. In the audience were such animation greats as Chuck Jones, Friz Freleng, Bob Clampett, Bob McKimson, Artie Davis, and others. I was terrified until I heard laughter from the other side of the curtain. They must have liked what they heard because when I came out they all applauded and crowded around. Chuck Jones put his arm around me and promised to use me soon. Bob Clampett as well. Friz Freleng looked up at me and said, "Why haven't I heard of you before now, Stan?" I shrugged, "Gee, I don't know, I've been around." Friz said, "Oh, I didn't mean that the way it sounded. I mean, I'm sure you didn't just get off the bus."

Three days later, I was at Warner Brothers Studios in Burbank with a new Screen Actors Guild card in my wallet, standing next to Mel Blanc, doing the first of many Warner's cartoons.

Over the years I was honored to work for such legendary animators as Chuck Jones who animated me as the Baby Bear in *The Three Little Bears,* and also as one of the two house-wrecking mice, Hubie and Bertie, which Mel and I did as well as the two polite gophers. Friz Freleng hired me to do the little dog Chester who jumped around encouraging the big bulldog. "Attaboy, Spike. You can do it, Spike!" I also sang a hip version of the three little pigs for Friz in *The Three Little Bops.* When Bugs Bunny was teaching his nephew to catch a puma in *Rabbit's Kin,* I was the voice of Pete Puma ("Gimme a whooooole lotta lumps!"). I worked for all the Warner's animation directors in over 50 cartoons and was also honored to work for Tex Avery, Bill Hanna and Joe Barbera, George Pal, Walter Lantz, and Walt Disney. In addition to creating the voice of the beaver in Disney's *Lady and the Tramp,* who frees Lady by chewing off her muzzle, I created a character called The Jabberwock for *Alice in Wonderland.* Disney himself directed me along with Ben Sharpsteen in that seven minute sequence. I also did a number of UPA cartoons working for Art Babbit, and Ernie Pintoff, the very original cartoonist, animator, and author of this book.

In addition to my other work today as a commercial producer and syndicated commentator on radio, I still do voices on several animated series like "Tiny Toons," and "Garfield." In the only animated episode of Steven Spielberg's "Amazing Stories: The Family Dog," I was the voice of the father. "Bad dog. Baaaaad dog!"

A Capitol CD of mine is called *Stan Freberg Presents The United States Of America.* Over the years, it has built a cult following throughout the world. Recently, I've been considering having it animated as a feature film. Animation is the perfect medium for comedy. Animated actors can move a lot faster than live ones, and so can the jokes. A young cartoon freak in England recently took it upon himself to compile a computer database of the cartoons in which my voice appears. It totaled more than 100 cartoons.

Apart from my work as a voice-over actor in animation, the real thrill came when as a producer of commercials I could, as often as possible, convince clients to go with animation. Even though I've worked most of the time in live-action over the years, I was never happier than when working with first-rate animation directors who could transpose what I'd written to that greatest of art forms: animation.

I was thrilled to be able to hire such great animation and design talents as Saul Bass, John Hubley, Bill Melendez, Ade Woolery, Emory Hawkins, and Bill Littlejohn. Littlejohn, working with Melendez, animated a series of commercials for Kaiser Aluminum Foil for my company, Freberg Ltd., that won the Venice Film Festival grand prize for best series of animated commercials. Hawkins animated a coffee commercial for my company in association with John Wilson's Fine Art Productions that won the New York Art Directors Club Gold Medal, and I am proud that many of my animated commercials have won Clio awards. But even without those honors, I would have been happy just writing and producing animation. Working along with the artists and animation directors, laying down the tracks with great actors, waiting for pencil tests, making modifications, then finally seeing the finished art of animation. I love everything about it. Long live animation, a true and original American art form!

Al Brodax
Animation Writer, Producer

■■■■■■■■■■■■■■■■■ ■ ■ ■ ■ ■ ■ ■ ■

I have had the good fortune to dance through a good deal of the media. Broadway, television—live and filmed—theatrical feature production, video, and especially animation for television as well as theatres. Promiscuous? Perhaps. But they are all connected in a positive, almost incestuous way. However, as in the case of wives, lovers, and children, in your heart of hearts there is always one very special love. Mine is clearly animation.

As a child of the depression years, I found *Snow White* to be a memorable break in the clouds. Sitting in the dark coolness of the theatre and breathing in the vague aroma of air conditioning, I fell in love. In the Fifties, with the war and university behind me, I eased my way into a graduate course in show biz, the mailroom of the William Morris Agency, a veritable fantasyland, where as a writer/producer I was "discovered."

One of the agency's clients was attempting to adapt some of Sherwood Anderson's short stories into a play for Broadway. Luckily, I knew Anderson's stories by heart, finding them brilliant in their poetic simplicity. One day, while the client was seated in our reception area puzzling over his adaptation, I had the chutzpah to critique his play. I had brought home the office copy to read over the weekend, not having enough money to do much else. I had found lots of shortfalls and didn't hold back. He seemed stunned but interested. A week later I received news that my critique had substance and was asked to help out with a final draft. I did. Six weeks later, I was one of three producers sitting in a rehearsal hall in New York City with Dorothy McGuire, Leon Ames, and James Whitmore. I was in heaven. I was also out of breath, running back and forth from rehearsals to my day job. Plays close overnight, and I still needed a steady income. This play, entitled *Winesburg, Ohio,* didn't close overnight after all. It lasted 13 performances. On closing night, the publicist for the play offered me an odd piece of advice. I could have a future in show business but had a tendency to be drawn towards the poetic, the esoteric. He suggested I expand my vision by taking on something "dumb and popular," something like *Popeye* for instance.

The Fifties were boomtimes for television. Promotions from mailroom to agent came fast and happily. By mid-decade I was dubbed "program developer." My mandate was to develop television programming for the agency's many stars. Along with two colleagues, I sat in a windowless room late into the night developing programs that did indeed make it to prime time, i.e., *Pulitzer Prize Playhouse.* Among the "stars" on my list was King Features Syndicate, a division of the Hearst Corporation, copyright owner of such properties as Krazy Kat, Barney Google, Beetle Bailey and Popeye. King Features was impressed by my interest and asked me to create a television and motion picture department for them. I did, and it was enormously successful. Ironically, my initial production involved the completion of 220 Popeye five-and-a-half minute episodes within 18 months. Anyone with a modicum of experience in animation would deem this impossible to pull off. It took Paramount 35 years to produce 225 Popeye theatrical shorts. But thanks to the Hanna-Barbara technique of "limited animation" and my naive approach to an impossible schedule, it somehow worked. With the strictest controls over model sheets, the creation of writing teams, the utilization of several studios (domestic and foreign), and most importantly the voices of Jack Mercer and May Questel as Popeye and Olive Oil, we came in on time and on budget. The project was a success and brought joy to the keepers of books at Hearst Corporation, and will do so forevermore.

In the Sixties, I followed suit with Krazy Kat, Barney Google and Beetle Bailey. It was time to try new things. And I did so with 39 half-hour episodes of Beatles cartoons. The group's music was undeniably perfect for animation. The beat was right, the timing for production, all perfect. A three-year run on the ABC network garnered a fifty percent share for its Saturday morning time slot: a rare number in ratings shares. By mid-decade, my grasp of the basic art form was secure. The marriage of music, movement and story was something I wanted to expand upon. To create an animated musical became my goal. *Fantasia* was a masterpiece without story. To recreate that excitement with story and perhaps a non-Disney look resulted in the production of *Yellow Submarine*. The music was at hand, the story yet to be written. I summoned the best and the brightest to complement the wonders of the Beatles' music. Seventeen treatments were written for and dismissed by Brian Epstein, the Beatles' manager, although at least 10 of them would have made marvelous motion pictures. Ringo insisted that, whatever the story, the title had to be *Yellow Submarine*. So we worked backwards. In the end, together with Eric Segal, a Yale professor who later went on to write *Love Story* and other motion pictures, I wrote the screenplay that became the movie. The design by Heinz Edelmann was outstanding and not at all grounded in Disney tradition. While Disney's characters were designed on a structure of circles, we thought rectangles should become our foundation, based on Edelmann's first renderings. As for backgrounds, the order of the day called for a move toward fine art wherever possible, any form that would best present the mood of a scene, be it impressionistic, abstract, realistic, or painted photo negatives. It was the genius of the Beatles' music and the images rendered by the artists that conjured up the magic of *Yellow Submarine*.

Animation, both traditional and computer-generated, along with a full measure of imagination in the hands of extraordinarily talented artists, provides a glorious canvas. Currently, the project *Strawberry Fields* is on my agenda. There are already three years of work behind this production. It will be a live-action, two-dimensional and computer animation hybrid. And indeed there is a wonderful story. There is also the bureaucratic madness of studio machinations to sort out. But that's another story, and the beauty of the dream is worth all the downside.

Debra Kaufman
Animation Journalist

■■■■■■■■■■■■■■■■■■ ■ ■ ■ ■ ■ ■ ■ ■

How would you like to go to the movies and see Arnold Schwarzenegger paired with Marilyn Monroe? Or how about a brand new Marx Brothers movie? The new frontier for computer animation seems impossible, but what's on the minds of computer animators nowadays is the digital actor.

In the six years that I have been covering the entertainment industry for the trade press, I have often written about computer animation and graphics and how they have been used in feature films. And it seems hard to believe how far we've come in a relatively short period of time. While each step forward in feature film use of computer animation has been exciting and generated public appreciation and good press, we obviously ain't seen nothin' yet.

A quick look at how computer animation and graphics developed in feature films shows the logic of an idea seemingly as farfetched as the digital actor. Prior to *Star Wars,* computerized effects were largely dismissed as being clumsy, unrealistic, and not very artistic. But *Star Wars* featured a digital motion control system that enabled that film's astonishing visual effects: it was the first indication of what was to come. When the film was completed, George Lucas went to San Rafael, California and founded Industrial Light and Magic and, shortly thereafter, established a nascent computer graphics division. But in the early 1980s, computers still didn't have enough processing power to create imagery fast enough to be realistic and economical.

Then, in 1986, *The Adventures of Young Sherlock Holmes* was ILM's first foray into bringing a computer-generated image onto the silver screen with a scene in which the knight depicted on a stained glass window "comes to life" and breaks out of the 2-D window into 3-D reality. At that moment, ILM's investment in CGI research and development came to fruition.

The same technique for generating computer images and compositing them with live-action sequences on film that had been scanned into the computer was further developed and used again to even greater effect in the film most experts consider to have been a visual breakthrough: *The Abyss.* In that film, audiences could only marvel at the shimmering water tentacle that imitated human faces. Created as a wireframe model with photos mapped onto the geometry, the water tentacle imitates water qualities by reflecting and refracting the environment around it.

In a similar fashion, ILM created the chrome man in *Terminator 2,* the film that proved without a doubt the power of computers to create dramatic and believable imagery and seamlessly integrate such imagery with live-action footage. The computer-created chrome man was only one of the film's many computer-aided effects, which included the creation of totally new images (3-D CGI), alteration of existing images (2-D image processing), and skillful combinations of both.

As CGI began to appear in a multitude of other places, from morphing faces in Michael Jackson's music video *Black and White* to the revivification of long dead actors in the Diet Coke commercial, some people began to tout the computer as the future's primary visual effects tool. Indeed, some predictions have come to pass very quickly. Though traditional effects have certainly not disappeared in not much more than a decade, the computer has been transformed from the unlikely to the omnipresent in Hollywood.

Jurassic Park was another huge leap forward. Until that film, the computer had been used to create objects and creatures that were obviously invented, sci-fi, unreal. Living, breathing creatures are a whole different ballgame.

Biologists or computer animators will readily explain that sentient beings are incredibly intricate machines, with a detail nearly impossible to replicate. Did you believe the dinosaurs in *Jurassic Park?* The degree to which you were able to suspend disbelief, to accept them as real, is the degree to which the effects team succeeded. Huge effort was put into the details large and small, from skin texture and dirt to movement. It was a first, but it certainly won't be the last effort we'll see to create a living being. Creating a human being, however, is likely to be a much bigger and more difficult undertaking.

Animators are at work right now creating completely digital actors. Probably not Marilyn Monroe at first, since we have a means of comparison, a reference point. But you can expect to see more anonymous examples in the not distant future. Another technique that we'll probably see again was that used in the Diet Coke commercials, which rotoscoped old stock footage and integrated it with new footage.

Can it be done? We'll all be witness to the attempts. The implications of the digital actor, its potential uses by politicians, corporations, and the media are almost too awesome to imagine. Viewed in the context of an era in which the capability of all digital media is dramatically expanding into new and unconventional arenas, staying informed about what technology can do assumes a new, urgent importance. The fat lady hasn't sung yet, but when she does, she'll almost certainly have been created in a computer.

Noel Blanc
Animation Director, Producer

■■■■■■■■■■■■■■■■■■ ■ ■ ■ ■ ■ ■ ■ ■ ■

Imagine you're in a darkened theatre. You're eight years old. It's Saturday morning. And up on the giant screen to the cheers of your friends in the packed house comes the Warner Brothers logo and the zany theme song introducing the greatest collection of cartoon characters the world has ever known.

"Eh, what's up, doc?"

"Boy, take it from me, Foghorn Leghorn, you're all washed up."

"Ooh, I taut I taw a puddy tat."

"How about we just talk about, about zee love, mes amis?"

"My life story... A Duck Is Born!"

"You'll be seein' stars if ya don't shut that beak a yers..."

"A thee, a thee, a thee... a that's all folks!"

These are just some of the close to 1,000 characters my dad brought to life during his more than 50 year career. By any measure, my father, Mel Blanc, was and still is thought to be the greatest voice artist in film history.

Together with my mom, Estelle, my dad encouraged me to study hard in school, but growing up in the house that Bugs built also meant being exposed to some of the true legends of the entertainment business on a constant basis.

Jack Benny, George Burns, and Al Jolson were just three of the superstars my dad worked with during the golden age of radio. I guess those giants made a great impression on me because after graduation from UCLA and a stint in the army, I came home and formed a production company and creative think tank with my dad. I've been in the animation and film business ever since.

Watching and listening to my dad become each character was as fine an education as any animation director/producer could ever hope to have. He said that in order for a character to be accepted by an audience, that character must be totally believable within the context of the production. And he stressed that achieving believability began with creating the right voice to match the scope and subtle shades of the proposed character. Considering that any animated character usually begins with a two-dimensional drawing, how should one go about creating the right voice for that character? As simple as it may sound, if you're the voice artist, you ask questions. If you are the creator of that character, hopefully you're prepared with answers to those questions. In other words, the collective question and answer session leads to the establishing of the subtext or story of the character. Like method acting in real life, knowing "what's my motivation" when putting a voice to a drawing is of primary importance. Let me use a few of the Warner Brothers characters as examples.

Let's start with the big cheese himself, Bugs Bunny. Bugs was actually the second Warner's character for which my dad was asked to create a voice (Porky Pig being the first). Originally, Bugs was known as Happy Rabbit and had kind of a rounded look, big buck teeth, and a dopey voice. When Warner's decided to change the character drawing of Happy, they asked my dad to create a new voice as well. After suggesting that the producers name the character after the animator who drew him, Bugs Hardaway, my father wanted to know what kind of a person Bugs Bunny would be, how would he react to others and what would be the primary storyline for each Bugs Bunny cartoon? The directors told my father that Bugs would be kind of a tough but lovable stinker who always won out no matter what. So Mel decided a combination of Bronx and Brooklyn accents would suit him perfectly. The signature line, "Eh, what's up doc?" was a popular phrase of the day and my dad suggested it be adopted for Bugs as well.

Creating memorable animation characters depends on combining all the elements of design, story, and voice. Regardless of the format, these principles remain constant. In other words, what you're doing in an ultra-modern, computer-based production lab really isn't any different from what Bob McKinson, Friz Freleng, and my dad were doing in a cavernous building on the Warner Brothers lot, affectionately dubbed "termite terrace," some 50 years before.

Carl Rosendahl
Computer Graphics Teacher

■■■■■■■■■■■■■■■■■■ ■ ■ ■ ■ ■ ■ ■

Having grown up in Los Angeles, I made a few short films in high school that piqued my interest in the entertainment industry. Later at Stanford University, I received my Bachelor of Science degree in Electrical Engineering. When I began working with computer graphics in 1980, it was with the simple dream of creating innovative images for the entertainment industry. At that time, there was no software available, very few computers capable of displaying anything other than simple text, and virtually no market for computer graphics. I assumed that I would spend the next five years learning about the media, writing software, and creating business slides for technology companies. The first year was spent doing exactly that. Then, in 1982 with two partners, we purchased a larger computer and set out to write a computer animation software system that would eventually allow us to sit at the beach with portable computers, while a large mainframe back at the home office slaved away rendering our visions. The dream of kicking back at the beach never became a reality, but the dream of creating imaginative images for entertainment did.

In 14 years, the industry has changed radically. High-quality graphics software is available off-the-shelf and runs not only on large computers, but also on Macintoshes, PCs, and Amigas—machines that didn't even exist in 1980. A dozen companies are creating computer graphics and animation for the high end of the market, with hundreds more following.

It has been fascinating to see the television and film industries adopt digital technology. As a first step, computers had to be able to do things that were already being done with other techniques, but computers had to do it better, faster, and more economically. When clients became comfortable with the technology, they opened up to using it to do new things. Only in the past few years have filmmakers been using computers to do things that could not have been done any other way, and thus they have been able to begin creating imagery that was previously impossible to create. In addition, whole new markets are opening up. Faster processors, better graphics hardware, and CD-ROMs have sparked a whole new generation of interactive products. Games with richer environments and more realistic characters, interactive stories, and electronic books are reaching the market. The majority of these have a base in high quality computer animation. Theme parks as well are using computer animation to create the visuals for spectacular simulator rides.

With all this development and change, I still look at this as an industry in its infancy. Even with the fastest computers available today we still aren't able to do everything we know is possible. Computers will continue to get faster and less expensive, and software will become more sophisticated. Because of this, the tools that animators will have at their fingertips will enable them to create incredible characters, environments, and stories that we can only dream about today.

When on-line computer services are capable of delivering video, and when interactive TV reaches our houses, whole new applications again will begin to emerge. There are enormous possibilities for these interactive services beyond current visions of home shopping, movies on demand, and ordering pizza on your TV. Via these connections into our homes, we will be able to enter computer-generated environments and communicate, explore, learn, and play games with other people in far away places.

Clearly there is a huge demand for computer animation and effects today, and there is a shortage of talented people to do it. Animation companies are growing, new ones are being formed, and movie studios and game companies are creating computer animation divisions. As interactive services come on-line, there will be an even greater demand for designers, animators, directors, and programmers to create the content and the front ends. The opportunities are clearly there for talented people to make their mark in this industry.

Maureen Furniss
Writer, Publisher

■■■■■■■■■■■■■■■■■■■ ■ ■ ■ ■ ■ ■ ■ ■

Until the late 1960s, it was rare to find women working in American animation production other than as inkers or painters. Still, several women played
key roles in animation history. The first person to distribute Disney films was
a woman named Margaret J. Winkler. And throughout the early years, other
studios employed women as artists. Among the best known today are Mary
Blair and Sylvia Holland, both of whom worked for Disney. A small number
of women were even promoted to the rank of animator during this same
period—for example Lillian Friedman at Fleisher, La Verne Harding at Walter
Lantz, and Retta Scott Worcester at Disney.

Internationally, several women are renowned for having pioneered as independent artists. One of the most famous is Lotte Reiniger of Germany, who
began animating in 1910. In 1923, at the age of 24, she began work on her feature-length film, *The Adventures of Prince Achmed,* which utilizes intricately
cut-out figures and took three years to complete. Also well-known is the
American Mary Ellen Bute, who during the Thirties began experimenting
with color, light, music, and abstract imagery to make films based on precise
mathematical formulae.

Other women of note functioned as members of creative partnerships,
although they have also worked individually. American Claire Parker, for
example, collaborated with her Russian-born husband Alexander Alexeieff to
produce beautiful animation made with a unique pinboard technique they
had developed. American husband and wife team John and Faith Hubley
made a number of independent films, many of which dealt with themes
revolving around children and social issues. And Canadian Evelyn Lambart
worked on many productions with filmmaker Norman McLaren at the
National Film Board of Canada.

During the 1970s, there was a period of significant growth in American independent animation, initiated in part by an increasing number of university film
production departments along with the availability of inexpensive film equipment. It was at this time, paralleling a general rise in feminism, that women
artists in animation became more commonplace. Some of those artists who
developed during the Seventies and Eighties are Mary Beams, Sally Cruikshank, Christine Panushka, Suzan Pitt, Joanna Priestley, Kathy Rose, and Mau-
reen Selwood. Many of this new generation of women animators have since
become owners of their own studios, and several teach production courses at
art schools and universities. In these positions they have the opportunity to
encourage other women to excel. In addition, women are now working in all
aspects of production at the major animation studios. Contemporary designers

and animators of note are Elaine Bass, Delores Cannata, Charlotte Peterson, and Sterling Sturtevant.

Throughout the years there have also been several outstanding women who have provided voice-overs for animated characters including Mae Questrel (Betty Boop), June Foray (Rocky), Julie Kavner (Marge in "The Simpsons"), Pat Carroll and Patti Deutsch (numerous films and commercials).

As for myself, I am the editor/publisher of *Animation Journal,* which I founded in 1991 to publish scholarly research dealing with animation history, theory, and criticism. With this journal, I promote awareness of animation in all its forms, including the works of studio and independent artists from America and throughout the world.

Chuck McCann

Actor, Animation Producer

■■■■■■■■■■■■■■■■ ■ ■ ■ ■ ■ ■ ■ ■ ■ ■

I have been creating voices for puppets and cartoons since I was 12 years old. Voices for animation are important in that they help to move the story forward and establish an attitude for the character on the screen. Surely an animated piece can stand on its own, silent, without dialogue or music. But when the marriage is right and the combination is working together in perfect sync, it's a joy. Especially when you add humor as a premise, the spoken word may help influence the animator in choosing the attitude and movement of a design, if the creative involvements are allowed to happen early enough in the project. Usually the storyboard is set in granite by the time the voice talent gets involved, so that the actors must carefully interpret the board and tailor their voices and nuances to fit the already established artwork.

Growing up in New York City, I was fortunate to have a father who was musical arranger at the Roxy Theatre. Every afternoon after school, I was ushered through the stage door and permitted to sit in the auditorium to watch the show. I guess my taste in humor was developing, and in all the right directions too: Laurel and Hardy, Buster Keaton, Charlie Chaplin, right along with Bugs Bunny, Daffy Duck, and Porky Pig. Those Warner Brothers cartoons stood out for me particularly due to the artistry of Mel Blanc. His vocal antics tickled your funny bone. To me, they were gut-wrenchingly funny, and only amplified what was happening up on screen. Combined with the writing and direction of a genius like Friz Freleng or Chuck Jones, you had cartoon heaven. Little did I realize at the age of seven, listening to Mel Blanc there in the darkened theatre, that 30 years later I would be standing alongside him at a microphone in Hollywood working with him. I guess everybody who ever wanted to do voices in animation has borrowed freely from this man. He truly has been an inspiration to every new successful vocal actor. Other great vocal influences in my career were Daws Butler, Stan Freberg, Hans Conried, Bill Scott, Paul Frees, and Don Messeck, just to name a few. Looking back, I suppose I was fortunate to have grown up before television when, through radio, you created the images in your imagination. Radio was rightly called "the theatre of the mind." It sharpened your senses and allowed you to create visions surpassing anything on screen because it dealt directly with your own individual emotions.

I always felt that animation not only meant drawn images that moved, filmed from cels, but also meant the movement of any inanimate object, i.e., clay (claymation), rubber sculpture with armatures inside, all forms of puppetry, whatever was used to create the illusion of life, whether live, on stage, or recorded on film. Perhaps the earliest form of cartoon was played against the back-lit silk screen of the Chinese, with rod puppets, thousands of years ago. They told entire stories in silhouette. Because I'm such a ham and like to play all the roles, puppetry has always appealed to me. Not unlike radio, it allows you to play multiple roles. Paul Ashley, the famous puppet maker, was a good friend of my father's, and I began to work with him in my early teens. Because

I was able to do impressions of many stars from film and television, we built a specialty act around this premise. Eventually, this led to my creating original characters that we used on my own television show that lasted for 14 years. It was on for four hours, from nine o'clock in the morning to one o'clock in the afternoon. Necessity being the mother of invention, I developed new techniques in shooting the puppets, by matting them against miniature sets and chromakeying them through a cut-out. When tape was in its infancy, I also devised a way to record tape backwards by inverting the heads of the Ampex 1000, switching the control track head with the cue track head. This allowed me to create fabulous backgrounds to mat the puppets against.

In the early days of movies, the cartoon replaced the short one-reel comedies simply because the drawn image could do things its human counterpart could not. Cinema is the amalgamation of all the arts, and it is important to understand the significance of this. It is becoming even more so with the development of new technology. Digitally recorded images can be projected with thousands of lines of resolution that far surpass the clarity of chemical crystals on celluloid. Today I am using sophisticated electronic computerized backgrounds and creating fantastic images with three-dimensional puppets. Artists graph the puppet models and feed them into the computer, arriving at lifelike, mind-boggling visual images. The progression of effects can go as far as the imagination can travel. There is nothing one cannot create on the screen today if it is in one's imagination. In some computer laboratory right at this moment, what is on the "drawing board" would boggle the mind of the ordinary man, but would fire the imagination of a true storyteller. Now with developing techniques of virtual reality, whereby we can see in true dimension, and can "virtually" hold and rotate an object while sensing its form, texture, and weight, storytellers have at their disposal tools that will take us to unheard of, vastly exciting horizons—providing we remember William's Shakespeare's words, *"the play's the thing."*

Linda Simensky
Animation Executive, Teacher

I began my career in the Nickelodeon animation department, as an intern in 1984. And one of my first tasks was working on the layback of the dubbing of the Japanese cartoon "Belle and Sebastian," about a boy and his dog in the French-Spanish Pyrennes, which we had dubbed in Canada. We laughed about how international it had become by the time we ran it in the States. At this point, most of our animation programming was acquired from other countries, which was unusual for American television. Although many of us had grown up watching Japanese cartoons such as "Speed Racer," Americans generally assumed that any good television show was probably produced in Hollywood.

While finishing my graduate studies at New York University, I moved from the Programming Department at Nickelodeon to the newly-created Animation Department, where my position included developing and assisting in the production of animated pilot episodes and series. And I found that working on American cartoons required full knowledge of the international animation scene.

There are many levels of international involvement for each program that we produce, starting with the script and storyboard. We go into each production with the knowledge that our International Program Sales Department will probably sell the show internationally, and that the show will be dubbed into many languages. When we work on a specific episode, we keep this in mind, watching for details such as making sure there are no written words or signage in the backgrounds crucial to the plot, and that there is no slang in the dialogue since it can be almost impossible to translate.

We also have a Program Enterprises Department, which focuses on international coproductions and involvement. Because animation is so costly, it often is beneficial to find an international coproduction entity willing to finance a portion of the program. Most recently we worked with Ellipse, the production arm of Canal + (the French television channel and program producer) to coproduce the animated series "Doug."

Television animation production generally involves an additional international layer. Most animation produced for television in the United States is animated, inked, painted, and filmed in Asia. There are a number of studios in Korea, as well as in Taiwan, Hong Kong, China, Thailand, and the Philippines, that are set up to do this work quickly and for less cost than we could do it in the United States or Europe. For the production of four different programs, Nickelodeon and its associated production companies use four different Korean studios: Sunwoo, Han Ho, Anivision, and Rough Draft.

In dealing with the various Korean studios, we have had to learn to communicate clearly and directly about animation with foreign artists who may not understand our show's culture-based sense of humor, or certain elements of our plot, or even our basic content, such as a story revolving around the game of football. One of our program's production bibles reminds art directors and storyboard artists to keep in mind that their storyboard and direction notes should be written in clear, succinct English because they will be translated into Korean. Generally, this lends an additional challenge to the production. However, the overseas directors do work very closely with the Korean animators to make sure they understand both our stories and directions. Ironically, this gulf often tells us when the slapstick and movement are really working. If the Korean animators laugh from looking at the action without even reading the stories or dialogue, then we know the gag is okay. In fact, one reason animation has been successful internationally is that it can transcend so many boundaries, even the cultural and linguistic ones. So much of animation is based on action, movement, and physical humor that it can work in many different cultures. And it helps that it can be easily dubbed when needed.

In terms of animation production centers, the international hot spots change periodically, often influencing styles and attitudes worldwide as well as changing the character of animation festivals. For the past few years, the United Kingdom has been a key trendsetter, with companies such as Aardman sweeping the awards at festivals, and Channel 4 in London producing consistently innovative shorts for television. The art schools in the United Kingdom have been instrumental in contributing to this groundswell of creativity.

In the course of my career as Supervising Producer of Animation, I have found it crucial to keep up with international animation and have included a stop at a local studio whenever I am on vacation abroad. Some of my more interesting excursions have involved visits to animation studios in Shanghai and Dublin. And as a professor at the School of Visual Arts, and lecturer at New York University, I also feel it both important and stimulating to help introduce my students to new trends from abroad.

Animation has always been part of the global village. Progressive video channels have played a key role in bringing more international animation to television screens in the United States than ever before. No doubt there will be even more involvement internationally as more cable channels are created. If you are about to start a career in animation, it seems inevitable that no matter which area you specialize in, at some point your focus will be international.

Philip Denslow
Teacher, Animation Technician

■■■■■■■■■■■■■■■■■■ ■ ■ ■ ■ ■ ■ ■ ■ ■ ■

I lost interest in everything else the first time I was exposed to the possibilities of creating animation. I had been studying commercial art and photography at the Art Center College of Design in Los Angeles. Animation was merely an elective subject taught in an obscure upstairs room. This semi-secretive aura appealed to me, as well as the noncommercial instructional approach. These days, some 20 years later, animation and its methods of creation have become such an everyday popular commodity that I wonder if I would now find it so appealing. I'd hoped that I would find out about animation's more esoteric and interesting aspects.

I have been working as the Animation Technician at the UCLA Animation Workshop for over a decade. This is a unique job, where I get paid to learn about animation and to share that knowledge with students. The salary is modest, but it is steady. Getting the job was a case of being at the right place at the right time: I had learned a lot about animation technology by making short films and building a computer-controlled camera stand, and happened to be visiting the campus when the job unexpectedly opened. Although this was obviously not the result of diligent career planning, I would like to discuss some pertinent ideas.

First, I feel that the most important thing one can do to learn animation is to make films. By making a complete film you learn about the entire process, not just a particular task within it, and you have a chance to show others how you think. The films can be experimental or traditional, cartoon or computer, funny or puzzling. Demonstrating your ability to make things move in an interesting way, perhaps to tell a story or set a mood, will let potential employers or project funders know what you are capable of, and you can complete the job. Attending an animation program at a university or college can expedite the process, but it is not the only way. I had made several short animated films as a student and as a professional. Schools can provide equipment, instruction, and motivation. Today it is possible to invest in a personal computer that can supply much of what is needed to make a film. And that leads to my second point.

It is continually more important for potential filmmakers to learn about computers. This is not just for those who seek work in what we now think of as computer animation, the movement of objects within a three-dimensional space. More and more areas of animation and film/television production are becoming computer-based. What was an industry of specialists, working with specific equipment and functioning in an assembly line manner, is now becoming a mixture of generalists who can accomplish several stages of production at one computer workstation. The ways computers input, manipulate, and output data and images are constantly changing with improvements in technology. And a significant part of my job is keeping current with the evolution of animation technology.

Multimedia, an overused term that few can define, is a new and growing area that incorporates many production tasks into one job. A multimedia project may include live-action recording and editing, traditional and computer animation creation, audio recording and editing, story development, historical research, interactive game design, and much more. The person who knows how to put all this together, how to create and manipulate bits of image and sound, and how to take a project from storyboard to completion is the *animation filmmaker.* So whatever multimedia is, people are buying it, companies are investing in it, and you may be working in it before long.

If you are pursuing a career in computer animation, I recommend learning about character animation, and if possible, making a film using traditional means. The techniques of realistic and caricatured motion are common to all forms of animation. Most computer animators are constantly struggling to infuse more cartoon-type motion into their mechanical simulations. It can be easier and more fun learning to make a squishy bouncy character walk using pencil and paper than fighting the limitations of computer software. Even if you gravitate toward the computer because of uncertain drawing skills, manipulating cut-out pieces of paper or small objects like paper clips can give quick and entertaining results.

I wish now that I had taken acting lessons or theatre classes. No matter what kind of animation you end up doing, a knowledge of how to communicate ideas with body motion and voice emotion can be very useful. These kinds of classes can also explore the importance of dramatic lighting and set design, and how to present a concept with an economy of visual information.

Whatever you do, don't get caught in the trap of thinking "If only I had a _____ (insert camera, computer, or other expensive technical device here), then I could really be creative and make lots of exciting films." I spent years building a complex piece of equipment for just that purpose. And although I did benefit from the learning involved, the equipment could not help me with primary ideas. My last film, *Madcap,* used as little technology as possible (drawn directly on 16mm film) and was by far, by eons, my most successful. *Serves me right!*

William Moritz
Animation Teacher, Writer

■■■■■■■■■■■■■■■■■ ■ ■ ■ ■ ■ ■ ■ ■ ■ ■ ■

Since much animation involves filming graphic artwork, styles of painting and drawing naturally influence animation films, either by involving a painter in filming his own brushstrokes in order to give them life in time, or by adopting the look of various paintings for the graphic style of a cartoon, or by making painting itself the subject of an animated film.

The painter Walter Ruttmann extended his abstract canvases into the realm of time through animation in 1919. His first film, *Light-play Opus I,* premiered in theatres April 1921. Ruttmann had painted on glass, shooting a single frame of film after each brushstroke—or changing the image by wiping something away. Since he had to use black and white film, Ruttman hand-tinted the prints to restore the color values of his painting. Oskar Fischinger, who was present at the premiere of Ruttmann's *Opus I,* devoted his whole career to abstract animation. Fischinger's color films from the 1930s are often referred to as "living Kandinskys." His last film, *Motion Painting,* which records in 10 minutes the many layers of thought and experimentation that went into the making of one particular oil painting, won the Grand Prize at the Brussels Experimental Film Festival in 1949.

A parallel tradition in abstract filmmaking involves painting directly onto the film's surface. Len Lye and Norman McLaren began doing this in the mid-1930s in England. Harry Smith in the 1940s, Hy Hirsh in the 1950s, and Stan Brakhage in the 1980s have continued exploring direct painting on film with great success.

In a representational mode, the great Polish animator Witold Giersz began animating oil painting on glass in 1960, creating a range of impressive films from the vivid *Forest Fire,* to the hilarious *The Red and the Black.* Caroline Leaf used painting on glass as the medium for her film *The Street,* which shows a child's perception of his grandmother's death in sophisticated images that simultaneously seem childlike as well as artfully stylized in the mode of Marc Chagall or Picasso.

The conscious use of modern art dates back at least to the early 1930s. Berthold Bartosch adopted the expressionistic woodcut look of Belgian artist Frans Masereel for his 1932 film *The Idea,* which, in its exploration of poverty, strikes, and political protest, was the first animation film dealing with a tragic theme. His friends Claire Parker and Alexandre Alexeieff invented a pin-screen to create the finely-shaded images for *Night on Bald Mountain* in 1933, which suggests the pointillism of Seurat as well as Picasso's supple rendering of the human form. British painter Anthony Gross brought the elegant, loose-lined abstraction of Matisse and Bloomsbury artists Duncan Grant and Vanessa Bell to his witty films *Joie de Vivre* (1934), *Fox Hunt* (1936), and *Around the World in 80 Days* (1939).

The UPA studios in the 1940s and 1950s consciously attempted to integrate the standards of modern art into the design and color of their cartoons, giving each film an individual character, including choosing movement suitable to a particular graphic style. This commitment to modern art culminated in a series of TV cartoons aimed at teaching young people about the works of selected well-known artists.

Painting has also been the subject of several celebrated animated films of the last decade. Frederic Back's *Crac!* traces the changing history of French Canada over the last century using a rocking chair as the protagonist and surrounding it by animated reproductions of famous Canadian paintings. Estonian animator Priit Pärn's *Déjeuner sur l'herbe* in 1987 chronicles the extremes through which four poverty-stricken people must go in a totalitarian bureaucracy to have a picnic in the park, culminating in their momentary transformation into the famous Manet painting. Dan McLaughlin's *God is Dog Spelled Backwards* flashes countless great paintings in three minutes by shooting single frames of reproductions as depicted in Janson's *History of Art.* And Joan Gratz's stunning *Mona Lisa Descending a Staircase* reproduces numerous famous paintings transforming one into another with single frames shot as she made modifications in colored clay—breathtaking proof of the degree to which so many masterpieces of art live in our minds.

Having received my doctorate degree from the University of Southern California, I made numerous live-action and animation films that have been screened in Paris, Amsterdam, Stockholm and Tokyo. I currently teach animation history and writing at Cal Arts. Also, I am on the editorial board and a frequent contributor to *Animation Journal.*

Vijay Patel
Program Developer, Teacher

Almost every minute we are blown away by spectacular computer-generated effects, seen hundreds of times on television and at the cinema, whether in MTV flying logos, Coke commercials, the Pillsbury doughboy, NFL and NBA events, the unreal morphing effects in *Terminator 2,* or the realistic recreation of enormous dinosaurs.

In the last couple of years, computer and video imaging has firmly entrenched itself in a variety of fields, including architecture, textiles, industrial design, scientific visualization, corporate education, bio-medical research, fine arts, and litigation arts. This growing demand for individuals fluent in this emerging technology led to the development of the program at Cogswell Poly-technical College where I am presently the director and chair. Several years of experience in computer graphics led me to design and conceptualize the Computer and Video Imaging Bachelor of Arts degree program at Cogswell.

Having grown up in India, I obtained an undergraduate degree in business administration and my master's degree in advertising from Xavier's College in Bombay before becoming an executive producer at a small advertising agency. Life passed slowly through hours in the darkroom working with editors while gulping sandwiches and tea. In order to superimpose a text slide on video, it was common practice to use handmade supers. We would glue the text on a black paper and point the camera to key the text on the subject, which would take approximately 45 minutes to align and impose on video.

In 1985, while in England, I was intrigued by a computer display in a small shop on Oxford Street. I bought my first eight color Sinclair Spectrum ZX, a British computer, and thus had my first character generator. The following year, on another trip to England, I purchased my first Amiga 1000 computer from Commodore. From eight colors, I moved on to 32 colors. It became an addiction. From an eight bit display, I progressed to 16.7 million colors with Vista boards from Truevision. I then moved to America for further studies in computer graphics. Unfortunately, I couldn't find any schools that offered a degree program in that area. By studying at a vocational guidance school, self-training, and networking, I eventually created and designed an imaging program.

Today, I am a partner in Digital Canvas India, a complete computer graphics facility serving the corporate and broadcasting industry in Bombay. I am also involved with software development, and affiliated with Digital Designs, an integrated media company serving corporate businesses in San Jose. Our clients include: Intel, Mitsubishi, Epic Design, Software Turnkey Systems, Metcal, Intersource Technologies, Siemens, Autodesk, Sierra Semiconductor, and Laserscope. Among other projects, we produced animation sequences for the movie *Mojo St. Charles,* which was presented at the San Francisco Film Festival.

Obviously there is enormous demand for the kind of program offered at Cogswell and for professional careers in computer graphics. The number of applications we receive each year are actually beyond imagination.

Jan Lenica

Artist, Teacher, Animation Director

■■■■■■■■■■■■■■■■■■■■■ ■ ■ ■ ■ ■ ■

I have always liked moving on the outskirts of art, on the perimeter of various spheres, penetrating regions situated far from the main routes. I used to find it amusing to rebel against or entirely ignore the rules—to blend together elements from opposing and unconnected fields—in other words to blur the boundaries. I also find myself attracted to many of the commonplace forms held in disregard by those who work in more "refined areas."

These remarks may seem surprising today, with the general integration of visual arts in such fields as graphic art, photography, etcetera. But I remember the time when painters and critics despised graphic art and when there was something contemptuous about the title "graphic artist." Where are those days? In the Fifties I was accused of using nongraphic techniques in my artwork that apparently disagreed with the printing technique. I was scorned for introducing subjects into my posters that originated from painting, such as portraits. Today, there are few techniques that have not been influenced by poster art, thus eliminating once and for all the isolation of graphic design. Posters have returned to their source; once again, they integrate multiple pictures on a set subject.

The situation in films is somewhat different. I must admit that I have chosen a rather difficult position for myself. Rebellion against accepted rules often results in painful consequences. The ruling principles of supply and demand are ruthless in that they repudiate everything that does not find its commercial place in the market. In the past, I thought that the animated film could become an instrument of fantastic possibilities when dealt with by an artist. Film appeared to me as the most contemporary raw material, an unparalleled means of expression and a fruitful area of activity. I was not fully aware then of the enormous difficulties experienced by those who do not want to bow to the commercial system of filmmaking.

Cinema as an object and manifestation of art in time and movement has not yet found its sponsor or collector. But I see a chance for film, with the development of new techniques of reproduction in video cassettes and laser disks now appearing on the market. This may result in the distribution of all sorts of films that up to now has been the privilege of works of literature and music.

Having been born and brought up in Poland, I studied music and architecture in Warsaw during the late Thirties. Since 1950, I have been an artist, poster designer, and animation filmmaker, and am now teaching in Germany.

Fred Wolf
Animation Director, Producer

A career in drawing can start very early in life. In my case it was at the age of seven when I won second prize for the best drawing of an Easter Bunny. The contest was held by the local movie theater in Brooklyn, New York. As fate would have it, Disney's *Pinocchio* was featured that same week, and it was to have an everlasting impression on me and the career choices I eventually made.

Approximately 10 years later, a summertime job opportunity came to me through a neighbor who was a background artist at Paramount's New York-based animation facility, Famous Studios. The job consisted of painting and polishing cels. At first it was hard to connect my destiny to this workplace. After all, cel polishing on Popeye theatrical shorts was okay, but it didn't exactly shout "cartoon career."

Upon graduating from high school, I took another lunge at the Popeye cel painting job until the Truman Administration personally reminded me about the war in Korea. Two years later, out of the Army after a tour of duty and still in one piece, I returned to Famous Studios to get serious about Popeye—this time as an in-betweener. From this point on I was convinced one could actually make a living in the animation industry. The biggest factor in this conviction was the explosion of television. Television in the early Fifties was brand new and had an insatiable appetite for films and commercials, especially animation. It was a time when anyone with a little animation experience was in demand. I fulfilled the requirements and got a job as an assistant animator with Shamus Culhane and later on as a full animator with H.F.J. Productions, working on numerous animated spots in the early Sixties.

My subsequent move to California gave me opportunities in television programming as an animator on such series as "Alvin and the Chipmunks" and "The Flintstones." Three years later, Jimmy Murakami, a very talented filmmaker, and I opened an animation studio called Murakami Wolf Films. Our newly-formed company was fortunate in gaining immediate attention, and we were flooded with bids and contracts from major advertising agencies to produce animated television commercials. Some of the most memorable for me were Frosted Flakes' Tony the Tiger and Green Giant's Little Green Sprout.

Simultaneously, both Murakami and I produced our own highly-personalized theatrical animated short subjects, although the market for such films was minimal. But the important thing for me about those shorts was making the tremendous leap into a totally creative endeavor. One had to capture all the arts in one project. To my mind, the best way to explore animation in all its complexities is to produce your own short film, from story idea, design and animation, to sound effects and music. For the aspiring animator, such a short production will enhance any portfolio of still art that you will be using in job-hunting.

Throughout, my background training in animation consisted largely of on-the-job experience. While I was still a cel painter I attended in-betweening classes at Famous Studios, which were excellent. In the late Fifties, with the exception of these in-house classes, there were few schools offering instruction in animation techniques. I found that assisting the best animators provided me with the most significant education. And with films of the animated classics on videotape today, the ambitious student can study the great animators' best scenes over and over again to approximate something of that apprenticeship experience.

A career in animation is a difficult one to plan because animation art calls upon so many specialized skills: drawing, writing, animating, directing, painting, designing, acting, and dancing. So if formal courses are available to you, by all means take them. And whatever school you choose, try to keep your studies as diversified as possible. While starting out, I attended Brooklyn Community College, where I took classes in advertising design, life drawing, illustration, and composition art. They were tremendous aids to me, as were courses in music, literature, and mathematics. But my career really took off once my first animated short, *The Box,* was completed. It won an Academy Award. Drawing, drawing, and more drawing along with thumbnail storyboard ideas should become the aspiring professional's pastime as that first personal film comes to life...like *Pinocchio.*

Gene Deitch

Animation Director, Producer

To date, I claim over 45 years in the field of animation—being involved at one time or another with every form and style from UPA shorts and television films, Bert and Harry Piel beer commercials, "Tom Terrific" shows (the first animated serial on network television), Terrytoons, Tom and Jerry revivals, Popeye, and a string of children's picture book adaptations of which I am most proud. I have always worked just beyond the edge of the spotlight. My films have not burst upon the wider public scene, but they have won many awards at specialized film festivals. Five of them have been nominated for Oscars, and one, *Munro*, actually won. Along the way, I have thought a lot about what it is we filmmakers are doing, and perhaps even why.

The word animation is derived from the Latin *anima*, "the breath of life." That is what animators are trying to create. In this regard, what is most difficult to achieve is the effect of reality and truth, although to speak of realism in a film is impossible in the literal sense. The realism we strive for is rather the realism of meaning. Cinema is a technical trick, an illusion. Whether in animation or live-action, realism and truth cannot be achieved merely by using realistically drawn animation figures or realistically costumed actors, but by presenting a story in which the characters are true to their situations. In writing for film, sometimes a character may take you on a difficult journey, but if it rings true, you're on the right path.

Even violence at times may be a valid element in storytelling if it occurs in a way that is consistent with the character's motivations and goals, and that includes animation created for children. As an animator, I have no faith in the call to purge all violence from children's fare. Violence is a part of life. Confronting this fact on a child's level of comprehension is far less dangerous than bland evasion of reality. They will surely face these things in their own lives. We should make clear the difference between fantasy and reality—in reality, violence is usually self-defeating. Film violence—a fantasy, can be an important vent for life's very real fears and pressures. The highly symbolic violence in the great traditional folk tales rings a deep and positive response in children. We cheat children if we take the menace and conflict out of stories we tell them.

As for technical considerations, animation requires special patience, preparation, and imagination. There is such a long time between conception and birth of an animated film, or even to reach the stage of viewing uncut scenes on screen, that it requires an intense effort to keep the film's planned tempo in one's head. In animation filmmaking, there is no action taking place until projection. We draw still phases of action—imagined action. Because film is an art that must be constructed in the dimension of time, I find that completing the soundtrack before animation begins allows me to envision the production in that time dimension. This requires imagining every detail of the action and timing it before it exists. I do not know a better discipline for developing that vital timing sense any good director must have.

But filmmaking is inevitably a process of compromise. Woody Allen once stated, "If my original idea represents 100 percent, and I end up with 60 percent, I consider that a roaring success." There is never enough time, enough money, the right conditions, etc., to ever achieve all we dream of in our very first conception of a film. This is why it makes no sense to start on a project unless we are convinced we have a truly great story, so that even after the compromises and failures of detail, enough will still be left to have made it worth the effort. Even though we may never achieve more than 60 percent of our goal, there is tremendous satisfaction in finally seeing the result.

Now how old is the idea of cinema? I figure about 35,000 years. The root idea for a dramatic sound and light presentation in a darkened room goes all the way back to our beginnings, and actually fulfills humankind's earliest artistic and storytelling cravings. My friend Alexander Marshak, an expert on cave paintings, in his research reminds us of the weird feeling we have when inside a cave. If you've ever been deep inside a cave without a lamp, you will know what darkness is. It is a total blackness and silence we can experience in no other way, especially added with the deathly feeling of being under tons of rock. Mr. Marshak points out that those beautiful paintings are often at least a kilometer deep inside the caves. Why? Obviously this would have been most difficult. It certainly proves that they were able to produce light. Hollowed stones have been found inside the caves that were probably oil lamps. They also had to be able to bring in drawing and painting utensils and to mix colors on the spot. Flattened areas of stone have been found with enough residue to indicate they were used as palettes, and it can be assumed that they did not drag all those animals in there to use as models. Yet these paintings are marvelous creations by any standard, and must have been made by trained artists. From this we have to assume that these so-called cave men had a more advanced social organization than we might have thought, and that societies 35,000 years ago could support artists!

All these deductions by Mr. Marshak got me to thinking that these people had a culture and lore they wished to preserve and pass on. And it struck me: What better way to inculcate their youth with the legends and lore of the community than to lead them into the icy, vast darkness of these caves, and in these deep forbidding galleries, with flickering oil lamps illuminating wondrous images, tell their tales in an atmosphere of terrifying attention? Such a childhood experience could never be forgotten. Could this not have been the first audio-visual presentation? Was it not the primeval beginning of our great art of cinema?

John Callahan
Writer, Cartoonist

■■■■■■■■■■■■■■■■ ■ ■ ■ ■ ■ ■ ■ ■ ■

I grew up in a peaceful Oregon town and underwent a strict Catholic education. From early on, I liked drawing and took delight in ridiculing the nuns with my caricatures. But when I started drinking in my teens, my interest in cartooning waned. Then, one July night in 1972, shortly after my 21st birthday, I was out on a spree with a pal and we hit an exit sign at 90 miles an hour. My spinal cord was severed and I have been paralyzed from the neck down ever since. I find the hardest thing about being a quadriplegic is the dependency one has on other people.

After leaving the hospital, I lived in nursing homes and then moved into an apartment. It was tough, but eventually, I felt like trying to draw again. Since I had some movement in my fingers, I started doing cartoons with my right hand, my left hand guiding. From the beginning, I have dealt with all sorts of touchy subjects—religion, anorexia, alcoholism, paralysis, blindness—you name it. The only criteria for me has been that my cartoons be funny. It took awhile, but eventually some newspapers and magazines began to run my work and I've since had six collections published. I still get flack about my choice of material but I believe there is a double standard for humor in America and I try to skewer that. Pity and patronizing attitudes are detestable to me and to others I know in my situation. I find humor in all aspects of life. People who are suffering from a disease so often create their own private jokes as a way of coping with pain. Why not share the joke in print? The question of what is off-limits should not be defined by some over-protective special interest group. The audience itself should decide.

I've started adapting some of my cartoons into animated short films—my first being a twisted version of the "doggie in the window" query. Most recently I wrote, co-directed, and narrated a black and white short titled *I Think I Was An Alcoholic*, which was shown as part of the 24th International Tournee of Animation. It's a pretty honest film about me and my problems and probably came out of a desire to be self-incriminating. My work in general is very unconscious and dark. One of my favorite cartoons showed Jesus on the cross thinking "T.G.I.F.!" The newspapers that printed it received quite a lot of mail.

Most recently, Robin Williams optioned the film rights to my autobiography, *Don't Worry, He Won't Get Far On Foot*. Visiting Robin in San Francisco, I found him to be this incredibly normal, nice guy. I just hope he can sit still long enough to play a quad. Meanwhile, I still draw several cartoons a week and am planning another animated project, while remaining patently uninterested in traditional views of how I should live the rest of my life. The idea promoted in rehab of the socially well-adjusted, happily-married quad does not appeal to me. But I might get married one day. It would be fun to hear the whir of little wheels around the house.

Fred Patten
Writer, Reviewer
■■■■■■■■■■■■■■■■■■ ■ ■ ■ ■ ■ ■ ■ ■

Having been a professional writer and reviewer of both American and foreign animation since the 1960s, I was the co-founder of the first American fan club for Japanese animation in 1977, and now work with Streamline Pictures, a company that acquires Japanese animation and dubs it into English for American theatrical and video distribution.

Japanese animation has recently emerged as a new cult category in American popular entertainment. It is especially popular with audiences who enjoy the action-adventure science fiction movies and super-hero comic books.

This unique art form was introduced into America in the late 1970s, when the Japanese community TV channels in several major cities began showing giant-robot super-hero cartoons with English subtitles. The first commercial VCRs also appeared at that time, allowing high-school and college fans to record them. During the next decade, the popularity of Japanese animation spread quickly.

The Japanese produce as much juvenile cartoon programming as the Americans do. But there is also a tremendous amount of adolescent and adult animation, including pornography. What has become known in America as "Japanese animation" is the science fiction and adventure extravaganzas, which would cost a fortune in special effects to produce in live-action.

After World War II, Japan was flooded with American movies, TV, and comic books. The first Japanese postwar animated films were feature-length dramatizations of the best-known Oriental folk tales adapted for children with lots of humor and cute animals. On the other hand, the TV animation emulated the American super-hero melodramas. And many of those Japanese cartoons were brought to America, such as "Astro Boy," and "Kimba, the White Lion." Then, American and Japanese television animation began to diverge when American TV animation came under greater restrictions against violence in childrens' programming, which was perceived as encompassing all animation, while the Japanese public demanded animated storytelling that was suitable for adults, in addition to childrens' cartoons.

The most simplistic dramatic animation depicts a story that could be told just as well in live-action as in cartoon form. A common cinematic gimmick in these films is an animated lens-flare in brightly-lit outdoor action scenes. More imaginative direction takes advantage of the potentials of animation, even when the stories are mundane. The feature, *Golgo 13*, is a hard-boiled crime drama with no fantasy element other than the protagonist's super macho ability to survive innumerable death traps. But a nighttime automobile chase through downtown San Francisco is a surrealistic light-show of the reflections from neon signs wrapping themselves exaggeratedly around the speeding cars. *Fist of the North Star* is a martial arts drama in which the fighters often move in extreme slow motion, with colored streaks flashing from their fingertips, color-coded to indicate the moves of the different warriors, while the backgrounds fade into obscurity so that the focus is entirely on the battling antagonists.

The directorial reverse of this is the use of animation to present seemingly straightforward action in futuristic or fantastic settings which would be impossible to film in live-action without elaborate special effects. There are numerous inexpensive animated science fiction adventures that resemble cheap sci-fi movies. But the "Mobile Suit Gundam" TV and theatrical series remains popular because of the attention to detail and the realism of the space battle scenes and space-station environments, which reinforce the sophistication of the complex interplanetary geopolitical melodrama.

This Japanese animation is beginning to have an influence in American animation. Peter Chung, creator of the "Aeon Flux" cartoons on MTV's "Liquid Television," has been a fan of Japanese cartoons since his student animation days. Many of the top Japanese cartoon directors, such as Hayao Miyazaki, Rin Taro, Katsuhiro Otomo, and Yoshiaki Kawajiri, are studied by the new animators in the cartoon industry. The Japanese influence has been acknowledged as one of the components of the "dark deco" look of the direction in "Batman: The Animated Series."

More and more Americans are importing Japanese cartoon videos and laser discs to study the animation techniques, even when they cannot understand the language. It seems as though America is edging closer to the popular realization of what the Japanese have long known, that "animation is not just for kids." And when that finally happens, a vast new market for animated action-adventure storytelling will open up.

Jon W. Sharer

Computer Animator, Teacher

■■■■■■■■■■■■■■■ ■ ■ ■ ■ ■ ■ ■ ■ ■ ■

For me, computer animation is a challenging and fulfilling lifestyle. However as a young artist in Chicago, the word "computer" was not part of my vocabulary and animation meant traditional cel animation. It was not until graduate study in the early Seventies that I learned the meaning of input by keypunching hundreds of data cards for a dissertation. With the availability of graphics hardware and software in the Eighties, I immersed myself in the technology as a tool for art and design, and began teaching courses in computer imaging and motion in the mid-1980s. In 1990, I developed a small video animation production facility for the purpose of creating fine arts and commercial animations while continuing university teaching.

The commercial, fine arts, and educational dimensions of computer animation complement each other. For example, technical innovations developed in a commercial project may be subsequently used in fine arts projects. Conversely, expressive effects used in fine arts projects may then be used in commercial applications. Yet while commercial projects are sequential in process, fine arts projects are more like jazz improvisations in which experimentation with passages of motion and light gives rise to animation sequences on a theme or concept. Each working process contributes to the other in generating innovative imagery, and each provides insights which are shared by students.

The focus of my work is 3-D video animation, which incorporates paint system imagery, 2-D animation, image processing, and morphing, using mirco and mini computers. Three-dimensional animation has historically focused on the simulation of objects in space with a geometric look and feel. In contrast, my work emphasizes expressive qualities. In fine arts applications, these qualities are incorporated into animations, which are windows to social issues. For example, presently I am working on a social commentary project regarding poverty and politics. In this project, hours of video shot on location in Chicago are integrated into the 3-D models and motion, using mapping, morphing, and image processing. The emphasis in this project is to visualize the hidden landscape of poverty and to contrast the feelings of people and the political rhetoric about poverty. The use of humanistically-oriented imagery and themes is atypical in the world of 3-D animation.

On the commercial side, the challenge for me is to be inventive using the cultural iconology of the times in design applications. The ability to communicate through motion sequences of these icons stems from the associations elicited in the viewer. In both fine arts and commercial applications, it is important for young animators to study how artists and designers have used relationships among image associations and qualities to convey that which the individual images cannot, and to study how people respond to these images. The power of the design stems from these form-content relationships.

The ability to create effects for 3-D animation requires a knowledge of both the technical and aesthetic dimensions of animation. To produce a new look requires a technical comprehension of software and hardware, and the ability to use an effect well requires a knowledge of art and design. My advice to young animators is not to become only the artist or only the technician, but to embrace both. You can realize more of your creative potential by having each interact with the other.

Lisa Baytos
Animation Student

■■■■■■■■■■■■■■■■■■ ■ ■ ■ ■ ■ ■ ■ ■ ■

I suppose that some people are lucky enough to know from a young age what their intended career will be. Perhaps it hits them like a flash, and filled with a strong sense of purpose, they go about their lives in pursuit of their ultimate career goal. I am not one of those people.

The path that led me to select animation as my career choice is long and twisted, filled with wrong turns and dangerous roads. But the one aspect of this confused journey has remained clear from the beginning. It all started with horses.

When I was a kid, I was animal crazy. This mania manifested itself in many forms. My family had to put up with a menagerie that started, quite innocently, with a parakeet. As I became older, my ambitions could be gauged by the ever-increasing size of my pets—from lizard to rat, cat to dog. Finally, I had my first horseback riding lesson. The stable was teetering on the brink of bankruptcy, and the mount I rode was a fly-riddled nag. But none of that mattered. I was hooked.

Horse fever had descended, and I succumbed to it willingly. Of course, following the pattern set earlier in my life, my next step was clear—to ask my father for a horse. The asking turned into pleading, the pleading into begging. But to no avail. The answer remained "No."

Daunted by my father's stubborn refusal to assist me in my dream of horse ownership, I channeled my equestrian-centered energies into another pursuit: I began drawing horses. My first efforts were humorous at best— the drawings looking more like blobs on sticks than the majestic beings I was so painfully trying to represent. The standard "how to draw horses" books proved to be frustrating. The progression of diagrams proceeded as follows: Step one; draw a circle. Step two; attach some lines to the circle. Step three; the circle with lines is magically transformed into a fully real-ized, magnificent drawing of a horse's head. Although I could never figure out what happened between steps two and three, I persistently continued my efforts.

My next big step was when I took my first art class in high school. It took only a few days to realize that drawing horses was not going to win me a spot in the Louvre. But through four years of plain hard work, I began to learn about the finer aspects of drawing.

Around this time, a friend and I began to experiment with a Super-8 camera. We created little stop-motion dramas, and I had my first taste of animation when I drew a 16 frame cycle of a speeding greyhound. By the age of 18, the seeds of an interest in animation were already present. I enjoyed drawing immensely, and filmmaking intrigued me as well.

Still unclear about which direction I wanted to take, I majored in film at Northwestern University, then went on to pursue a master's degree in film production at USC. It was there that I took my first animation class, and the long winding search for a career choice came to an end. Slaving over a drawing desk, I discovered that certain aspects of the craft fit my personality perfectly. I found that I actually preferred the precision of drawing motion frame-by-frame to the uncertainty of working in live-action. And I couldn't cease to be thrilled by the sight of my drawing coming to life. My long search had finally come to an end. Animation was the answer.

Joe Siracusa
Animation Editor

■■■■■■■■■■■■■■■■■■■■■ ■ ■ ■ ■ ■ ■ ■ ■ ■ ■

My background was primarily in the field of music, ranging from performing as a percussionist with the Cleveland Philharmonic Orchestra to playing with Spike Jones And His City Slickers. And as Spike would have said, "That's quite a jump without a parachute."

I was only six years old in Cleveland, Ohio when I had my first exposure to show biz with my neighbor and pal, Herb Klynn, when we produced some marionette shows for our families. Twenty-five years later when I was the drummer with Spike's band and we recorded "How The Circus Learned to Smile," it was my job to create and perform the sound effects—squeaking clown shoes, dancing bears, galloping ponies, and performing seals—all accomplished musically and to tempo. About that time, Herb, newly associated with UPA, suggested we combine our talents to produce an animated TV film and although that project never came to fruition, my appetite for animation was whetted. Subsequently when UPA offered me the chance to "get off the road," I took it.

After some tutelage, I worked up to supervising film editor and was able to invite a few of my talented friends from the Spike Jones organization to help form one of the most creative sound departments in the business. For example, we supplied music for a Mr. Magoo film by making rhythmic loops of sounds, then mixing and dubbing them into a quasi-musical background. One of my favorite experiences was for a project at DePatie-Freleng, working with Ted Giesel (Dr. Seuss) on our second Emmy-winning TV special, "The Grinch Grinches The Cat In The Hat," for which I created many original sounds. After sharing in numerous awards, Klynn and a group of us decided to establish our own animation company, Format Films.

All in all, I consider myself fortunate that I have been able to truly express myself as an animation film editor. Whether editing music, dialogue, picture, or sound effects, I have always appreciated the opportunity to participate in such a creative industry.

Arch Leean
Animation Teacher

Wow! For 20 years we've been saying that. Especially those of us who learned animation on a light table. But "wow" is a little like responding to a cold shower. It surprises us, and then it's over until the next cold shower.

There is a dilemma here. The graphic computer's potential seems to be endless, especially to creative artist trained in the classic techniques of cel animation. Try another variation. Change some parameter. Every subtle move has the potential to significantly surprise us. And for a creative person, that surprise, that "wow," can be highly satisfying and rewarding. It's hard to stop playing.

So we counsel ourselves and our students, should we have any, to have a plan, to aim at some defined goal, to use only those experiments that build up to a unified whole. One often finds direction and success with such a simple critique. Yet it still may be only a "wow." We still may not have tapped anything very personal. Our content may still derive only from the medium.

I came to animation indirectly. I was doing graduate study in England, concentrating on drawing and printmaking. I was also assisting an international group that was providing space for refugee families that were displaced by events behind the "iron curtain." That was life in the Fifties. And I recall watching the children of those people. They were usually the targets of historical or cultural lectures. Almost all were bored or restless.

One day, perhaps in desperation, I was asked to conduct a session. With the help of an old Argus 35mm camera, a film strip projector, a former BBC radio announcer, and an overnight film processing lab, I made my first audio-visual film. The children were fascinated and I was intrigued by the apparent power of my crude images when combined with sound.

The next year in an effort to find out more about the about the audio-visual field I took a class in animation at Columbia University. This was the challenge I had been looking for. I then left for Hollywood to learn more about it. I learned the techniques of animation like others of my generation by working in animation studios like Jay Ward, Hanna-Barbera, TV Spots, and Disney. I realized I was only an actor hired to draw someone else's character but the process was fascinating.

Before I went to work at Disney, my teachers all seemed to be ex-Disney animators who had left that studio for various reasons, most of which were not flattering. Later when there were massive layoffs and a Disney job was my only option, I seriously questioned whether I wanted it. As it turned our, this tour was a highlight for me. I relearned some early lessons. Speed, which was highly valued in most studios, didn't seem to be that important at Disney. My scenes were often returned, and it was suggested that I spend some time in the library, which I did. Someone also said that my drawings reminded him of veteran Disney animator Frank Thomas, whom I promptly looked up, only to discover that his original sketchy lines always moved better than any of my

Xerox-ready drawings. I was back in school, but I quickly appreciated the way my drawing skills were challenged and improved.

I also learned the value of personal content. Regarding the art of animation, that lesson was perhaps best communicated by animator-director Robert Cannon, "Bobe," whom I had the good fortune to work with. I recall one lunch break stroll with Bobe in a back lot at the Disney Studios. Suddenly he stopped. There was a couple on a park bench directly in front of us. After a few moments Bobe backed up quietly, and when we were out of range he asked me if I had seen "that." I assumed he knew one or both of the people but it turned out he didn't know either one of them. Bobe merely observed a gesture, a gesture that he said was "perfect." I obviously wasn't watching in the same way. I still wasn't the student I needed to be of human actions and responses.

So what's the future of this business? How does one prepare to use this powerful new computer animation tool? The challenge for today's animator isn't that different from my generation. One needs more than craft. I chose to leave the studio scene and teach at a liberal arts college. I believe in education and advise as broad a background as possible. I look for students who are fascinated by their humanity and search every idea, every discipline, document, or gesture for answers. They are the students who make animation sequences that have holding power beyond "wow."

Jack H. Davis
Multimedia Art Director

Early in my formal training in the graphic arts, I learned that one of the most essential goals of graphic design is the elegant distilling of something dynamic, such as a company product or service, into something symbolic and static that can be visually communicated through the printed page. This "freeze-drying" process of reducing something "alive" into something that can be easily grasped and remembered, such as a company's identity, was an incredibly exciting challenge for me. But after years of working with the traditional tools in graphic communication, I came to a crossroads in my career. In the early 1980s I saw the advent of the use of computer graphics in the television industry, specifically, the infamous flying logos of the TV network IDs. For the first time I saw symbols, typography, and illustrations that were not static but vibrantly dynamic.

It was also at this time, in 1984, that a new tool appeared that had the future potential of putting these dynamic capabilities into the hands of individual graphic artists. In contrast to the extremely high-end computer graphics facilities of prior years, where designers had to work with scientists and computer programmers in order to visualize their concepts, the Macintosh computer provided the seemingly unlimited potential of a graphics processor, or image synthesizer, on the desktop of the artist. The advent of the Mac excited me to the point of starting graduate work to explore this brand-new area of computer imagery and design.

I began, as other computer-based designers did, by replicating traditional graphics techniques in electronic form. But as the graphics capabilities of the Mac eventually developed beyond black-and-white imagery, into color illustration, and then into complete prepress integration, it also evolved to the point of being able to manage those same 3-D animation and video effects that had enticed me earlier on. However, what has happened in the desktop design studio in the last few years goes beyond even this most contemporary area of the graphic design industry. Desktop computers can now produce not only the static representations used in printed communication, and the dynamic imagery used in video (both of these by their very nature linear and noninteractive), but also multimedia. Interactive multimedia is the integration of text, graphics, audio, animation, and video within the context of communication that is accessible in a nonlinear fashion. In other words, the user does not need to start at page one and continue on through the middle to the end of one continuous presentation of information, but has the option to navigate through the information interactively (usually by pointing and clicking selected words, images, or buttons) in a way that is most relevant to his or her individual needs. Interactive multimedia arose not from any act of forward-thinking leadership from within the graphics community, but almost accidentally through the interplay of independent technological advances such as interactive presentation software, digital video, and CD-ROM.

In regards to the roles of artists in this new arena, it is important to point out that the production process of creating something like a 600 megabyte interactive project is usually more like working in a movie studio than in a graphic design studio. In a traditional graphics setting, designers, illustrators, and photographers all contribute to the final printed piece, but even with these team requirements, most of the production can still be handled in-house by traditionally trained graphic artists. In the movie studio, however, an extremely diverse range of specialized talents is more essential. The titles of producer, director, art director, set designer, choreographer, composer, special effects personnel, and actors all have some counterpart in the field of interactive multimedia. All these roles were necessary to handle the components involved in creating The Journeyman Project (Presto Studios' photo-realistic 3-D adventure game).

This new medium, or combination of media, is a dramatic step in the evolution of communication. Because it draws upon the decades of work that have gone into optimizing the various components that make it up (such as text, sound, photography, animation, and cinematography), it starts with an incredibly robust and diverse set of tools with which to create. And it is obvious that the apex of this new technology is not simply the aggregation of the different media types, but their synthesis within this nonlinear environment. This active participation of the user in that dynamic communication process is likely to be the next radical shift in visual communication.

What will make interactive multimedia widely available is the popularization of new consumer devices that allow the playback of this information through a TV set rather than a dedicated computer system. Some of these devices such as CDI, CDTV, Photo CD, and 3DO are already on the market. Others are on the verge of release. All are similar to the VCR, in that they involve a black box that sits on or near the TV and allows the user to make selections and interact with different media types through a hand-held remote control unit. With the advent of these low-cost players, the number of possible participants in interactive multimedia will quickly expand from the hundreds of thousands of present CD-ROM owners, to a number in the millions. With the introduction of feature-length movies on these compact discs, as well as games and educational resources, not to mention the unrealized world of true virtual reality, there is a phenomenal potential for creating a whole new industry within the field of visual communication. It is into this future that I hope to continue to explore the boundaries of graphic design, illustration, animation, and cinematography. And I can't think of a more exciting or potentially earth-changing area of communication to be working on.

Irene Trivas
Animator, Designer, Illustrator

My animation career began in the Sixties after I had returned from an extended stay in Europe. I was in debt and jobless. My work experience up to that point had consisted of a few years at Tri-Arts, a small commercial studio in Los Angeles where I had designed record covers. I had also spent several years at the J. Walter Thompson Advertising Agency, working as an assistant art director. There, I was hailed as the Queen of the Scott Paper Company— my reward for the appalling cuteness I had contributed to their line of toilet tissue. In New York, I needed a job but I also badly needed to do something creative. Luckily, that's when the animation team of Pablo Ferro, Fred Mogubgub, and Lew Schwartz hired me. I knew nothing whatsoever about animation. All I could do was draw. But since I knew nothing, there was nothing to unlearn, and I learned animation techniques on the job from Fred Mogubgub.

In retrospect, I realize how extraordinarily fortunate I was. Not only was Fred a gifted original, but it was just the beginning of the Sixties. In many respects, the Sixties was a blank slate: television was the best new toy on the market, and we all got to play. For the first few glorious years, the ad agencies deferred to the production companies for all ideas and storyboards. They only insisted that the product looked perfect. Otherwise whatever craziness we came up with was okay by them, especially in animation, probably because they didn't know anything about it.

Eventually, I developed into an animation designer. I drew storyboards, designed characters, painted backgrounds, and little by little tried to shed the conventional skin imposed on me by a conventional education. To this day, I harbor a profound distrust of the purely academic approach to any form of art. Of course, school is the appropriate place to learn the possibilities and limitations of everything from a tape recorder to a tube of oil paint. School is the place where one should learn the alphabet, the tools of the arts. But what you do with those tools—the films you make, the poems you write, or the paintings you paint, can really happen anywhere. I remember certain teachers in art school whose personalities were so powerful that one's own fledging ego hardly had a chance. The right academic environment takes as much care in allowing a student's own personality to flower as in providing technical instruction.

Later, Fred formed Mogubgub, Ltd., and together with one other animator, I worked in a ramshackle suite of rooms on 46th Street. For the next few years we produced dozens of offbeat commercials for major clients such as Ford and Coca-Cola, as well other innovative projects such as a promotional film for the School of Visual Arts. During those years, I ended up doing a lot of drawing. Fred was one of the pioneers in the use of quick cuts, and he was convinced that projecting an image for only two or three frames was quite long enough. To him, an image was an image: it could be a drawing, a photograph, a piece of old footage, whatever. It was enormously liberating to be able to look at film that way: any picture in any form that propelled the story was valid.

Toward the mid-Sixties, things began to change. Many of the hot-shot outside TV producers went inside, hired by the ad agencies to produce the commercials. More and more often we were handed ready-made storyboards with very little room to play. Then the agencies realized they could get their message across in 20 or 30 seconds as effectively and much more cheaply than in 60 seconds. By now there was too much money at stake. Playtime was over.

Eventually I moved to Vermont and became a children's book illustrator and sometime writer. Yet I do miss animation terribly. It was simply the best work experience of my life—collaborating with three or four other creative people in a noncompetitive way in order to produce one final work of art. Being employed in the Sixties, when the medium was new and the rules minimal, our little team had the opportunity to do our jobs well, with hardly any interference. And as long as we got away with it, I considered myself extraordinarily lucky to have been part of it all.

Erik Loyer

Computer Graphic Artist

■■■■■■■■■■■■■■■■■ ■ ■ ■ ■ ■ ■ ■ ■

Animation is all about motion, so in its broadest sense, computer animation could be considered any motion that is electronically controlled or generated. When defined like that, computer animation appears to be permeating the American lifestyle. From the flashing cursor in your word processor to the relentlessly advancing hours of your digital alarm clock, electronically regulated visual change surrounds us. Of course, these examples seem pedestrian when compared to the convincingly real dinosaurs of *Jurassic Park,* or the metamorphosing faces in Michael Jackson's "Black or White" video. These instances of computer-generated motion, produced by some of the current masters in the field, have captured imaginations all over the world.

For its more than 30-year history, computer animation for the most part has lacked the public enthusiasm it enjoys today. Probably the most important factor in this recent upsurge of interest is that computer animation technology has developed to the point where it can now provide visual wish fulfillment for the masses. Monsters of liquid metal, metamorphosing faces, and other hyper-real images have been easy for visual dreamers to conceive, but until now difficult to bring convincingly to life. It is still difficult, but computer animation is making quantum leaps in visual expression, allowing us to create visions never before seen outside the mind's eye.

Computer animation had a much greater effect on me while I was growing up than television did. When I say computer animation, I don't mean the kind of work you might find in one of today's blockbuster films. Hardly. No, I'm talking about the clunky, low resolution stuff that came from my family's beloved Apple II computer, which was purchased in 1978 when I was six years old. Television may have pumped the occasionally-interesting show into our living room, but our computer was always ready and waiting for us to type in a new program, write a song, play a game or draw a picture. And while the technology was not yet sophisticated enough for me to easily create my own animations, my interest was definitely aroused. With the introduction of the Macintosh computer in 1984, the ability to create motion graphics became much more accessible, and my best friend and I produced silly computer animations by the truckload.

For my family, computer animation evolved as something we had the power to shape and control in our own home. I feel the term "computer animation" and all it implies will never have reached its fullest expression until the individual can create visual poetry with as much creative ease (and as much productive creative difficulty) as one finds when writing. This attitude remains a powerful inspiration for me in my work in computer animation—a field whose promise fascinates me. The things that are becoming possible today for the average person with a computer will deeply affect how that individual relaxes, plays, works, and even thinks.

There is a catch, however. We are a society obsessed with technological promise and tormented by technological failure and if the old saying holds true about computers only being as smart as their users, then humans are the only ones to blame. Progress becomes empty and wasteful without an enduring vision to support it and at the moment, our typical experience with computer animations is indissolubly linked to the commercial interests of those who produce them. An overly commercial approach has already distorted the affective potential of much of our electronic media. How then can we prevent computer animation from going the way of the boob tube, the blockbuster action flick, or the shoot-'em-up computer game?

As in other visual media, the art of computer animation is closely linked to the art of illusion. But the illusion, the trick that makes one thing appear to take the form of another, is little more than a parlor game if the image being created has no relevance to its audience. What kind of emotional or (God forbid) intellectual response do you have to dancing LifeSavers? Making computer graphics relevant to people involves integrating it into their everyday perception, while at the same time using it to provide striking new perspectives on the world in which they live.

Words surround us constantly. We use them every day to communicate with each other, not to mention all the thousands of verbal messages our culture sends us telling us what to do, buy, or think. Once in a while, however, there comes that certain individual who can transform the phrases of everyday conversation into sounds and rhythms of high emotion and intellect. These artists take the everyday and the common and render it creatively divine through the conduit of its very familiarity. This is the link that gives their art its power.

So it must be with computer animation. More than flying logos and perfect reflections, we need computer animations that function on the same level as your word processor or your digital clock, taking the visual components of an everyday environment and combining them with wholly new visions and perspectives. They need not be didactic, need not serve a higher "purpose" or a broader "market," need not cater to the lowest common denominator nor serve the highest "cultural elite." Creatively, they should be in the hands of as many people as possible. Artistically, they should take every form imaginable. Intuitively, they should be relevant to our personal experience.

The field of computer animation holds more creative room for expression than any one of us can currently imagine. To the person eager to enter this field, I would ask you to remember this: The average person who has heard of computer graphics today probably thinks it is best used to morph a pop star or create highly-reflective, three-dimensional objects in action films and commercials. It's always good to prove people wrong.

Hans Jaggi
Animation Equipment Executive

The term "animation" was not even in my vocabulary as an American immigrant fresh from Switzerland in the 1950s. After getting off the ship at Hoboken, New Jersey I managed to find a job as a lathe operator at a sweat shop in Mount Vernon, New York. After some time, I set out with the vague notion of finding something a bit more interesting to do. I hoped to find a position that might somehow involve photography or mechanical engineering, as that had been my passion since my childhood. In my search for employment, I happened to walk into a small garage that was equipped with a primitive but ingenious machine shop. The owner turned out to be John Oxberry. At that time he was a struggling young inventor with great ideas but little money. We started experimenting together, and from the very beginning, I sensed he was a genius. He was in no way an eccentric. Indeed, I found him to be an easygoing man, and most stimulating to work with.

Fortunately, I was able to help John put together an optical printer, and later we collaborated in developing the prototype for the Oxberry master animation stand. We watched in amazement as the product grew to become renowned and used in countless colleges and universities throughout the world. Over 1,000 Oxberry animation cameras and stands are now used internationally for commercial purposes.

Eventually John Oxberry retired, but we of Photographic Equipment Service, Inc. have continued to research, develop, and service the best animation equipment possible. Innovations like Aerial Image, which is a camera accepting interchangeable film movements in 35mm, 16mm, and 8mm, the Automator, a digital mirco-computer created for the animation stand cameraman, and the Image Expander, a device designed to overcome problems inherent in the copying or animating of small transparencies, have become particularly exciting accomplishments in the field of animation engineering.

Emru Townsend

Animation Filmmaker, Writer

■■■■■■■■■■■■■■■■■■ ■■ ■ ■ ■ ■ ■ ■

Recently, there has been considerable furor over what is acceptable or unacceptable in the visual media, especially regarding cartoons. The rise of political correctness and general paranoia as to the effects of cartoons on children have led to classic animation being pulled or expurgated on television, to be replaced by cartoons that are painfully bland.

Being both black and a lifelong fan and student of things animated, I confess to sometimes feeling torn when it comes to the depiction of ethnic groups in animation. Blacks, Asians, and Native Americans have received the short end of the caricature stick in cartoons, with blacks taking the brunt of the blows over the decades. However, to censor every animated cartoon with a potentially offensive racial stereotype would be to eliminate a large portion of some of the wittiest and most innovative works created. Some studios and networks have turned to editing out offensive scenes from their libraries, but this is tantamount to revisionism. Still, there are some wonderful shorts out there that have never been viewed because of various blackface gags or politically incorrect characterizations.

For example, James Stuart Blackton's 1906 cartoon, *Humorous Phases of Funny Faces,* employs rapid-fire sketches—one of which features an unflattering black caricature labeled "coon," followed by an unattractive Jewish caricature called "Cohen"—after which Blackton is heard to emit a quiet chortle.

The question is, does this make him particularly evil? By late twentieth-century standards, maybe so—but in 1906, slavery had only recently been abolished in the United States. And Blackton's attitude was a reflection of the times. Some would say that this is immaterial, that he was a racist and therefore his works should not be shown. But one must be reminded that many useful inventions were created by people who would be considered racists today. The creator's intent, therefore, must be evaluated within its historical context.

I suppose I can forgive Winsor McCay's monstrously-lipped, nappy-headed, spear-chucking Impy from 1911's *Little Nemo,* considering that every character, save the princess, was absurd. And I also imagine that Harman and Ising can be forgiven for Bosko in their early 1930s *Sinkin' in the Bathtub,* if only because it didn't take them long to alter Bosko's voice so that he was no longer a black stereotype.

After the mid-30s, things got stickier. Many cartoons used blackface gags or deprecating images of Africans, but few stick out in my mind more than Friz Freleng's 1938 short, *Jungle Jitters.* The first half of the cartoon has massively-lipped tribal Africans dancing around, with many gags centering around bones and rings in their hair or noses, among other things.

Chuck Jones directed a handful of shorts starring a pygmy by the name of Inki, who is depicted as being tiny, of course, with a bone in his hair, big puckered pink lips, and a dazed expression on his face. I saw my first Inki short, *Inki and the Lion* (1941) just one year ago. And in that, Inki is the subject of a carnival attraction, totally oblivious to the insane goings-on throughout.

Tex Avery could present quick word and visual association gags the likes of which still can't be topped. Unfortunately, some of those led to obnoxious characterizations, as in his screamingly funny *Musical Maestro* from 1951. An opera singer is at the mercy of a vengeful magician. With a wave of his wand, objects magically appear that affect the singer's performance. At one point he gets a faceful of ink, and . . . well, you can guess what transpires.

I mention these shorts particularly, because they present some of my personal internal conflicts. My earliest memories of watching cartoons as a three-year-old involve spotting director's credits such as Jones, Avery, or Freleng and instantly knowing I was going to enjoy what was coming next. These three men kindled my love for animation. Imagine my dismay when, over 10 years later, I saw some of their works with jokes and visuals that were at the expense of my people. It's hard to have your idols not only become human, but to do so in a way that hurts.

On the surface, Bob Clampett's *Coal Black and de Sebben Dwarfs* from 1942, a blackface, jive-talking send-up of Disney's *Snow White*, is one of the most blatantly racist cartoons ever to see the light of day. But dig a bit deeper, and you find an interesting story. Clampett wanted to not only skewer *Snow White*, but filter it through the black nightclub scene of the day. So he grabbed some gag men and animators from the studio and they went to various predominantly black dance clubs and observed. The result was one of the fastest, wackiest, and jazziest Warner Brothers cartoons ever made.

Of course, Clampett uses the same sort of stylization for the black characters as Jones did for Inki. The character animation, designs, and voice work are all essentially that of black people seen through a white man's perception. The big difference is the intent of the director. *Inki and the Lion,* though superbly animated, essentially makes fun of blacks, though Inki could have been a cat, a dog, or any other cartoon staple without changing the plot line. Clampett's cartoon may poke fun at blacks, but it does so from a more informed perspective, and requires that the characters be black. Clampett's intentions can be said to be more valid than those of his predecessors.

So where does this leave us? To broadcast or not to broadcast? I don't think that can be properly answered here, but I do believe that we, the people, should discuss the subject rationally before it is decided for us. Knee-jerk reactions, whether for censorship or freedom of expression, will not work.

Karen Kreider

Multimedia Producer

■■■■■■■■■■■■■■■■■■ ■ ■ ■ ■ ■ ■ ■ ■

Animation is one of the purest sources of joy I can think of. It can transport young minds to exotic lands and once-upon-a-times more eloquently than almost any other form of entertainment. An added bonus is that it can affect adult minds as well. How many times have we grown-ups taken along a child as an excuse to see a cartoon movie?

Remarkably, adults today are walking alone into G-rated animated films more than ever—without shame or embarrassment. Animation has arrived. So too have all the ancillary pursuits: toys, T-shirts, towels, blankets, coffee mugs, books, and the newest frontier, CD-ROMS.

I came to developing animated movies into animated storybooks on CD-ROM for Disney Interactive through a circuitous path. Having majored in theatre at Rollins College in Florida, I had dreams of becoming a Broadway star. But in my heart, I really wanted to write, direct, and produce projects that had dynamic women's roles for a Broadway star. Acquiring an MFA from Tisch School of the Arts at New York University afforded me the opportunity to study playwriting and directing along with acting.

At first glance, an advanced degree in theatre is not the most appropriate preparation for an assistant producer of CD-ROM titles, nor an editor and writer of children's books before that. But then again, why not? The theatre environment is an extraordinary exercise in observation. And it is through observation that we find the raw materials to create a good story. The stage is where stories come to life. The leap then isn't so large from the stage to the theatricality of an interactive animated retelling of a story. It's like putting on a show in a different format and allowing the audience to participate in the fun!

As an assistant producer, I feel all my life's experiences have found a raison d'être. At last, creating animated storybooks and activity centers on CD-ROM brings together the elements of good storytelling, imaginative directing, creative producing, and courage to push the envelope of learning through technology. It offers the child a chance to linger a little longer with his or her favorite characters from the films, explore the worlds of those characters at the child's own pace, click on people, objects, or animal friends and watch them giggle over and over again!

It becomes clear that there's more to animation than simply creating a film. There's a whole life beyond the movie screen. My goal is to help children relive that tummy-tickling, wide-eyed experience that bombarded their senses in a darkened movie theatre and enhance it beyond a linear scope on the screen of a computer. And, along the way, help them to think and learn and forge their own path into the new century.

Irwin Bazelon

Composer, Conductor, Writer

After graduating from the School of Music at DePaul University and completing my studies in composition with Darius Milhaud at Mills College, I arrived in New York City to begin my musical career and recall writing over 300 letters to schools all over the country inquiring about teaching positions in music. Subsequently I received one response, and that was negative. So I took a job as a reservation clerk with the Atlantic Coastline Railroad and worked there for seven years while writing music at night.

Finally I decided to quit my job, and through a series of fortuitous introductions, managed to meet the chief executive for UPA, who was looking for some offbeat music for a series of animated commercials they were producing for the Alfred Hitchcock TV show. Hearing my music, which I played on the piano, using my voice to illustrate and imitate musical instruments, UPA hired me to write the score. I vividly recall how I presented my composition utilizing piccolo, xylophone, trumpet, piano, and tuba. This was a radical departure from the "jingle mentality" of numerous sound tracks written for commercials during that period, but my work was accepted over the objections of the account executive in charge.

UPA coordinated my score with the animation. Instead of the usual tracks for animation, I began to write compositions scored for various musical combinations. Soon I found my work in demand on a scale I never dreamed possible, and was collaborating with highly creative art directors, eager to employ contemporary solutions featuring diverse music. All of this led me to embrace documentary films, art films, industrial films, commercials, music for theater, and television programs. Probably most recognizable was my signature composition for NBC News which ran throughout the '60s. In fact, those eight seconds of music supported me while I composed my initial three symphonies, and NBC became my chief sponsor during that time of my life. Fortunately, I found myself working with people eager to tap native resources, people who were aware of the difference between a composer and a noncomposer, a score and a nonscore. I was allowed the freedom to write anything I determined appropriate, and in almost 95 percent of the scores I created, I was able to duplicate my concert hall style and bring my own personal signature to the music I composed. I also had the chance to write my music quickly and with assurance, without the benefit of running to the piano for trial and error compositions, but to hear it played immediately by the best musicians in the world, including in many cases, members of the New York Philharmonic. In short, I became a professional composer with confidence and a sense of pride. I had the opportunity of conducting my music with orchestras throughout the world, and I am grateful for the experience I acquired in conducting my music for documentary and animated films.

My beginnings as a composer literally commenced with the compositions I wrote for animated commercials and short subject films. That gave me the opportunity to "hear" my music and grow creatively. In 1975, I wrote my first book, *Knowing The Score/Notes On Film Music.* Recently I have been a guest composer, lecturing, and performing my music at several universities and colleges.

Brian Sawyer
Film School Graduate

I participated in a lot of community theatre while growing up in Santa Barbara. It was easy to get roles, since there were only two or three other kids in town auditioning for parts. To me there was nothing more exciting than theatre, watching the rehearsals, seeing characters develop, and having the audience react to performances. But once I reached my teens, there were lots of others competing for roles, and I stopped getting parts. So I abandoned theatre and became interested in computers, eventually spending most of my free time writing programs on a home computer.

In college, the sensible major was computer science, especially since a high-paying job was almost guaranteed upon graduation. For years after graduation I worked in the computer industry as a software author, and co-authored a number of books on artificial intelligence. I developed an "expert system" software product called VP-Expert, which used techniques from artificial intelligence to let computer users create programs using English-like rules, rather than having to write cryptic computer codes. I found a publisher interested in marketing the product, and spent three years adding new features to it.

While I had enjoyed creating the project, I gradually lost interest in maintaining it. People around the country would call me with strange and elaborate requests for features to add to VP-Expert. Others would call to proudly tell me about obscure bugs they had found in the program, which would take me weeks to track down and fix. I began to grow tired of the hours and hours of life spent in front of a computer, typing strange symbols, debugging, and writing thousands of lines of computer code. I had even started dreaming in languages like "C" and Pascal. While it was gratifying to have created a successful product, the cost of maintaining it had become too much, and I decided to try something new.

So I searched for a field that was more universal and human, a field with qualities I remembered in theatre, and finally entered a graduate program in film production. I very much liked thinking of the world in terms of characters and stories, rather than programs and data. Although there was an occasional temptation to return to the computer industry for financial security, I decided to commit myself to cinema, and for three years made films and wrote scripts before graduating.

Since my own background is a combination of storytelling and technology, I am naturally curious about the future of interactive media, where computers and films are combined. It seems the obvious uses of this new technology are in education and games. I am not sure how interactive technology will affect storytelling in narrative films. I don't think people who go to movies really want to "interact" with a film and press buttons to control the flow of a story. I believe interactive technology will fail where it is used gratuitously. People go to films to experience emotions, to empathize with characters, and to stimulate their imaginations. If interactive technology can be used to achieve these ends, only then it will have a big impact on filmmaking. For the moment, I am continuing to write traditional screenplays and make traditional films.

Barbara Carrasco

Artist, Muralist

■■■■■■■■■■■■■■■■ ■ ■ ■ ■ ■ ■ ■ ■ ■

When my sister Frances opened a small computer company with her friend, I didn't realize the potential computers had to enrich the graphic sensibilities in my artwork. At the time, I was painting large-scale banners for the United Farm Workers Union. I had often met with Cesar Chavez, the president of that union, who would suggest I design images that were relevant to the theme of a particular convention or event where the banners would be displayed. He preferred simple art work that was self-explanatory. Condensing numerous ideas into an effective banner was not easy for me, especially working under time constraints. Also, most of the banners contained text that was difficult to integrate with art. My sister pointed out that I was using an archaic method of measuring the letter spacing and demonstrated how my artwork could be scanned in the computer, then added and positioned onto the dimensions of a banner. The combined printout would then be enlarged by an opaque projector and transferred directly onto the banner material. After taking some computer training, I was soon able to reduce production time on the banners by half, and the text was situated accurately.

In 1989 I was one of 12 artists selected to create an computer animation display to be shown on the Spectacolor, Inc. lightboard in New York City's Times Square for an entire month. It was the most exciting art project I ever had the opportunity to work on. First, I made a storyboard sketch, which was submitted and approved for production. Then, after completing the planning, I observed and consulted with the Spectacolor animation programmer. I had decided to create an animated sequence that would support the Farm Workers of America who were fighting against the use of pesticides in the fields. The title of my piece was *Pesticides,* and it illustrated a farm worker picking grapes while a crop duster swept down and sprayed pesticides over him. The worker was then shown flat on his back next to a crate of grapes. In the next scene, the crate appeared in a supermarket where a woman bought the grapes. After washing them, she tried to feed the grapes to her children, but they refused to eat them, implying they were afraid of the health risks. The mother threw the grapes into a trash can that moved toward the viewer revealing the grapes inside. The trash can rim encircled and crossed over the grapes. The shot then zoomed in revealing skull-like faces on the grapes, and ended with a repeat scene of the crop duster spraying pesticides.

Coincidentally, Cesar Chevez was in New York gathering support for the union-waged grape boycott. I called to tell him about my computer project and he was very supportive. He even referred to the 15 years I had volunteered my artistic skills for the union on a National Public Radio interview he subsequently gave. I was honored that the person I most admired as a student had publicly acknowledged my work as an artist.

Within a year, I began to integrate computer generated images in my paintings and drawings. And because many of my paintings are flat and hard-edged in style, utilizing software programs such as Freehand and Illustrator offered on the Apple Macintosh was a natural step to refining my techniques. I began to realize that the computer was more than a vehicle for production and technical assistance. It was a tool for creating art, just as a brush is used to create a painting. Scanned art work could be placed over a grid, then removed to work with the art on the computer. Applying color, reducing, enlarging, and repeating images is simpler, faster, and more efficient.

When working on the computer to create complex geometric or contour lines I recall comments made by my UCLA art professors about the limitations of trying to draw "perfect pictures." The late artist, Jan Stussy, who taught anatomy and life drawing, observed that my lines were more fluid and expressive when I wasn't focused on being precise. He felt that drawings must never be "perfect," because there are always ways to improve them. For me, the computer allows for experimental variations in creating the "perfect picture," and through its use, I have been documenting and categorizing relevant information about all my artwork.

There have been many influences that have affected the development of my work, such as the powerful expressiveness of the line drawings in traditional Japanese prints as well as the use of motion to achieve an emotional response in the viewer by using many of the animation techniques from the Forties and Fifties. Currently, I am working on animation with young patients at Childrens Hospital Los Angeles, where I have been the visual artist in residence for two years.

Creating art with the computer has been extremely rewarding, and has added new dimensions to my work as an artist and muralist.

Leslie Iwerks

Film Director, Producer

■■■■■■■■■■■■■■■■■■■ ■ ■ ■ ■ ■ ■ ■ ■ ■ ■

A couple of circles, movement, voice, personality—and what you have is the most popular cartoon character in the world. As with any beginning venture, Ub Iwerks was far from realizing the impact a few sketches of a mouse would have on millions of people, generation after generation.

1928 was a big year for Walt Disney and Ub Iwerks, as they traversed a series of successes and failures in the animation industry by creating a character called Mickey Mouse. Those early days of animation had to be exciting ones, where challenges were posed daily and inventions were constantly being created. What those early days of loyalty, friendship, and a focus for success evolved into was a multimillion dollar industry of animation and family entertainment. But it goes without saying that all that excitement as well as fame and fortune did not come into being without its trials and tribulations, including the fierce competition from rival animation studios.

Ub Iwerks started out in Kansas City working on ads for the Pesmin-Rubin Commercial Art Studio, where he did airbrushing and lettering. And it was there in 1919 that he met Walt Disney. After being laid off from work following the holiday rush, the two of them decided to venture out on their own and form the Iwerks-Disney Company. Feeling the strain of the competition and economic hardships of the time, the business didn't last long and they were soon back working for someone else, the Film Ad Company. Animation was still a baby during those years, but as time and technology progressed, so did the two partners. Finally, Walt and Ub moved to California to embark on new goals, where Ub created Mickey Mouse, and became the fastest animator of his day. He animated the legendary *Steamboat Willie,* and *Skeleton Dance,* and his many technical advances included the simple animation peg bar, the multiplane camera, and refinements on the optical printer.

Although there has been an explosion of animation and film technology, which has affected the entire entertainment business, the importance of good writing has remained. Unlike live-action, where actors can express emotions with subtle gestures, many cartoons are physical and aggressive in nature. Debates and discussions have often raged over the content of cartoons—whether or not they are good lessons for young children. Believe it or not, even the early Mickey Mouse cartoons were considered "too violent." So as an animator, study and refine all aspects of story and character, not only your drawing and computer skills, but what you want to contribute and what kind of impression you wish to make.

Growing up hearing and learning about Ub Iwerks, my grandfather, has given me immense inspiration. Having been involved in art since I was young, I started a commercial art business in high school, designing murals, logos, T-shirts, book illustrations, and store-front windows. What grew out of that initial venture were numerous clients and diverse projects that expanded my education and challenged my artistic abilities. Following that, I studied cinema and television directing at USC, then formed a film/video production company, which also makes short dramatic films.

As I continue my career in directing, I realize that art and animation will always be a part of the films that I make. There are so many opportunities and so much to learn from the daily events that inspire my stories. I believe there is more room for great filmmaking by just experiencing and appreciating life to its fullest. After all his accomplishments in animation and film processes, this is one belief I know my grandfather would agree with.

Jun Falkenstein

Animator, Storyboard Artist

■■■■■■■■■■■■■■■■■■ ■ ■ ■ ■ ■ ■ ■ ■

I was always fascinated by cartoons and cartoon characters. This may not be unusual for a kid growing up in America, but I was not content to merely observe. I had to see if I could draw them as well. My mom encouraged me to pursue my interest in art from the moment I could hold a pencil. Although I attempted to copy what I saw on television and in the movies, most of the time I was creating my own characters and writing stories for them to act in.

When I was 11, a neighbor showed me how to execute a limited style of animation and lent me his Super-8 camera. Racing to the library, I read everything available on how to make animated films, and was soon creating short experiments thatencompassed a variety of styles including claymation and pixillation. It was a constant source of amazement to me to see that drawings I devised could actually come to life. So I pursued animation throughout high school, gradually creating longer films with more complex stories.

After high school, I was accepted to the University of Southern California's School of Cinema and Television. Although the undergraduate curriculum emphasized live-action filmmaking, I found myself more interested in animation, and produced four short films. One was a black and white pencil test, and the others had full color and sound. I also added animation whenever possible to enhance my live-action projects.

Upon graduating, I applied for a job at Disney (like everybody else) but was rejected (also like everybody else). Then a friend suggested I try Warner Brothers. As it turned out, they had one slot open for a character layout artist, and I was hired. After this, I was offered a position on the animation team. This in turn led to a directorial position at Hanna-Barbera. But my first love has always been theatrical feature animation, so I left television to rejoin Warner Brothers in their new feature animation unit. The future looks bright right now for the industry. It's an especially exciting time for us all.

There is much to be said for short films, and they are one of the reasons I praise my education. Some say it's more practical to just go out there and get a job in the industry. It is true that connections can be made faster that way, but on the downside, you start immediately as one of the "workhorses," who must then move up the ranks in order to get a chance to work on your own projects. However, if you start out in film school, you have the opportunity to create and complete your own films, to develop some of your own ideas and execute them the way you want. You can establish your own style and experiment freely without worrying about whether the film will make money or appeal to the right demographic age group. In my humble opinion, the films you create in film school serve to demonstrate the various aspects of your individual talents much better than a portfolio of still pictures—the proof of this being that some people get hired on the strength of their reel alone!

My studies were most valuable to me in that they allowed total freedom. I hope one day to resume creating my own films on a full-time basis, just like I did in cinema school.

Howard Schmitt

Graduate Student, Arts

■■■■■■■■■■■■■■■■ ■ ■ ■ ■ ■ ■ ■ ■

I had not planned to study animation or even go to film school. I felt I didn't draw fast enough to consider animation because in design class I spent hours on assignments thatother students would finish in 30 minutes. As for film school, I was admittedly intimidated by cinema departments. But the odd thing is that I have accumulated experience that seems particularly well-suited for animation.

Having written a good deal in high school and wanting to study playwriting, I set out to be a theatre major at Northwestern University. There, in a costume design class, I made a revealing discovery: I knew what the characters looked like. So I stayed with costume design.

My background in designing costumes has been invaluable in learning how to animate characters. Designing costumes entails delineating characters by their visual image, whether obvious or subtle. All my studies in art, architecture, literature, and the history of fashion required for costume design have helped me enormously in animation classes. In addition, anyone who deals with costumes spends a lot of time attending dress rehearsals. You learn how directors deal with scenes or characters to make them work. It is surprising what a skilled director can accomplish in a couple of rehearsals. By watching actors perform through dress rehearsals and previews, you discover how to breathe life into what might have been a series of static scenes.

Soon I became aware that I needed to assemble a portfolio of my production work in design. So I spent some time studying photography. Cameras became my new "toys" and I learned the importance of controlling what is in frame and what is not.

Finally, I took a course in computer graphics, and that is where I first dealt with animation. I liked moving an image around a computer screen. When drawing, I had always thought in three dimensions. Now, using a computer I could make 3-D models, then position them. The graphics process now matched my thought process and I no longer had to concern myself with drawing speed. I set about to make models for stage sets and costumes using graphics software.

Now I am writing animation scripts. I still think of each prop and costume accessory as an individual character and find that if I can imagine the placement of props and define characters by their clothing, I can solve most script problems.

Judi Cassell
Animation Inker and Painter

■■■■■■■■■■■■■ ■ ■ ■ ■ ■ ■ ■ ■ ■ ■

Have you heard the one about the three men and the elephant? Each man was introduced to a particular part of the animal, then walked away with entirely different impressions. To me, this is a perfect description of the animation process.

Each person involved—designer, animator, inker, painter, or someone in one of the numerous other positions—sees it from a different perspective and brings his own expertise to the process. Somehow all this melds to produce something marvelous and creative, something that appeals to the child in all of us, something called animation.

During the 30 years I have been in the animation industry, I have witnessed the popularity of the medium wax and wane. I have seen production sent out of the country, return to the country, then leave the country once more. I have observed the first primitive attempts of computer animation develop into the high technology of today, a process that evolves so quickly that techniques can be passé almost before a film is completed.

Contrary to the belief of those who see this new world of animation as threatening, I view it as a renaissance. Each new introduction expands the perimeters and opens new creative avenues. (Compare the special effects of *Aladdin* with those of early Disney classics.) For me, this is probably the most exciting era of animation.

The amazing aspect of animation is that each new introduction does not replace an existing entity, but rather offers additional options. Xerox did not replace inking, but complemented it. While computer animation enhanced and expanded the concept of animation, classic animation still thrives and always will. There is a niche for all, because the only limitations of animation are the limitations of the imagination and the budget.

I am not using the term "budget" lightly, for it is the budget that establishes the boundaries of any given project. Being head of an ink and paint service, I must be aware of cost at all times. The work must be completed as quickly as possible with the highest quality and within the projected budget. At the same time, we strive to provide the clients with exactly what they want.

The activity can get extremely hectic when there are as many as three or four projects in production at the same time. Each job has specific requirements, each client wishes things done in a most specific way, and the demands of various projects are often at odds with one another. Without proper attention and management, results could be disastrous. But calm is maintained by assigning a different crew to each job. Each team works only on a specific job until it is finished. Only then will that crew move on to the next project with its own special requirements. As you can imagine, careful records must be kept to identify each cel so that at any given time it can be located. Detailed records are also kept of each client's instructions and preferences.

Years ago, there were no school courses offered in animation. The training we received was all on-the-job, but we all had fine art backgrounds. Today, many colleges and universities offer not just animation courses but full majors in the field. Animation and computer graphics are even being taught in some high schools and elementary schools.

I highly recommend that anyone interested in a career in animation seek formal training. Job competition is stiff and being well-grounded makes all the difference in obtaining your goals.

Probably one of the few areas where formal training is not necessary is the field of inking and painting. But even here, I look for some art background when choosing candidates for training, especially when it comes to inking. Without raw talent, however, it is virtually impossible to become a top inker.

Painting is another story. Some of the best painters I have trained had never picked up a brush before. Fortunately, they learned the technique quickly and proved themselves. Don't get me wrong, I am not saying that anyone can paint! For every person who becomes a top painter, there are very many who just cannot do it, despite their desire and will.

The ink and paint department of a large studio is but one avenue that graduates might use to break into the industry. Even with extensive training, that may be the only available way to enter. Once in, it is possible for neophytes to seek advancement in the direction of their chosen field by making contacts and showing their abilities.

In the early days, the industry was particularly sexist. Women and men were relegated to certain positions. With few exceptions, females, oddly enough, did not animate, and males, oddly enough, did not paint! But that has changed now.

Throughout the years, the projects I have worked on have been varied, each offering different challenges. And there is great satisfaction in seeing a stimulating feature, commercial, or television special knowing the enormous effort that went into its making.

Animation is an art form I was attracted to from the start—and its fascination never ends.

Bill Plympton
Animation Director, Producer
■■■■■■■■■■■■■■■■ ■ ■ ■ ■ ■ ■ ■ ■

When I was three years old in Oregon, my mother could never figure out why the drawings on the walls of my crib were upside down, until she finally realized that I was drawing on my back.

I always had a love for drawing, and when I saw my first Warner Brothers cartoon, I became hooked on animation. Of course I would redraw all the popular characters, as every kid did. And when I was eight, I created my own character called Stew the Shark. In my head, I would create endless storyboards of chase sequences and fight scenes. However, I always felt that to make a real animated film one had to move to Hollywood and work for Disney, but I just wasn't cut out for the corporate art world. Besides, I was bursting with other artistic notions, like painting, illustration, and caricature.

Upon graduation from Portland State University, where I took all the art classes they had (but no cartooning or animation), I moved to New York City to become a serious illustrator. Fortunately, my work caught on, and soon appeared in such publications as *Rolling Stone, House Beautiful, Vogue,* and *The New York Times.* But as my illustration career progressed, I discovered to my amazement that my serious and high-minded illustrations began transforming themselves into humorous gags. It was then I realized that the ultimate joy for me was to make people laugh with my drawings.

Once I became aware of that fact, I felt a real sense of freedom and mission to my work. So I dove headfirst into creating gag cartoons and started to think again about animation. It was around that time that the whole independent film movement took off with people like Spike Lee and Jim Jarmusch. I thought if they could make films outside of "the system," so could I. Realistically, I was then too old to go back to film school so I joined an international animation organization called ASIFA and talked with as many animators as possible. I also learned that the film festivals were excellent places to ask questions and find out about new techniques. And of course I referred to my Bible—Preston Blair's classic book on animation.

My first full-length feature, called *The Tune,* is the only one I know of that was animated by one person—me. Exhausted but grateful, I reawakened my first love. It's marvelous to be able to make a living doing animation because there are few joys in life equal to seeing one's drawings 20 feet high, moving and talking and being laughed at by happy gobs of people.

Bill Littlejohn
Animator

■■■■■■■■■■■■■■■■■■■■■■■■■■

Animation came to my rescue in grade school. To keep from falling asleep in class, I'd draw stick figures on the page margins of newly-issued books. The resulting flip-book animation kept me awake so I would just learn enough to squeak through the system.

And it's been that way ever since I got into animation. Working with directors such as Burt Gillett, Friz Freling, Hugh Harmon, Rudy Ising, Milt Gross, Joe Barbara and Bill Hanna, kept me on my toes. While at MGM I got involved in the unionizing of the animation industry, resulting in the famous Disney strike of 1941. That strike was an education in itself. The forces involved ranged from politics, economics, public relations, the media, personalities, world events, and most of all, human nature—sort of what bad movie scripts are made of.

The war busted up things and when I came back to animation again, TV was already in the picture. I started working on commercials for various studios with voice talents such as Daws Butler, Stan Freburg, June Foray and other greats. That's also when I met Bill Melendez and the "Peanuts" gang—whom I'm still with. Also, I started working with John Hubley, whose pioneering style started a revolution. I worked with John until his untimely death, doing the Trudeau "Doonesbury" special. Fortunately, I'm still working with Faith Hubley.

During this time, I got involved in ASIFA and other international festivals. Seeing films by worldwide artists really woke me up to the awesome potential and scope of the animation medium. The work is so varied that I realized one had to be a student full-time or be passed by. And now we have the mighty computer to contend with!

The ASIFA exposure brought about The International Tournee of Animation, organized by Les Goldman, Ward Kimball, and myself. The Tournee is in its 25th year, and brings to audiences the outstanding works of world independent filmmakers such as Yuri Norstein, Yoji Kuri, Frederic Back, Peter Lord, and Luzzati, among many others.

Animation is no doubt the most stimulating art form since cave drawings. In fact, the medium is so exciting that it has kept me awake long enough to write these comments!

David Steele
Animation Student
■■■■■■■■■■■■■■■■■■ ■ ■ ■ ■ ■ ■ ■ ■

My life did not start out auspiciously. I was just another teenager who hated school and liked to party. I was a shy kid and developing bad habits was my way of trying to fit in. I barely graduated from high school and went on to a series of boring and meaningless office jobs, which simply enabled me to pay a variety of bills and fines from week to week.

Yet I had always liked to draw. The crew at work, including my supervisor, were appreciative of the comic flyers I circulated spoofing life on the job. When I found that one of my co-workers was going to film school at night to become a sound editor, it began to dawn on me that I was frittering my life away, and I decided put my drawing skills to better use.

I started out by attending a community college part-time, and in five years earned an A.A. degree in technical illustration. It was an important achievement for me, the kid who had sworn off school forever. But later I realized the choice of technical illustration was made to escape from a boring life, not because I really cared about it. It was a start, but I needed creative freedom more than simple financial security. That's when I decided to go for broke and pursue a B.F.A. in film animation.

Now that I am completing my degree, I'm anticipating entering this highly competitive field. I have always loved cartoons, but until college had never considered that I could become part of their creation. I suppose I thought they were created by superior beings somewhere. But the beings are real, and I am about to become one of them. Until recently, I had forgotten how as a child in kindergarten my best times were spent alone stacking brightly colored blocks of wood, building them into my own imaginary world. I remember the pleasure I felt as the other kids would come over to see what I had created. It is no wonder that after 30 years I can recall those times so clearly, because now I have the opportunity to feel that way again. I am creating a world of my own and then showing it to others, hoping they'll see what I've seen.

Kim Deitch
Cartoonist

■■■■■■■■■■■■■■ ■ ■ ■ ■ ■ ■ ■ ■ ■

I've been around the animation business all of my life. Being the son of Gene Deitch, an animation director/producer, I was poking around cartoon studios even before I quite realized what cartoons were.

I was also exposed to animation's rich history on a daily basis via television in the early 1950s. Outside of B Westerns, old cartoons from the 1920s and 1930s were about all they showed on TV for kids then. By the time I was a teenager, my best friend, Tony Eastman, who went on to be a successful animator, and I were drawing our own cartoons, both individually and collaboratively. Tony's were outstanding. Mine were, well, okay for a kid. But mainly they proved to me was that I really didn't have the right stuff to become an animator. Instead, I eventually became an underground comic strip artist— and I love it. In a sense I've been creating my own movies on paper for more than 20 years, having had my work published in *The East Village Other*, along with colleagues Art Spiegelman, Robert Crumb, and Bill Griffith. Actually, I miss not having music and sound effects to work with, but I get to do things my own way, and get them done. But I never have quite shaken animation off my shoes. And during the 1970s, I worked on and created voices for three cartoons by Sally Cruikshank: *Quasi At The Quackedero, Make Me Psychic,* and *Quasi's Cabaret.*

What brought me closer to the animation realm occurred a few years ago when I was kicking comic strip ideas around with my brother, friend, mentor, and sometimes collaborator, Simon. We wrote a story about two brothers in the animation business. It starts in the early Winsor McCay (creator of *Little Nemo*) pioneer days and follows the industry's ups and downs as well as its quirks and trends, all the way to the present—including animation's legends and folklore, politics and personalities.

Happily, our first installment was published by *Raw Magazine.* The second episode has been published by *Fantagraphics Books,* who will also publish the final episodes under the title *Waldo World.* Of course in the end it's merely fiction, but like most good fiction, our story has a solid ring of truth. I believe it tells about the creative process in general and animated cartoons as well as those who make them in particular.

Ted Sullivan
Screenwriter

■■■■■■■■■■■■■■■■■■■ ■ ■ ■ ■ ■ ■ ■

I grew up in the Dark Ages of animation. The 1970s were a time when experimentation was minimal and quality was abysmal. But being a television
junkie, I didn't know any better and eagerly devoured each episode of "The
Superfriends" or "Battle of the Planets." Yet I was lucky. I had a brother who
acted not only as my best friend, but as a fellow dreamer as well. Together we
created our own stories, and ultimately our own animated films.

We started by playing out adventures and scenes with *Star Wars* figures.
This continued until one momentous Christmas, when we were given a
Super-8 camera capable of stop animation. In just days, our attic was trans-
formed into a sound stage and our action figures had become actors.

Film, mixed with animation, became my total obsession. I had an intense
desire to become a renowned filmmaker like George Lucas, Terry Gilliam, and
Steven Spielberg, whom I idolized in the same manner as other kids my age
worshipped Larry Bird and Magic Johnson.

My goal was clear: go to the best film school in the world and just "do it." I
was accepted by a myriad of film schools: Northwestern University, New York
University, the University of Santa Barbara, and the University of Southern
California. I ultimately decided the fastest route to success was studying in Los
Angeles, so I chose the four-year Filmic Writing Program at USC. I'm embar-
rassed to say that like most of my classmates, I never expected to graduate. I
imagined my "brilliance" would be immediately identified, and that in a year
or two I'd be working in the industry. Thankfully, nothing could have been
further from the truth.

Film school should be just that—school. It's a place to learn, a place to discover, and a place to develop. The main problem with film school is that most
people, students and professors alike, think of it as a trade school. They teach
you how to load a camera, how to structure a script, or how to critique a film.
But this is only a small aspect of the filmmaking process. Making movies isn't
simply composed of the technical mastery of a few basic elements. It is an art,
as intricate and personal as poetry or painting, and in order to achieve the
various shadings of art, one must have some sort of understanding of the
world. There was nothing more boring than those monotonous technical lectures defining the differences in individual film stocks or explaining how digital sound was developed. The most valuable classes in my four years wound
up being, for the most part, outside the film school. Nothing fascinated me
like psychology, educated me like European literature, or opened my mind like
Chinese history. Those classes ultimately prepared me to fully utilize the
upper-level film writing classes. With a wider base of knowledge, classes like
Adaptation for the Screen or Writing for Animation came alive, and my thesis
screenplays became more intensely personal than I ever could have hoped. It
was this merging of knowledge and experience that ultimately made film
school incredibly worthwhile.

Location is less important than one might think. While Los Angeles is indisputably the heart of the film community, there are great film schools all over the country. I studied at Northwestern's film school for a summer and found it both exciting and educational. And my brother is one of the best student directors and editors in the film school at NYU. Both of us have had completely different experiences on completely different coasts, but we couldn't be happier with the choices we've made. Each program has allowed us to grow, develop, learn, and explore.

Since the start of my love for film was due to animation, and the last part of my formal education focused on it, I have some passionate opinions concerning the majority of animation produced today. Nothing is more frustrating than to watch an animated film that dazzles us with visuals, but has nothing more than an unsatisfactory hole for a story. No matter how many visual tricks an animator employs, he cannot convince the audience they are watching something interesting if the story is nonexistent. At USC, we were made to first study writing for animation without working on the actual illustration of the action. That way, there were no pretty pictures to hide behind or dazzling special effects to mesmerize the audience. There's no greater embarrassment than to read a paltry piece of writing out loud and try to use that old, dry excuse, "Well, the animation will make it work." It never will. And a total diet of celluloid won't sustain an education in film school. Only a well-rounded experience can make the dreams of a 10-year-old boy huddled over a Super-8 camera in an attic turn into reality.

Gerald Potterton

Animation Designer, Director

■■■■■■■■■■■■■■■■■■■■■ ■ ■ ■ ■ ■ ■ ■ ■

Like a lot of other people, I grew up in wartime London. The 1930s passed in a haze of comic books, adoring young show-biz aunts, uncles and parents (I was the first-born), and Saturday morning movies at the nearby Odeon: exciting westerns and adventures such as *Buck Jones and the Riders of Death Valley* and *Buck Rogers and the Undersea Kingdom,* as well as a gloriously funny, colorful, inventive, never-ending supply of animated cartoons. Even now I can hear the joyous roar of anticipation that erupted whenever Uncle Walt's Mickey Mouse logo burst onto the screen. It wasn't until long after the biggest and most vicious war in history was over that I was shown another way to appreciate animation—the UPA way: Magoo, McBoing Boing, Frankie and Johnny and all the rest. In the drab London of the early 50s with its bomb sites and smog, those films were like fresh Rocky Mountain air.

I went to art school because a kid told me you didn't have to do mathematics, which I hated. He lied. Following a few years at the school and a few more in the Royal Air Force, I plodded along as a clean-up assistant on the Halas and Bachelor feature *Animal Farm.* I say plodded because I didn't think I was very good at drawing and besides, the animals in the film seemed to plod everywhere. While at art school, I worked as a child extra at some of the main British film studios. I enjoyed both acting and drawing, and animation seemed to combine the two. I think what impressed me most about the UPA films was the simplicity and freshness of the stories, the design, the characters, and the acting. I thought then, and still do, that most commercial cel character acting was overstated and 'over the top.' Why antic a character around with a few hundred drawings when you could usually double the impact with only a few dozen or less?

As I in-betweened my way though *Animal Farm* surrounded by some very talented animators, wondering why we had to keep drawing so many different steps, I discovered the National Film Board of Canada. Suddenly, my hazy ambition of slaving away for Uncle Walt went out the window, even though I believed, and still do, that no one will ever improve on *Snow White* or *Pinocchio.* Like Orson Welles' *Citizen Kane* or Buster Keaton's *The General,* those two are seemingly out of reach of contemporary mortals. Two NFB films in particular knocked me off my feet: Norman McLaren's *Neighbours* and the cel-animated masterpiece *The Romance of Transportation.* Once again, as with the UPA work, simplicity and directness shone like a beacon. Somehow, I had to go to Canada. I had to work with those guys at the National Film Board. I borrowed the boat fare from an *Animal Farm* colleague and went. It was the best thing I ever did. Armed with a portfolio of old art school sketches and newspaper and magazine cartoons I'd done on the side, I hammered on the door of Mecca until they let me in.

They were all there—in an old saw mill overlooking the Ottawa River, Normal McLaren, fresh from the glow of his recent Oscar for *Neighbours* (he used it as a door stop), nonchalantly animating away in color onto raw film stock and creating his own sound by scratching into the emulsion; Wolf Koenig, who shot *Neighbours,* and designed and animated the characters in *The Romance of Transportation.* Koenig, along with Roman Kroiter (the co-inventor of Imax) would soon shoot, direct, and produce some of the finest documentary films ever made—films like *City of Gold, Lonely Boy, Corral* (with Colin Low), *Stravinsky, Glenn Gould: On and Off the Record,* and so on.

Headed by Colin Low, a fine graphic artist and filmmaker, whose special F/X film *Universe* would one day influence Stanley Kubrick's *2001: A Space Odyssey,* the animation department of the NFB experimented with every kind of animation: puppets, cel, cut outs, pixillation, the works. With much help from the aforementioned, as well as other talented NFBers like Grant Munro, Bob Verrall, Sid Goldsmith, Stanley Jackson, and the scholarly producer/editor Tom Daly, I managed over the years to eke out some films on my own. The Film Board taught me to try everything, and I did, eventually.

I mention these co-workers because without their multiple talents and support, I would never have had the chance or know-how to be so "eclectic" in my own work. I've always tried to whittle things down to their simplest form and occasionally I have succeeded. Among my preferred works is *Pinter People,* based on several characters from the pen of Harold Pinter, in which I used the voices of Pinter himself as well as Vivian Merchant and Donald Pleasance. I particularly have enjoyed working on surrealistic pieces which mix live-action with animation. As long as I remind myself of some of the really inspired work of others I've seen over the years, I'll keep on whittling, armed with the knowledge that in today's hi-tech world, we animators have never had it so good.

Karl Cohen
Writer, Filmmaker, Teacher

■■■■■■■■■■■■■■■■■■■■ ■ ■ ■ ■ ■ ■ ■ ■

One lesson that isn't always taught in college is how to get your career in animation off the ground. Your instructors have given you the basics, but now you have to learn to package yourself so you can walk into that big job interview and shine.

Before you begin, you should have some idea where you want to be in the industry a few years from now. Most people do not start out as directors, producers, heads of companies, or creators of their own television series. There are exceptions, but most people start with entry level jobs and work their way up. Knowing your eventual career objectives will help you direct your job search in the right direction.

The job market for people with animation skills is quite varied and growing. Animators work on a variety of productions including television series, theatricals, commercials, videos used as evidence in courtrooms, video games, CD Rom books, multimedia projects, virtual reality software and in other ways that didn't exist a few years ago. You may find a job doing exactly what you want to do, but in an area where you never expected to find work.

It isn't hard to find businesses to contact when you are ready to look for work. The best directory of animation companies in the USA is published by *Animation Magazine* in California. Some cities have regional directories covering film, video and computer companies. Trade magazines and newsletters carry job listings. And don't forget the yellow pages and your local newspapers.

Trade publications are not hard to find if you know where to look for them. They are not often on news racks or available at public libraries. Instead they can be found at many film, video, and computer production companies.

Ask around to find out about professional associations that have meetings you can attend. If you live in a city with an ASIFA and/or SIGGRAPH chapter, join it so you can network with people and obtain job leads and other information. There are also a growing number of computer user groups. They too can offer the opportunity to meet people and to learn about companies that might hire you.

Keep in touch with your friends from school. They may be your best source of information. Some classmates will also be looking for work and will share information about companies that get large contracts for big projects that require them to hire several people. Another reason to keep in touch is that later in your career you my be hired by somebody who knew you way back when, or you may be in a position to hire a former schoolmate. Animation is a field in which friends often help each other to find jobs.

Many positions with large production houses will start you off as an art assistant or in-betweener. When you call them the first time they will tell you who the contact person is that reviews portfolios. That person expects to be called frequently by job seekers, so a once-a-week call is not out of line. Studios also hire people to answer phones and do other clerical work. Nonartists may become producers, while assistants and in-betweeners could move on as animators and eventually directors. Often, studio work is on a freelance or temporary basis. If you are hired to work on a TV commercial the job is likely to last a few days. On the other hand, work on a television series could last for several months. Expect to be laid off when the project ends. If the company is interested in hiring you back, you might ask for a raise. Whatever you do, don't burn your bridges behind you. I know a talented animator who has trouble finding work due to his poor attitude and bad temper. His abilities find him work, but people who work with him rarely want to rehire him.

When you are ready for your first interview, make sure your portfolio is well organized. Know ahead of time what the company you are going to specializes in, and pick samples of your work that will show them what they want to see. Few employers have time to peruse examples of your work that does not relate to their needs.

If you want to work for Disney on an animated feature, they will want to see life drawings, quick sketches, drawings of people and animals in motion, painting samples, two or more flipable drawings, etc. They do not want to see cartoons with Disney characters.

Most companies want to see the same kind of material that Disney requests. So if you did not save the life drawings you made at college, take a life drawing class, or consider spending some time sketching at your local zoo.

Computer animation companies also want to see samples of your drawing skills if you want to work with them as an animator. The head of the animation department at a well known games company says he prefers to see about eight samples of a person's work in their portfolio. He also tries to hire people that can relate to their clients, describing the clients as "14-year-old kids with acne who hang around malls" and love violent coin-operated computer games. A friend who worked for this company was happy to leave them for a CD Rom company doing children's books. She grew to hate moving tanks and missiles around and then blowing them up.

People in the computer graphics business often say they can teach animators the computer, but they do not have the time to teach computer trained people how to draw. The head of one award-winning company recently declared "many of our animators can't tell you what is going on inside a computer." Many traditionally trained animators are now being hired to work for computer companies. They do the drawings on paper and their work is then scanned into the computer. Technical operators then complete the project.

College graduates with a background in computers who do not draw well often become technical directors at computer graphics companies. Special technical skills are needed on almost every computer project and the artist rarely possesses the technical background to create new effects and other special elements.

If you are not skilled at drawing and do not have a computer background, consider a career in stop-motion animation. Many companies are seeking people with experience "moving ball and socket puppets." There are other companies that look for set and model builders, model makers, mold makers, machinists to make armatures, costume makers, and other skilled talent.

There are many success stories in animation. When Joe Murray graduated from DeAnza, a small community college with just a few animation instructors, his film *The Chore* won the student Academy Award. It was also shown on television by Dick Clark. Next, Murray produced and directed *My Dog Zero*. It has greater production values than his first film and it showed Nickelodeon that he was capable of producing a TV series. The pilot Murray made for the network was a hit and was turned into the series *Rocko's Modern Life*.

As for my own work in animation, I am essentially a writer, and have been an experimental animator/filmmaker. I have taught at San Francisco State University and the University of California at Berkeley. Presently I am researching a book on the censorship of animation in theatres and television.

A final word. If you are about to enter the animation profession you are doing so at a time when job opportunities are growing. Television has a voracious appetite for animated series, and cable TV as well as networks are now producing animated shows. Computer firms are constantly finding new uses for animation. The market for animated TV commercials continues to grow and it appears this trend will continue for many years. Animation is certainly one of the greatest art forms of the 20th century and it looks as though it will play an even more important role in the arts of the next century.

Index